HISTORY
AND
MEMORY

Books by Charles W. Yost

The Conduct and Misconduct of Foreign Affairs
The Insecurity of Nations
The Age of Triumph and Frustration: Modern Dialogues
History and Memory

HISTORY
AND
MEMORY

Charles W. Yost

W. W. NORTON & COMPANY
NEW YORK   LONDON

Copyright © 1980 by Charles W. Yost
Published simultaneously in Canada by George J. McLeod Limited,
Toronto. Printed in the United States of America.

ALL RIGHTS RESERVED

FIRST EDITION

Library of Congress Cataloging in Publication Data
Yost, Charles Woodruff.
  History and Memory.
  Includes Index.
  1. Yost, Charles Woodruff. 2. World politics—
1945–   3. United States—Foreign relations—
1945–   4. Statesmen—United States—Biography.
I. Title.
E840.8.Y63A34 1980   973.9′092′4 [B]   80–14216
ISBN 0–393–01408–8

1 2 3 4 5 6 7 8 9

To my grandchildren,
Daniel, Chad, and Aubrey,
and to their generation.

Acknowledgments

Without the understanding and tireless help of three people, who deserve to be called co-authors, this book could not have been written:

My wife, Irena, who during its long gestation carried most of the family burdens and protected me indefatigably from the intrusions and distractions of everyday life;

my editor, Evan Thomas, whose wise and ever tactful suggestions made it a far better book than it could otherwise have been;

my assistant, Moselle Kimbler, whose contribution both to my research and my peace of mind was considerable and who cheerfully and faultlessly typed and retyped the several drafts from an almost indecipherable script.

Finally, I should like to express my profound gratitude to all those wise men and women, living and dead, quoted in the book or only present in spirit, whose insights into the riddles and paradoxes of life in the twentieth century contributed so much to enriching and refining my own perceptions.

Charles W. Yost

Contents

Photographs on pages 189 to 198.

Introduction

George Santayana, the Spanish-American philosopher, has often been quoted as remarking that those who cannot remember the past are condemned to repeat it. Unfortunately, that has usually been what has happened. Sons mistrust their fathers' experience and, after a decent interval, repeat their fathers' mistakes.

No sensible person would wish to repeat exactly, despite its fantastic achievements, the history of the first three-quarters of the twentieth century—two immensely devastating world wars, a full decade of profound economic depression with disastrous political consequences, a global mobilization of new weapons certain, if used, to wipe out much of humanity, an explosion of human populations straining critically the biosphere and the resources of our small planet.

There is therefore every reason, in the sense of Santayana's warning, not only to remember this history but to reflect upon it most earnestly, to analyze it with the greatest possible objectivity in order to determine, whenever possible, where we and our fathers went wrong, how and why we brought upon ourselves these catastrophes, all of which were avoidable. It is possible that, to the degree we do so, we and our children may escape another revolution of the dreary wheel of human error, needless conflict, and man-made disaster.

It would be well also to recall a similar warning that Henry Kissinger voiced in 1978. "It is dangerously arrogant to believe," Kissinger said, "that foreign policy can be conducted effectively without knowing something of how other generations have faced comparable problems—the compromises they had to make, how their best judgments turned out, and how limited foresight is, even in the best of men and under optimal circumstances. We always tend to think of historical tragedy as failing to get what we want, but if we study history, we find that the worst tragedies have occurred when people got what they wanted . . . and it turned out to be the wrong objective."

So one of the most critical objects of our reflections on history should be not only how and why statesmen failed to achieve what they were seeking but how and where, *having* achieved it, they nevertheless so often failed miserably because they had overlooked the side effects of that kind of success. This was what led Georges Clemenceau, who presided over the allied triumph in 1918, to entitle his memoirs *Grandeurs and Miseries of a Victory.*

To explore these unlearned lessons, in some cases these unasked questions, of the twentieth-century experience is the chief purpose of this book—from which several other purposes flow.

In his speech to Congress after signing the SALT II agreement in June 1979, President Carter said: "The truth of the nuclear age is that the United States and the Soviet Union must live in peace—or we may not live at all. . . . In the age of the hydrogen bomb there is no longer any meaningful distinction between global war and global suicide."

Indeed it has for some time been clear that a level of international violence that was customary and tolerable in human affairs since the beginnings of civlization had already by the third year of World War I, thanks to new weapons, become far more costly than profitable to either victor or vanquished, and that such a level of combat with the weapons deployed today could cripple or destroy civilization itself. An exploration of the causes and consequences of the two world wars of this century, and of the elemental unsubdued impulses toward a third, is another central purpose of this book.

Still another is the following. Ours is an age of specialization. Someone has remarked that the only generalist in a modern hospital is the patient; there is often no one else looking at the whole man or woman. Similarly, few are examining the whole body politic, particularly since this body has become global rather than merely national.

Men have, at least since the age of classic Greece, been endeavoring to make their systems of government more just, reliable, and efficient. In the seventeenth century they began to question the legitimacy of autocracy and to experiment with various forms of representative or democratic government. At about the same time they began equally to question the utility of economic systems directed or manipulated by the state and to free the individual entrepreneur to produce, trade, consume, and accumulate as he pleased.

These new political and economic systems prospered brilliantly in the nineteenth century and spread, along with the imperial domains of their inventors, around the world. In critical ways, however, they have proved unable to cope with the challenges of the twentieth century. Capitalism or free enterprise, already under attack as unjust by socialists and progressives, suffered a stunning psychological blow in the crash of 1929, from which it has never entirely recovered. The democracies were victorious in 1918, in the war that was supposed to make the world safe for them, but since that time the area of democracy has tended to shrink more often than to expand. Even where it is still ascendant, it is frequently said to be in crisis. Meanwhile new authoritarian and totalitarian systems have sprung up and overrun vast territories. Some have collapsed, others have flourished for a time, but none seems to have provided any more reliable prescriptions than their predecessors for the successful management of human affairs.

In the thirty-five years since World War II, the vast British, French, Dutch, Belgian, and Portuguese colonial empires have dissolved, and more than a hundred nations that were submerged or nonexistent are free and sovereign today. They are, however, in the throes of an explosive process of transition in which they are trying to leap, politically, economically, and culturally, from the seventeenth or eighteenth century into the late twentieth. Compressing this process into so short a space of time creates enormous stresses and strains, in which civil wars and external conflicts are inevitably epidemic and will become more so, and in which great powers find themselves constantly tempted to intervene and often yield to that temptation.

Yet at the same time, owing to revolutions in technology and communications, the bonds of interdependence between developed and developing countries have been tightening and are now practically indissoluble. Nothing of major significance can happen in any part of the world without affecting every part of the world. Never have great powers been militarily so overwhelmingly strong. Yet since so much of their military strength is in practical terms unusable, global power is in fact more diffused than it has been at any time since the European colonial empires were established.

These two phenomena—the danger of general war of unimaginable destructiveness and the imperatives of interdependence among 150 nation-states claiming sovereignty and independence—are further themes this book explores.

Men and women have almost always been badly governed. Yet they have survived, created great civilizations, even gradually—with many ups and downs—progressed. This book argues, however, that mankind cannot much longer afford government, either in the political or the economic sphere, as disorderly, as careless, as inequitable, as shortsighted, as most governments have been and still are today. Earlier centuries could patiently endure governments that were despotic or ineffectual or both; our more vulnerable time, it more and more clearly appears, cannot safely do without governments that possess authority, competence, and consent of the governed.

The book will therefore conclude with a chapter of concrete recommendations for dealing with these predicaments: for the more prudent and rational conduct of international relations, for arms control and conflict control; for the more competent conduct of government in the democracies; for the better management of interdependence between developed and developing countries, and for the further elaboration of international institutions for that and other purposes.

The power lies almost entirely with us, I shall argue, to cope effectively with the ills we have for the most part inflicted on ourselves. Our grandchildren's future depends on the degree to which intelligent human choice is or is not exercised, to which leaders and peoples accept the discipline of technological, ecological, and social constraints, or alternatively the degree to which leaders and peoples, eyes fixed on the next meal, the next bonanza, the next crisis, or the next election, let the accumulation of mismanaged evolutions and revolutions overwhelm them and sweep them away. If doomsday should ever come, it would be because we ourselves blew the trumpet and opened the gates.

Finally, a personal note will be introduced from time to time in the following pages. After all, I have the good fortune to be nearly as old as the century and, through the accident of my profession, to have witnessed a number of its great events.

I joined in celebrating Armistice Day at the end of World War I. I was in Washington through most of the New Deal, World War II, the outbreak of war in Korea, and the administrations of Nixon, Ford, and Carter. I was at the San Francisco Conference that founded the United Nations and the Potsdam Conference that ended World War II and ushered in the Cold War. I was at the United Nations in New York for seven years during the conflicts in the Congo, the Middle East, and Vietnam. I was in Peking in 1917, 1973, and 1977, in Stalin's

Russia in 1929 and 1934, and in Brezhnev's several times in the 1970s. I was in Paris for the funeral of Foch in 1929 and the birth of the European Community in 1957, in Hitler's Germany, Mussolini's Italy, and Pilsudski's Poland. I lived in Egypt while it was still under British dominion, in Prague under Beneš and Masaryk, in Vienna under Four Power occupation, in Athens at the end of civil war, in Thailand just after liberation from the Japanese and Laos before the Communists, in Syria when it united with Egypt and Morocco just after its independence. I served and knew seven Presidents from Hoover to Nixon and was for two years in the latter's cabinet.

In order to recall history as vividly as possible, I shall begin with a few snapshots of what the world looked like to a student in Paris fifty years ago and proceed from there to an account of how it got that way, how World War I came about, and how it in turn generated World War II.

HISTORY
AND
MEMORY

≫ 1 ≪

1929 – A Personal Memoir

The years that stand out in one's memory do so more because of one's own state of mind than because of the state of the world. Youth, if it is not too grossly mistreated, inclines to happiness in both good times and bad. Still there are fortunate moments when personal and public felicity seem to coincide.

Such a moment was in my case the year 1928–29 when, having just graduated from Princeton, I led a student's life in Paris and wandered footloose through Europe from Granada to Rome, from Leningrad to Istanbul. That was also when—not only to the naïve eye of a young man of twenty-one—Europe seemed to have recovered from the debacle of World War I and to be once more resuming the triumphant progress it had so stupidly and unnecessarily interrupted by this wholesale fratricide.

In Paris from November 1928 to June 1929 I lived in the Latin Quarter at the Pension Thélia behind the Panthéon. The pension stood shabbily around a little courtyard, hemstitched with bedraggled trees. The proprietress was a small, hunchbacked lady with sharp eyes and tongue, who fiercely though barely preserved the respectability of her house and set a table more notable for austerity than gourmandise, horsemeat being the usual Sunday treat. Parties among the inmates were permitted but were of the utmost innocence and candor, nourished solely on sparkling Vouvray and sweet cakes.

I went to school intermittently at the Ecole des Hautes Ecoles Internationales near the Deux Magots, concentrating on an exploration of why Europe fifteen years before had allowed itself to slip into four years of carnage no one had dreamed of or sought.

That winter was one of the coldest in man's memory. The Seine was frozen over, and the puny radiator in my room was quite insufficient to defrost the blood in my veins. I spent many a morning in a neighboring café huddled in an overcoat beside a charcoal stove, nibbling brioches, sipping cafés au lait, and reading the memoirs of Poincaré or Paléologue, the incredible correspondence between Nicholas II and the czarina who destroyed him, the "Willy-Nicky letters," Ludwig's *July 1914,* Remarque's *All Quiet on the Western Front,* or, for a change, *A la recherche du temps perdu.*

I led a double life between Right and Left banks of the Seine in those intoxicating final months of the great Wall Street boom and its European reverberations. Many of my nights were passed in Montparnasse sitting on sidewalks at the Dome, the Rotonde, or the Coupole, perhaps beside Foujita, the impassive, black-banged Japanese artist and his famous model, Kiki, somewhat overblown now, who had slept with every school of painters for the past twenty years. Once in "South Sea" costume—a burlap bag around one's waist and brown grease elsewhere—I went to the "Quatz" Arts ball and danced all night in ascending rhythm and diminishing costume.

By a stroke of good fortune I was introduced to a school for Rumanian girls at Fontenay aux Roses and there met Nellie Stirbei and Magda Jorga, lovely daughters of notables in their country. Sweet blond Nellie I took to art museums—she was herself a gifted artist— or skating on the lake at Versailles that icy winter, swinging arm and arm its sunlit length beneath the vast edifice of the Sun King. Whatever happened to Nellie and Magda, I wonder when first the Nazis, then the Communists, swallowed up their country?

At the same moment the affluent Americans were flooding through Paris in their last wild binge before the crash. Often on winter's nights I donned black or white tie and, thus metamorphosed in body and spirit, crossed the icefloed river to join compatriots in Montmartre, cavorting among the mirrors at Pile au Face, jubilating to the rhythm of black trumpeters and drummers at Florence's, dancing with the pale, powdered girls at Zelli's.

Sometimes I took a bright young thing, unconstrained in the thigh-high sack dress and boyish bob of the day, to a White Russian restaurant where emigré princes and generals served us caviar, blinis, and champagne and sang to us of dark eyes and Volga boatmen, or to a more cozy boîte where Lucienne Boyer or Cora Madou sat on a piano in the smoke and darkness and, in a sad, sulky voice, sang of love, and bitterness and death.

In more cultured if less ecstatic moods I frequented Sylvia Beach's bookshop near the Luxembourg, bought and plunged into the paperback *Ulysses,* still forbidden in America, and on occasion rubbed elbows with Scott Fitzgerald. I never saw Zelda; perhaps she never came there. The American colony buzzed with tales of their nocturnal doings, bathing nude at dawn in the fountain on the Place de la Concorde or driving misappropriated milk wagons up the glittering Champs Elysées. Alas, I was not invited to these childlike entertainments.

Throughout this winter I had other more serious distractions. I frequented the French Assembly at the Palais Bourbon and saw the great men of the day—Poincaré, Briand, Tardieu, Loucheur—in passionate and eloquent, if unproductive, debate. I called with a group of fellow Americans on Marshal Joffre, the victor of the Marne; he was majestic and benignant but clearly had no more idea what to say to us than we what to say to him. I rose at dawn one March morning to watch the spectacular funeral of Ferdinand Foch roll up the Champs Elysées, colorful contingents from all the armies of the Allies and their empires parading silently behind the black-draped caisson and the prancing horse without a rider.

I watched Igor Stravinsky directing his *Histoire du soldat* and playing a piano sonata. I can still see in my mind's eye Serge Lifar, prone and taut in remorse, miming the *Prodigal Son* in Diaghilev's last season with the Ballet Russe. I was in the Paris Opéra when Maurice Ravel directed the first performance of his *Bolero,* Ida Rubinstein and her company dancing to those new pulsing rhythms on a great table that filled the stage. I heard Paderewski at his piano in old age, and Yehudi Menuhin, a small, plump prodigy in velvet pants and bare knees.

No doubt each "younger generation" for the past two hundred years has imagined it was playing an unprecedented role in the liberation of mankind from the abuses and constraints of a worn-out society. A persuasive case could be made that the generation that experienced or just escaped the First World War mutinied most spectacularly, making the sharpest break with the established order.

Conventions that had corseted Western society for a hundred years evaporated in half a dozen. Sexual freedom proliferated farther and faster in the ten years after 1917 than in the subsequent fifty. Skirts rose from ankles to thighs with the speed of light. In America Prohibition brought on an exuberant consumption at almost every social gathering of bathtub gin or straight alcohol, with predictable effects on the behavior of the participants, male and female. Europe merrily followed suit. Chaperones went up in smoke. "Necking" and "petting" among enthusiastically consenting adolescents, not infrequently "going the limit," became as socially acceptable as ballroom dancing a generation earlier. All that distinguished it from the liberation of later times was a reticence about public and pictorial nudity and the frustrations imposed by cruder contraceptive devices than the pill.

The dominant politics and economics of the 1920s, except in such odd places as Russia, China, and Mexico, tended to be conventional, even reactionary, a last effort by the shocked establishment to return to "normalcy," to the safe haven of Victorian dogmas. To the young, however, who had lived four years in the shadow of death, all the old verities seemed lies and all the old moralities empty. As Hemingway said later: "In those days we did not trust anyone who had not been in the war, but we did not completely trust anyone." After stumbling over the battlefields and cemeteries of Verdun, however, I could not help but feel that it was there the real "lost generation" lay. The politics or literature the survivors made out of their alienation were not exactly what their comrades had died for.

In September 1929 I attended with a group of Princeton students the annual session at Geneva of the League of Nations, for which at the time I had enormous admiration and hope. It was the last untroubled session before the storms broke. We saw and heard the great men: Briand, who at a luncheon there sketched out a united Europe "between the cheese and a pear"; Ramsay MacDonald, the handsome, decent weathercock evangelist; Stresemann, a sallow, shrunken man who had restored Germany to respectability and was in a month to die.

In a hotel lobby we encountered Nancy Astor, a spry, vivacious lady, quick and sharp as a hummingbird, member of Parliament and godmother of women's liberation. She had just come back from climbing the Matterhorn, but, I wrote in my diary, one feels she would be just as breezy after a month in the hospital. She urged us to rouse the women of America to force Hoover to come out for the league. We suggested he was afraid of the Senate. Ah, the Senate, she exploded, I can manage them, let me at them. She mentioned a meeting with Coolidge at which they discussed a speech of his on America's participation in world affairs. I thought it was a pretty good speech, said Coolidge. Well, it couldn't have been worse, retorted Nancy.

From Geneva a friend and I traveled to Berlin and thence for three weeks through the Soviet Union, Leningrad, Moscow, over the Caucusus to Tiflis, across the Black Sea to Odessa, up to Kiev and out to Warsaw; thence Budapest, Bucharest, Istanbul, Sofia, Belgrade, Vienna, Paris, and home to New York in December. I shall come back later to some vignettes of Russia in the naïve, hopeful days of its First Five-Year Plan.

Here, however, I shall depart from these personal reminiscences and turn to the real subject of this book—an examination of what underlay the history I have seen unfold through more than half a century, why we men and women of this century conjured up calamities for ourselves, how we met and survived them, why and how we then, having failed to learn from them, repeated them, with seemingly tireless passion, again and again.

How in God's name did it come about that, only ten years after the "war to end war" had been won, after the world had been made "safe for democracy"—as I sat in my peaceful café in Paris learning the follies of the past, as I skated across the frozen lake beneath the palace of Versailles where peace had just been signed, as I came stumbling out of the Quatz Arts Ball into the bright dawn of the new age—how could it be that mankind was only a year away from the most disastrous economic crash of modern times, only four years from the coming to power in the heart of Europe of a régime of almost unimaginable barbarity, only ten years from a second world war?

Moreover, how could it be that, the second war having been fought and won, the barbarous anachronisms that had been spawned in Germany and Japan having been crushed, Asia and Africa having been liberated from domination by alien empires, our peace, prosperity, and progress still appeared as precarious as ever, and a third world war conducted with weapons capable of snuffing out civilization seemed to hang on the hair trigger of a few men's fear and pride? Was this blind repetition of proven errors and follies something writ indelibly in the animal nature of man? Was it caused by ambitious men and the tribal passions on which they so cunningly played? Was it an inevitable consequence of the fragmentation of mankind into a hundred and fifty nation-states and the international anarchy that prevailed among them? Did it arise from a clash around the globe of rival ideologies and their priesthoods, as dedicated, as hidebound, as fanatical as their religious forebears four hundred years before?

These will be the questions we shall be seeking to answer in light of the experience of our century thus far.

≈ 2 ≈

Origins of World War I
1900–1914

The ills of one's own time always seem worse than those of the past. It shocks all of us who stop to think about it that rarely in history have wars been so numerous, and never so destructive, as in our "civilized" twentieth century.

This may be an illusion. Thucydides' account of the dissolution of Greek civilization in the Peloponnesian war, Gibbon's history of the decline and fall of the Roman Empire, Barbara Tuchman's recent description of the almost incessant warfare that devastated Europe in the fourteenth century remind us of the deep-seated inclination even of civilized man to combat and fratricide.

Still, the catalogue of twentieth-century wars is an impressive one. Raymond Aron has called ours "the century of total war." No previous conflict has matched its two world wars either in geographical extent or in their ingenious capacity to produce within days or hours casualties numbering in the scores of thousands, among combatants at Verdun or the Somme in World War I, among noncombatants at Dresden, Hiroshima, and Auschwitz in World War II. Moreover, the sheer number and variety of wars in this century constitute a tribute to the imagination, indefatigability, and technological genius of our contemporaries.

In one of his last appearances as Secretary of State in January 1977, Henry Kissinger observed: "I would say that if there is a conflict between the Soviet Union and us, it is much less likely to occur as a result of a Soviet attack, deliberate attack on a vital interest of the

United States, than as a result of a conflict that maybe neither of us saw, into which we were drawn in a series of escalating moves. In other words, I think World War I is a better guide to our danger than World War II."

That observation explains the relevance of the origins of World War I to the perils that now confront and will continue to confront not only the United States and the Soviet Union but mankind generally.

With considerate timing Queen Victoria died three weeks after the twentieth century began. As "grandmother of Europe" and sovereign of the world's most powerful empire, she symbolized the era to which she had given her name. Her death was a shock, but no one imagined that much would change—except through the stately and beneficent march of human progress.

Yet, within fourteen years of Victoria's death, the whole of Europe, including its vast overseas empires, was involved in the most devastating war in history up to that time. Within another four years the three oldest and most powerful of its dynasties had been swept away. One was succeeded by a régime purporting to transform the whole of society. The domains of a second were split into seven fragments. The people of the third were so demoralized by the war and its aftermath that, after a brief interval, they turned over power to a régime so barbarous that it almost plunged Europe into another Dark Age.

How could all this come about? How could the unprecedented power and prosperity, the seeming rock-ribbed stability, the unbridled complacency and arrogance of an era, so quickly dissolve into almost universal conflict, chaos, and revolution?

In the opening years of the twentieth century Europe dominated the world, as it had since the age of discovery and colonization in the sixteenth and seventeenth centuries. The efficient civilization that it had evolved after the Renaissance out of freer scientific inquiry, artillery, pelagic navigation, centrally controlled nation-states, commercial enterprise, proselytizing religions, and industrial revolution had so far outstripped the social organization even of ancient and powerful empires, such as China, India, and the Ottomans, that it maintained unchallenged domination of the globe down to and even beyond the First World War.

Europe itself was ruled for the most part by a small minority of aristocrats, bureaucrats, and entrepreneurs. This was true not only of the autocracies of Central and Eastern Europe but of Britain and to some degree France and even the United States. An examination of the *New York Times* of January 1901, for example, conveys the impression that only the doings of a few hundred or thousand economically and politically powerful men and women were of any real significance or interest. From Vienna to New York the aristocracy and the Four Hundred waltzed, dined, cut coupons, and inveighed righteously against anarchists, strikes, sinful laxity, and neighboring countries. Only a handful of men in the various European capitals in July 1914 had anything to do with the decisions that led in a few days to general war.

Of course enormous changes had occurred during the nineteenth century, but these had been apparently digested by the traditional system and were assumed to have made it stronger than ever. In fact, however, many of these mutations, working away quietly under the skin, had, unperceived, eviscerated the body politic, so that in many countries it was drained of vitality and legitimacy—a walking corpse.

The most pervasive and insidious of these mutations was nationalism. Nationalism is a curious phenomenon, when one comes to reflect on it soberly, an overwhelming but nebulous sentiment that groups men and women in conglomerations of haphazard origin, inspires them with a passionate devotion to their conglomeration and an intense hostility to others, and relieves them of their usual obligations under the Sixth Commandment and the Sermon on the Mount whenever these conflict with the injunctions of patriotism, however irrational. The ease with which Europeans, at that time the most sophisticated and civilized of peoples, were twice within a quarter-century swept into "total" wars shows vividly how men as shallow as Count Berchtold or as mad as Hitler can pervert patriotism to bring about the destruction of their nations.

Nation-states in the modern sense began to emerge in Western Europe in the fifteenth century, but it was the French Revolution, Napoleon, the Romantic poets, and ethnic philologists who spread the vision throughout the continent in the nineteenth century. The wars of Italian and German unification left the process of "liberation" far from complete, as indeed it remains to this day. Particularly inside the Austrian Empire from 1848 onward Hungarians, Italians, Poles,

Czechs, Slovaks, Croats, Slovenes, and Rumanians were becoming conscious of their identity and striving for independent nationhood or association with compatriots outside the empire. This was the profoundest underlying cause of instability in Europe when the new century opened.

Europe was, moreover, both deeply divided among its members and grossly overextended vis-à-vis the rest of the world in terms of inherent and durable power.

A line could have been drawn through the center of Europe in 1914 separating autocracies from democracies, which would have diverged only slightly (by the shift westward of the Federal Republic of Germany) from the line of the Iron Curtain after World War II. The spoor of history is only very gradually erased.

There were, however, two curious anomalies distinguishing the line dividing Europe in 1914 from the curtain of 1946 or 1980. First, the line of 1914 was more permeable. People moved freely without passports from London to the Russian border. The movement of goods was also relatively uninhibited. The aristocracies of West and East, both of blood and commerce, were intimately interrelated. The Kaiser of Germany was Queen Victoria's grandson; George V of England and Nicholas II of Russia were first cousins.

The second difference between then and now was that until World War I had actually broken out, constitutional and ideological contrasts between West and East were muted. The European alliance system in 1914 did not group autocracies on one side and democracies on the other but opposed traditional and almost coincidental rivals. Republican France was allied to the most inflexible of the autocracies, Russia. Parliamentary Britain, before contracting an entente with France and Russia, first sought one with imperial Germany.

Lord Palmerston had said half a century before: "We have no eternal allies, we have no perpetual enemies. Our interests are eternal and perpetual, and these interests it is our duty to follow." This was one of those majestic oversimplifications that lead "realists" astray.

The first part of it is indisputably true. No one has eternal allies or enemies, as U.S. relations with Germany, Japan, and Russia in this century have so clearly illustrated. The second part is true in principle, but what statesmen *perceive* as national "interests," whether perpetual or not, varies enormously from age to age, even from year to year. During the first five years of the new century, British leaders' perceptions of where her interests lay and where therefore it was their "duty" to follow shifted dramatically. This shift contributed significantly to the polarization among the great powers of Europe and to the destabilization of the balance of power that led so rapidly and astonishingly to general war.

The underlying weakness was that in nineteenth-century Europe after the defeat of Napoleon, despite the so-called Concert of Europe, despite the Holy Alliance, despite the Metternichean and Bismarckian "systems," there was really no international system at all. There were national systems of varying degrees of effectiveness, but there was international anarchy.

Nevertheless, at the beginning of the new century there had been no great conflict since the battle of Waterloo in 1815. Men had almost forgotten that there could be one, or what war was like. The Crimean war, the wars of Italian and German unification, had engaged only some of the great powers and had ended rather quickly before they could spread. The last one, however, had left a cancer in the heart of Europe—Alsace-Lorraine.

Bismarck had wisely ended his victorious war with Austria in 1866 without annexations and without indemnities. As a result Germany and Austria were able thereafter to live in peace and to become allies. Had Bismarck chosen or been able to be as magnanimous to France after the Franco-Prussian War, he might have ended then, as his successor did eighty years later, the ancient enmity between France and Germany, and established a solid block of common interest in the center of Europe. The emperor and the Prussian generals, however, insisted on a "strategic" frontier to protect Germany's "security" against French revanchism. By doing so, and thereby profoundly affronting French nationalism, they created the revanchism and aggravated the insecurity they sought to forestall. In consequence, in the following decades Europe split into two hostile alliances, the Franco-Russian Alliance matching and confronting the Triple Alliance of Germany, Austria, and Italy.

Both alliances were ambitious and each was intensely mistrustful of the other; yet neither would have been likely to risk war as long as England, the doyen among the great powers, maintained the "splendid isolation" that had been her tradition for three-quarters of a century, enabling her to throw her weight in whichever direction seemed best calculated at any given time to preserve equilibrium on the Continent. In 1900, however, the majestic and uninterrupted expansion of the British Empire encountered its first serious setback in almost a century, from a "contemptible" little band of farmers, the Boers. Through the unconcealed glee with which their defeats in South Africa were hailed throughout Europe and most of the rest of the world, the British to their amazement discovered that they were not loved, indeed were almost universally detested. They reacted in uncharacteristic fashion—with panic.

First the Conservatives, and after their electoral victory in 1906 the Liberals, with almost no reflection abandoned the "isolation"—that is, the freedom of action—that had served them and Europe so well, and sought, mistakenly supposing it would strengthen Britain's security, to associate themselves with one or the other of the two continental alliances. In fact, this association subjected Britain's fate to decisions made in Vienna and Saint Petersburg.

What underlay this fatal decision was the overextension, after three hundred years of imperial expansion, of British ambitions and responsibilities. Britain awoke from the prolonged "fit of absence of mind" through which she had acquired her vast empire to the fact that she was increasingly on a collision course with other European imperialisms and could no longer sustain rivalry with all of them at the same time. The alternative of moderating her expansion and contenting herself with an empire on which the sun would sometimes set did not occur to her leaders at that juncture, or indeed till nearly fifty years later when the exhaustion induced by two great wars left her no choice.

In 1901 much the easier and more honorable alternative seemed to be to ensure the empire by joining one of the two alliances, accommodating with it respective colonial claims, and jointly resisting the ambitions and claims of the other alliance.

The first approach of the Conservatives, who were in office as the century began, was to Germany, with whom Britain had longstanding and intimate dynastic ties, whereas she had been fighting France off and on for centuries and had nearly gone to war with her as recently as 1898, when their sprawling empires collided at Fashoda on the upper Nile. The Germans, however, were a meticulous, inflexibly minded people, unprepared to adapt to the Anglo-Saxon disposition to contingency, imprecision, and offhandedness. They wanted signatures on the dotted line. They insisted on an elaborate treaty with specific commitments for which the British were not ready. They therefore, in what a later historian referred to as Holstein's "Grosses Nein," rejected the inestimable prize offered them.

The French were more subtle and more sensible. They accepted an entente, typically British in its vagueness, with no commitments except about the division of colonial spoils in Egypt and Morocco, and then devoted the next eight years to weaving a network of "defensive arrangements," known only to a handful of members of the British cabinet and General Staff. These so deeply and "morally" committed Britain that she became, in fact if not in form, a full-fledged member of the Franco-Russian Alliance, unable, even if it had wished, to divorce its fortunes from theirs. Asquith and Grey seem never to have fully understood where and how far they were going, though permanent officials at the Foreign Office, like Crowe, Hardinge, and Nicolson, certainly did, and indeed, because of their profound hostility to Germany, pushed their ministers steadily along this fatal course.

Thus, beginning in 1904 all the great powers of Europe, and with them well over half the globe, became divided into two hostile and heavily armed alliances. Both the hostility and the armaments increased steadily through the next decade. For this rapid and fatal deterioration of relations the governments of Russia, Germany, Austria, and France share, in not too unequal a measure, the responsibility. Britain's culpability was more negative than positive. By committing themselves to one of the two alliances, by coming to share the fears and condone the ambitions of their allies, they frittered away their great power and influence. When the critical days of July 1914 came round, their voice was largely ignored. The British proposed a conference, but neither adversaries nor allies were interested. The fatal decisions were made in Vienna, Saint Petersburg, Berlin, Paris. London hardly counted.

During the decade after 1904 the leaders on the Continent, for the most part as parochial, hidebound, and myopic a set of men and women as ever led great nations, indulged in a series of acts of folly that steadily exacerbated the antagonism between the two alliances and led them into one crisis after another, culminating in 1914.

The German Kaiser, who already had the strongest army in Europe, persisted in launching also a substantial navy, for reasons almost entirely of vainglory. The military uselessness of the German fleet was demonstrated throughout the ensuing war. Nevertheless, its creation alarmed and angered the British and had much to do with their drift into ever-closer military arrangements with their French and Russian allies.

The Kaiser's colonial ambitions, which were as legitimate or illegitimate as those of his French and British rivals, led him twice, in 1905 and 1911, to challenge their agreement and French hegemony in Morocco in a provocative and yet ineffectual fashion. Again the consequence was to sharpen his image as a warmonger, to stir up popular anxiety in Britain and France, and to cement their alliance. The total effect of Wilhelm's fatuous adventures was to make him more and more dependent on his single reliable ally, Austria-Hungary, so that paradoxically the weaker of the two partners came to be the one who, in a crisis, called the tune.

Austria was a danger to Europe not because of its strength but because of its weakness. Despite a grandiose façade, it was an unstable anachronism in an age of intense nationalism, its millions of Slavs and Latins increasingly restless under alien rule. Rather than conceding these nationalisms a fuller partnership in their governance, the Austrian and Magyar elite sought foolishly to check the centrifugal forces by suppressing them. The almost total dissolution of the Ottoman Empire in Europe in the Balkan wars of 1912–13, and the resulting aggrandizement and incitement of the South Slavs, created by 1914 a dangerous sense of panic in Vienna.

The Russian Empire continued during this decade to be externally insatiable and internally disintegrating. The inveterate expansionism that had carried it to the Pacific and beyond brought it at the opening of the new century into a war with Japan which, to the astonishment of the world, ended with the first defeat of a European by an Asian nation since the time of Suleiman the Magnificent. Government under Nicholas II, or more exactly under his paranoiac empress and her favorites, combined stupidity, immobility, and weakness to an almost incredible degree. Near-revolution in 1905 had little seeming effect. The more distracted the régime was at home, the more obsessed it became with its pretensions abroad, particularly its self-imposed role as defender of the South Slavs, even when the ambitions of the latter threatened the existence of the Austro-Hungarian Empire.

France, forty years after Sedan, remained hypnotized by German military might, with the recovery of Alsace-Lorraine, and with continuing colonial expansion in Africa no matter what the risks and costs. These were the central concerns of such pertinacious and single-minded leaders as Delcassé, Poincaré, and Clemenceau. Their determination to round out their empire in North Africa formed the basis of their bargain with Britain and provoked two confrontations with Germany which brought the two alliances to the verge of war. By generous loans they propped up the tottering Russian colossus. The two allies shared each other's chauvinisms. Russian grand duchesses carried pillboxes containing soil from Alsace-Lorraine. Like the Germans to Austria, the French became captive to the rash policies of their weaker ally, because they feared she might defect and leave them to confront Germany alone.

So through the decade 1904–14 one diplomatic crisis led to another, each further solidifying both alliances and reenforcing the loser's conviction that it could not afford to be humiliated again. Looking back on the whole decade and its appalling climax, one may say that a series of diplomatic victories for one alliance or the other ended in a fatal diplomatic defeat for both.

All these tensions, traumas, and follies, quite unexpectedly for all concerned, reached a critical mass in July 1914. No one—Wilhelm, Nicholas, Franz Joseph, Poincaré—expected or wanted a general European war at that time or indeed ever. Nevertheless, the passions and miscalculations of all of them, and of their rattlebrained governments, produced this catastrophe within a single month.

The Austrains felt that the murder of the heir to their throne by Serbian irredentists, the latest in what seemed to them a series of Slavic provocations and Austrian reverses, constituted such a threat to the survival of their empire that only a spectacular punishment of Serbia could forestall disintegration. They wanted a quick military victory over Serbia alone and fatuously gambled they could get away with it.

Russia felt it could not sit idly by while its small Slav "brother" was crushed. When the Czar sought to mobilize against Austria alone, he was told by his generals that this was impossible, since all their plans had been drawn up on the assumption of general mobilization. After vacillating for several days, Nicholas gave in, though he should have been aware that throughout Europe military men had long considered general mobilization tantamount to a declaration of war against Germany, since the latter would not passively wait while huge Russian armies were assembled on its frontiers.

Wilhelm, shocked by the assassination of his dynastic ally, at first gave the Austrians the famous "blank cheque" to do what they would in punishing Serbia.* However, when the Serbs accepted almost the whole of the Austrian ultimatum and the likelihood of general war if Austria persisted began to emerge, he concluded his ally had obtained ample satisfaction and belatedly sought to hold her back. However, the Austrian declaration of war against Serbia and the Russian general mobilization cut short these efforts and produced their predictable consequences—German declarations of war against Russia and France and the implementation of the long-established Schlieffen Plan whereby Germany, as its best military riposte to a two-front war, sought by an attack in the west through Belgium to knock out France before Russia could fully mobilize.

Diplomatic historians have judged, on the basis of the events of July 1914, that Austria's actions made European war probable and Russia's made it certain. In the diplomatic exchanges during that fatal month, Germany, France, and Britain each sought primarily to warn and restrain adversaries rather than allies, though they might have been supposed to have more influence with the latter than with the former. When Germany did seek to hold back Austria toward the end of the month, the intervention was too late and was soon overtaken by events.

Britain's timid intercession was equally ineffective. While it was secretly committed to France and Russia, it was not formally bound, and Germany could therefore cherish the illusion Britain might stay out. This aspect of the crisis, like many others, was for the most part

*During my assignment to Vienna thirty-five years later I was told by the son of Count Hoyos, the Austrian official who obtained the blank check from the Kaiser, that Hoyos subsequently, overwhelmed with remorse for his part in bringing on the fatal war and destruction of his country, ended his life in a monastery.

a charade, since the British government knew Germany planned in case of war to attack through Belgium (and indeed would have been enormously embarrassed if it had not), whereas the German government should have been aware that the invasion of Belgium, if nothing else, would certainly bring Britain into the war.

This chain of events, each almost inevitably following the other once the first two—Austrian declaration of war on Serbia and Russian general mobilization—had occurred, explains the historical judgment that Austria and Russia bear the chief responsiblity for the outbreak of general war. However, from the broader perspective called for under the circumstances, all five great powers were equally responsible for permitting a system—or rather an absence of system, two adversary alliances in extremely precarious balance—to grow up over the two preceding decades and for their failure to provide any mechanism for preventing catastrophe if the balance was upset, as it almost had been on several occasions between 1905 and 1914 and as it finally was in the latter year.

In retrospect the errors committed by all the leaders were clear and gross. Each alliance mistrusted the other, though the alliances were relatively new and Britain missed by only a hair being allied with Germany and Austria instead of France and Russia. There was a basic misperception of one another's real aims, compounded by both the escalating and unnecessary arms race and by persistent colonial rivalries. The intensity of newly released national feeling in the Balkans and the issue of life or death that this presented for the Hapsburg monarchy were grievously underestimated everywhere else.

There was a total misunderstanding of the character of a war between the two alliances if it should come. Each assumed it would end in a few months in a victory, after the pattern of the Franco-Prussian or Russo-Japanese wars. No one foresaw that national security required that war not be won but avoided, that general European war would be almost as much of a disaster for victors as for vanquished. No serious effort was therefore made to establish any machinery which, in a crisis, would forestall or delay hostilities until there could be a cooling-off and a reappraisal. Everyone relied on the frail expedients of traditional diplomacy, which became less and less effectual as one crisis followed another.

The whole edifice of nineteenth-century civilization, the Victorian

Age, was brought crashing to the ground in the short space of eight days—between the delivery of the Austrian ultimatum to Serbia on July 23 and the Russian general mobilization on July 31. The world would never be the same again.

≫ 3 ≪

Course and Consequences
of World War I
1914–1929

Only five months after the twentieth century began, on May 13, 1901, a fledgling member of the British House of Commons, fresh from the battlefields of South Africa, made a speech there. At this early date Winston Churchill warned:

> In former days, when wars arose from individual causes, from the policy of a Minister or the passion of a King, when they were fought by small regular armies of professional soldiers, and when their course was retarded by the difficulties of communication and supply, often suspended by the winter season, it was possible to limit the liabilities of the combatants. But now, when mighty populations are impelled on each other, each individual severely embittered and inflamed, when the resources of science and civilization sweep away everything that might mitigate their fury, a European war can only end in the ruin of the vanquished and the scarcely less fatal dislocation and exhaustion of the conquerors. Democracy is more vindictive than Cabinets, the wars of peoples will be more terrible than those of Kings.

These prescient words, if they were ever noted, were by 1914 long since forgotten, not least of all, one suspects, by the First Lord of the Admiralty himself.

The war began in 1914 with an enormous outburst of jubilation in each of the contending capitals. Young men flocked joyously to the colors; young women passionately embraced strangers in uniform; old men and priests spoke solemnly of king and country, *la patrie, Gott mit uns.* No one doubted the righteousness of his cause or the wickedness and guilt of his enemies.

Everyone expected to destroy the hostile armies and enter the enemy capital in very short order. Very few supposed the war would last longer than Christmas. Practically no one came remotely close to imagining what it would really be like.

There were presumably two principal reasons for this singularly inappropriate mood and these gross miscalculations.

No one alive had ever taken part in a great war, and very few had taken part in any war at all. Those wars that had occurred in the past half-century had illmatched contenders, ended quickly, and did not give modern artillery, particularly machine guns, a chance to wreak the appalling havoc of which they were capable. Probably the closest military paradigm of World War I was the U.S. Civil War, and only a handful of military historians had paid any attention to that.

The other underlying factor was more subtle and psychological, even psychopathic. The Victorians, as we now know only too well but they hardly suspected, were abnormally repressed and frustrated in many critical aspects of their personal lives and social relationships. Existence was drab for all but the rich, and boring even for many of those. War was to many a welcome relief from humdrum lives. It was an even more welcome opportunity to give vent to emotions and aggressions that had been unnaturally constrained by rigid social custom and by exorbitant conjugal, parental, pedagogical, and bureaucratic authority. Sex, youth, and spontaneity had all been bottled up during a century of Victorianism; they broke loose like a pack of hounds unleashed. National animosities, long fostered by "patriotic" elements in each country, inflamed by chauvinist writers and intellectuals, provided convenient scapegoats for the aggressive passions so long accumulated and suppressed at home.

In sum, from 1870 to 1914 European men and women had been unconsciously programming themselves for an enormous outburst of international violence. That is what now occurred. Only a rare human spirit recognized what was happening. In late 1914 Albert Einstein wrote to his friend Paul Ehrenfest: "Europe, in her insanity, has started something unbelievable. In such times one realizes to what a sad species of animal one belongs."

Once it became apparent, moreover, that neither side was going to win immediately and that a prolonged national effort of unprecedented scope would be required, the engines of contemporary propaganda—at that time essentially press and advertising—whose capabilities had never before been fully understood or used, were set in motion by governments to depict the enemy as beasts in human form, to contrast the viciousness of his war aims with the purity of one's own, and to exploit both idealism and jingoism to spur recruitment and war production. These extraordinary propaganda campaigns, mirror images of each other and yet mutually destructive, were in a sense the most successful campaigns of the war. By inspiring and mobilizing whole nations, they enabled foolish governments, caught in their own traps, to prolong the war far beyond the capacity of equally foolish generals to end it. Feeble attempts from time to time to negotiate peace without victory were indignantly scotched as treasonous capitulation to enemies metamorphosed by propaganda into unspeakable barbarians.

Almost worse, this too-successful propaganda so saturated the popular mind with false perceptions of reality that, after the war, it was impossible even for more enlightened politicians to make a real peace. The irresponsible propaganda of World War I was a major cause of World War II.

This is an egregious example of what I might call, following Parkinson's practice, "Yost's Law"—that side effects of human actions are not less important effects than those intended or expected but merely *other* than those intended or expected. They are "side" effects only from the viewpoint of the initiator or beholder; they may be in fact the principal effects. Much of history seems a catalogue of the overwhelming prevalence of unintended over intended consequences of what men say and do. The evolution of human society usually has been and probably will continue to be governed primarily by the inadvertent and unexpected consequences of actions designed to achieve other purposes.

The folly of the "statesmen" who led their people into catastrophe was equaled only by the folly of the generals, whose anachronisms made the catastrophe infinitely more bloody than it need have been. After the German repulse at the battle of the Marne, the entire

Western Front sank into almost four years of sanguinary and meaningless stalemate, as millions of men rotted in rain-drenched trenches
which they shared with rats, lice, and disease.

The generals could think of no way out other than to throw their
troops uselessly again and again against machine guns and barbed
wire. Maurice Hankey, secretary of the British Committee of Imperial
Defense, wrote in his diary at the time: "The General Staff are so
intolerably complacent and self-satisfied that they won't listen to any
outside view. Meanwhile they are bleeding us to death." The losses
were indeed appalling. The British lost 420,000 in the Battle of the
Somme in 1916, 70,000 on the first day. In the same battle the Germans
lost 440,000 and the French nearly 200,000. This followed shortly the
Battle of Verdun, where the losses were on a similar scale. The military utility of both battles was nil.

A substantial proportion of "the best and the brightest" young
Englishmen, Frenchmen, and Germans of their day was wiped out.
A decade and a half later Dick Diver, the hero of Scott Fitzgerald's
Tender Is the Night, visited the battlefield of the Somme and remarked: "See that little stream. We could walk it in two minutes. It
took the British a month to walk it—a whole empire walking very
slowly, dying in front and pushing forward behind." These were
indeed men who "died in vain."

Though the war began in a fit of passion and absence of mind,
unplanned and without a calculated object other than, on both sides,
defense against what was perceived as intolerable aggression, it very
soon acquired "war aims" that were far from high-minded and disinterested. As early as September 1914, in response to American offers
of mediation, Bethmann-Hollweg, chancellor of a Germany that had
gone to war to resist Russian "attack" and Allied "encirclement," was
drawing up a shopping list that included annexation of economically
important parts of France and Belgium and substantial additions to
the German colonial empire in Africa. The Entente, being a more
disparate alliance, took some months to negotiate among themselves
the anticipated spoils. In 1915 and 1916 Russia, France, and Britain by
a series of secret treaties divided up the whole of the Ottoman Empire,
including most of present-day Turkey, and, to induce Italy to enter
the war, promised her not only the extensive Austrian territories she
received in 1919 but Dalmatia as well.

Therefore, while the young men on both sides were dying in such colossal numbers, as they believed for defense of the fatherland, for a just peace, for an end to militarism, their rulers were behaving as though nothing had changed since the War of the Spanish Succession, as though the real object of this greatest of European civil wars, as of all before it, was merely the redistribution of territories and empires, without the slightest regard to the desires of their inhabitants, and the creation of a new "balance of power" favorable to the victors.

However, in the end the "statesmen" proved to be at least as deluded as their young men. No one won the war. Everyone lost: the Germans and Italians who fell easy prey to Nazi and Fascist minorities and followed them to disaster; the French who collapsed morally in 1940; the British who, despite the glorious interlude of 1940–45, lost their empire almost overnight. This European civil war was ultimately almost as destructive to all the combatants as the Peloponnesian war had been to the Greeks.

A prodigious side effect was the Russian Revolution, not the liberal revolution of March 1917, which was a century overdue, but the Bolshevik revolution eight months later whereby, thanks to the chaos into which Russia had fallen, a tiny minority of dedicated zealots was able to seize power, to nullify the results of free elections the following January, to perpetuate their rule over the compliant Russian masses, and thereby to introduce into the community of nations for the remainder of the century a violently disruptive ideological struggle of a kind largely absent from human affairs since the religious wars of the sixteenth and seventeenth centuries.

Another consequence of World War I was to bring onto the center of the world stage the United States, to call in the New World to redress the balance of the Old, as Woodrow Wilson saw it.

It is not at all certain that the national interests of the United States, or even the long-term interests of Europe, required that the United States enter the war. Had it remained neutral, a peace without the victory of either side might have been forced upon the exhausted European powers. Such a peace might not have given rise to another war within two decades. (My first recollection of a public event is being taken in November 1916 to the public square of our town to watch a rollicking torchlight parade celebrating Wilson's second election—under the slogan "He kept us out of war.")

In his great speech to the American Senate on January 22, 1917, Wilson called for "a peace without victory." "Victory would mean peace forced upon the losers," he warned with tragic foresight, "a victor's terms imposed upon the vanquished. It would be accepted in humiliation, under duress, at an intolerable sacrifice, and would leave a sting, a resentment, a bitter memory upon which terms of peace would rest, not permanently, but only as upon quicksand. Only a peace between equals can last."

Unfortunately, during the preceding two years Wilson had by gradual degrees maneuvered himself into a position whereby the decision whether the United States remained neutral or entered the war rested not with him but with Germany. Once the Kaiser and his military leaders decided to resume unrestricted submarine warfare, as in fact they already secretly had when Wilson spoke, he had little alternative, given the position he had repeatedly taken and the consequent state of American opinion, but to go to war. When a statesman seeks to deter another government by open threats, and it defies him, he must at some point carry out his threats or lose credibility, dignity, and the confidence of his people.

So only ten weeks after the speech quoted above, Wilson appeared before a joint session of Congress and asked for a declaration of war. He no longer, needless to say, called for "a peace without victory." "We are glad," he said, "now that we see the facts with no veil of false pretense about them, to fight thus for the ultimate peace of the world and for the liberation of its peoples, the German people included; for the rights of nations great and small and the privilege of men everywhere to choose their way of life and of obedience. The world must be made safe for democracy. Its peace must be planted upon the tested foundations of political liberty."

So Wilson offered the peoples of the world not only a just peace, not only national self-determination to assure their freedom from foreign rule, but domestic political rights to assure their freedom to govern themselves democratically. Those were promises, as the event soon proved, that America could not deliver, since they applied in principle at least to the empires of allies as well as adversaries, and to the internal behavior of scores of governments America could exhort but in no sense control. Nevertheless, these words—"liberation," "rights of nations great and small," "democracy," "political liberty"—were words whose time had come. They were now graven in the international political vocabulary and would echo around the world for the remainder of the century.

Another pregnant concept took public shape in that landmark speech of January 1917, though Wilson was not its originator. As early as the summer of 1915 Sir Edward Grey, the British Foreign Secretary, was writing to Colonel House:

> My own mind revolves more and more about the point that the refusal of a Conference was the fatal step that decided peace or war last year, and about the moral to be drawn from it: which is that the pearl of great price, if it can be found, would be some League of Nations that would be relied on to insist that disputes between any two nations must be settled by arbitration, mediation or conference of others. International Law has hitherto had no sanction. The lesson of this war is that the Powers must bind themselves to give it a sanction.

By the end of that year Wilson had espoused this idea. In a speech in May 1916 to the League to Enforce Peace, he announced that the United States was willing to become a partner in any feasible association of nations to ensure that the principle of public right prevails. In his Senate speech in January 1917 he declared: "It will be absolutely necessary that a force be created as a guarantor of the permanency of the settlement so much greater than the force of any nation now engaged or any alliance hitherto formed or projected that no nation, no probable combination of nations, could force or withstand it. ... There must be, not a balance of power, but a community of power; not organized rivalries, but an organized common peace."

Alas, other Americans, as represented by Henry Cabot Lodge, Sr., William E. Borah, and Warren Harding, were not yet ready to assume the global responsibilities Wilson had offered them. Nor were such brilliant anachronisms as Lloyd George and Clemenceau ready to accept an American peace based on liberation, democracy, and a community of power. Self-determination was acceptable to them only as it applied to the empires of adversaries, and an organized peace only if they organized and controlled it.

The enormous wave of popular enthusiasm and hope that greeted Wilson when he first arrived in Europe in 1918 was soon beaten back by the conventional "realism" and acquisitiveness of the European leaders and by their cynical pandering to the national passions they had aroused during the war. "We'll squeeze the Germans until the pips squeak," Lloyd George had promised in the "khaki election" at the end of 1918, and as a consequence astronomical reparations were demanded—which, as John Maynard Keynes predicted, could not conceivably be collected and would have ruined the economies of the Allies if they had been.

The settlement fabricated at Versailles had to be imposed on Germany, was neither just nor durable, and had all the demoralizing consequences Wilson had foreseen in his speech of January 1917. Its one element of constructive innovation, the League of Nations, was disavowed by the American Congress and thereby emasculated at birth. Wilson died a broken man; but he will probably be a hero to the twenty-first or twenty-second centuries—if civilization survives until then.

The victors' sins of commission and omission in the first five years after the 1918 armistice laid the groundwork for World War II, just as the attitudes instilled by wartime propaganda engendered the policies of those five years. The prolongation of the blockade of a desperately hungry Germany, the imposition in the Versailles treaty of a "war guilt" clause that every German passionately repudiated, the reparations that contributed to a runaway inflation which impoverished the German middle class, the French military occupation of the Ruhr—all these catastrophes, which the fledgling Weimar Republic could not prevent, had by 1923 discredited it in the eyes of half the German electorate. Yet the Allies, had they been wise should have been doing all they could to legitimize and strengthen this republic, repository of whatever hopes there were for a democratic and stable Europe. The immediate consequence of their failure to do so was the election of Hindenburg as president in 1925; the longer-term consequence, together with other causes, was the vertiginous rise of the Nazi party after 1929.

Other consequences of the war were equally destabilizing. The Austro-Hungarian Empire, not by fiat of the victors but through its internal contradictions, fell into half a dozen national fragments, completing the balkanization of Southeast Europe that the collapse of the Ottoman Empire had begun. While the new configuration accurately represented the hodgepodge of nationalities long established there, the new nations were so weak and divided that they easily fell prey first to the Nazis and then to the Soviets.

The Allies, even before the end of the war, attempted a military intervention in the Soviet Union which, particularly since it was in support of czarist generals and admirals who had learned and forgotten nothing, was considerably beyond both their military capabilities and the tolerance of their war-weary populations. The result was merely to intensify the siege complex of the Soviets and to widen the chasm already forming between East and West.

Finally, in obstensibly victonous Italy, seething with a popular conviction that its huge losses had not been adequately compensated and suffering moreover from chronic political and economic maladjustments, a new phenomenon, Fascism, appeared, born of the delusions, fears, and machismo of an embittered middle class.

In a sense every war is a primary cause of the next one. Victory induces hubris; hubris brings retribution. The German victory in 1870, their seizure of Alsace-Lorraine and the conspicuous display of "blood and iron" by both Bismarck and William II, inspired the alliance that brought about their defeat in 1918. The Allied victory in World War I and their crass treatment of the vanquished threw Germany into the arms of Hitler and led to the disasters of 1939–42 and loss of the British and French empires. The triumph of the Allies in World War II brought the Russians into the heart of Europe, where they remain. As French historian Rene Grousset has written: "There is no victory which, finally, remains unpunished, no conquest which, in the long run, does not conquer the conquerors."

In any case, by the end of 1923, five years after all was at last quiet on the Western Front, most of the tinder to ignite World War II had already been assembled. From 1924 to 1929 a hopeful and deceptive lull occurred; it briefly seemed that the scars of war might be healed and the main contenders reconciled. During this roseate interlude I reveled in the intellectual and fleshly delights of Paris. By the time I left, the smell of smoke was once more in the air.

The first bell that tolled, however, was not on a battlefield but on Wall Street, of all places. Recovery of Europe in the 1920s, less directly but as substantially as in the 1940s, was based on American economic prosperity. When that prosperity dramatically and inexplicably collapsed, the hollow foundations on which European, particularly German, recovery rested crumbled to dust, exposing the bodies, the putrefaction, the corruption of mind and spirit, so thinly buried underneath.

To understand a little of why this happened it is necessary, before leaving 1929, to look briefly at the economic theory and practice of those times. John Maynard Keynes wrote a few years later:

> The ideas of economists and political philosophers, both when they are right and when they are wrong, are more powerful than is commonly understood. Indeed the world is ruled by little else. Practical men, who believe themselves to be quite exempt from any intellectual influences, are usually the slaves of some defunct economist. Madmen in authority, who hear voices in the air, are distilling their frenzy from some academic scribble of a few years back. I am sure that the power of vested interests is vastly exaggerated compared with the gradual encroachment of ideas.*

Being an economist and political philosopher himself, Keynes was somewhat prejudiced, but there was much in what he said.

The political diversity characterizing the organization of nations in 1901—autocracies, constitutional monarchies, republics, oligarchies, military dictatorships—contrasted with a remarkable uniformity of economic theory and practice. The theory was capitalism or, as it was later baptised, "free enterprise." This system had indeed been practiced for centuries by the merchants and bankers of the Middle Ages, but it achieved legitimacy and liberation from strict government control—that is, from the preceding dominant theory, mercantilism—only with the progress of political liberalization in the eighteenth and early nineteenth centuries. By 1901 its triumph was complete almost everywhere.

The bible of capitalism, as it developed through the nineteenth century, was Adam Smith's *Wealth of Nations,* of which the central text was—*let the market alone.* Under the theory and practice he advocated, Smith wrote, "The sovereign is completely discharged from a duty, in the attempting to perform which he must always be exposed to innumerable delusions, and for the proper performance of which no human wisdom or knowledge could ever be sufficient: the

The General Theory of Employment, Interest and Money.

duty of superintending the industry of private people, and of directing it towards the employments most suitable to the interests of society."

The state need not, indeed must not, Smith declared, "superintend the industry of private people," since the benign operation of the "laws of nature," including "human nature," as the eighteenth century conceived them, would automatically ensure that the selfish behavior of "private people," in particular, the entrepreneur or businessman, would best serve the interests of society. "By preferring the support of domestic to that of foreign industry," Smith wrote, "he intends only his own security; and by directing that industry in such a manner as its produce may be of the greatest value, he intends only his own gain, and he is in this, as in many other cases, led by an invisible hand to promote an end which was no part of his intention."

Naturally businessmen were, and ever since have been, delighted with a doctrine that seems to provide them with license to do exactly as they wish with their property or business, and indeed to argue that to do so is in accord with the laws of nature and will best serve the interests of society. Unfortunately, businessmen, then and since, have tended to read and quote Smith selectively. As a matter of fact, in his defense of the free market, he was just as sternly opposed to private monopoly, in recent times so prevalent, as he was to public supervision. "People of the same trade seldom meet together," he wrote, "but the conversation ends in a conspiracy against the public, or in some diversion to raise prices."

In any case the doctrines of Adam Smith and some of his economic disciples, as interpreted by those who found them profitable and convenient, did produce during the subsequent Industrial Revolution the horrors with which history has made us familiar, such as small children working twelve hours a day in factories and coal mines. Ricardo's "iron law of wages" postulated that wages and profits were in inescapable competition, that profits could rise only when wages fell, that indeed, because of the incorrigible habit of the working class of having as many children as possible, wages would always tend to hover just above the level required for bare subsistence.

Industrialists therefore loudly clamored, when in the 1830s the first legislation to remedy inhumane conditions in mines and factories was proposed, that such state interference would violate economic "laws" and would drive them out of business. As Dickens wrote in *Hard Times* of "Coketown," his version of Birmingham:

> Surely there never was such fragile chinaware as that of which the millers of Coketown were made. Handle them never so lightly, and they fell to pieces with such ease that you might have suspected them of having been flawed before. They were ruined when they were required to send laboring children to school; they were ruined when inspectors were appointed to look into their works; they were ruined when such inspectors considered it doubtful whether they were quite justified in chopping people up with their machinery; they were utterly undone when it was hinted that perhaps they need not always make quite so much smoke.

How familiar it all sounds more than a hundred years later.

As the philosopher and scientist Alfred North Whitehead wrote in 1925: "It may be that civilization will never recover from the bad climate which enveloped the introduction of machinery. This climate pervaded the whole commercial system of the progressive northern European races. It was partly the result of the aesthetic errors of Protestantism and partly the result of scientific materialism, and partly the result of the natural greed of mankind, and partly the result of the abstractions of political economy."*

The growth of this lopsided "commercial system" throughout the nineteenth century produced, conjointly, an unprecedented upsurge in the production of material goods, the opening up and rapid exploitation of vast new territories in North America, Africa, and Australia, the enormous fortunes of the American robber barons and their European counterparts, a flood of economic homilies justifying and blessing these developments on allegedly scientific grounds, and a countervailing outpouring of tracts anathemizing and condemning not only the abuses but the entire economic and philosophic rationale of the new gospel. The latter ranged from the ultrarevolutionary doctrine of Karl Marx's *Communist Manifesto* and *Capital,* through the reformist social democracy that emerged in Britain and Germany, to the pungent ironies of the American economist Thorstein Veblen in his *Theory of the Leisure Class* (1899) and *Theory of Business Enterprise* (1904).

*Science and the Modern World.

A revulsion against laissez-faire economics, its abuses, and its irregularities had, therefore, before 1914 begun to shift the focus of political action in the Western democracies from complacent acceptance of the status quo to a popular assault on that generation of capitalists whom Theodore Roosevelt called "malefactors of great wealth."

In terms of production capitalism had been and continued to be enormously successful. Its munificence was bestowed, however, even in the democracies, on only a small fraction of the population. The "trickle down" theory, which postulated that the benefits accruing to the rich would by the automatic operation of the system seep down to the poor, proved a feeble instrument for the more general distribution of the much larger production capitalism had brought about. A few of the most successful capitalists, such as Carnegie and Rockefeller, began in their later years to dispense some of their great wealth in innovative philanthropies, but most of them preferred the conspicuous consumption that lined Fifth Avenue with imitations of French chateaux and Italian palazzi. By the beginning of the new century political democracy and economic oligarchy were coming to seem more and more inconsistent and incompatible.

So-called utopian socialism had been advanced as a remedy in the early nineteenth century by such men as Owen, Saint-Simon, and Fourier. Their schemes attracted zealous little groups of acolytes but had no impact on the system. Marx sounded the call for social revolution and founded a political movement that generated socialist or social democratic parties in most European countries, including a First and Second Socialist International. These frightened the bourgeoisie half out of their wits but by the end of the century had not won power anywhere, or even approached doing so. More successful was the trade union movement which also proliferated, though with painful slowness, and in Britain formed the underpinning of its own political party.

Already in the 1880s Bismarck, of all people, for political reasons of his own, had introduced national health insurance and old-age pensions in Germany. When the Liberals returned to power in England in 1906, they launched a most ambitious program of social reform to mitigate the rigors and gross disparities that laissez-faire had generated: free school meals and medical services, trade boards to fix minimum wages in industries where unions were weak, a supertax on high incomes and capital gains tax on land sales, unemployment and health insurance. All this, mild and natural as it may seem seventy years later, provoked such intense conservative indignation that the hitherto comatose House of Lords refused to approve the "Lloyd George budget," and two elections were required to return it to "innocuous desuetude."

Similar measures of reform were presented to the French parliament by Clemenceau and others but were for the most part defeated by an odd combination: the bloc of conservatives representing the middle class and peasants, and the refusal of the socialists to participate in "bourgeois" governments because of the all-or-nothing dictates of the Second International. French politics, moreover, had during this period been skewed by a recrudescence of chauvinism, envenomed by the Dreyfus Affair and the series of increasingly sharp clashes with Germany that culminated in World War I. The French have for two centuries had difficulty reconciling the Rights of Man with *la patrie* and *la gloire;* usually the latter have prevailed.

In the United States the setback the Populist movement encountered with the defeat of Bryan in 1896 was reversed by the fortuitous coming to the Presidency of Theodore Roosevelt in 1901. All the pressures for reform accumulating since the Civil War exploded during the next fifteen years. Roosevelt, declaiming from his "bully pulpit," the White House, breathed new life into the moribund Sherman Anti-Trust Act, forced arbitration of a great coal strike, subjected railroad rates to Interstate Commerce Commission control, and pushed through a Pure Food and Drug Act. How much farther he might have gone had he been elected in 1912 is suggested by his famous speech at Osawatomie, Kansas, two years before.

In words that would sound inflammatory to conservatives if uttered by a prominent political leader even today, Roosevelt said: "The essence of any struggle for healthy liberty has always been, and must always be, to take from some one man or class of men the right to enjoy power, or wealth, or position, or immunity, which has not been earned by his or their fellows. . . . At many stages in the advance of humanity, the conflict between the men who possess more than they have earned and the men who have earned more than they possess is the central condition of progress." He also said in the same speech:

"We keep countless men from being good citizens by the conditions of life with which we surround them."

Roosevelt was defeated in 1912 by the split in the Republican party, but his successful rival, Woodrow Wilson, rode in on the crest of the same progressive wave and sought many of the same reforms. In his first inaugural address in 1913 he said: "There has been something crude and heartless and unfeeling in our haste to succeed and be great. Our thought has been 'Let every man look out for himself, let every generation look out for itself,' while we reared giant machinery which made it impossible that any but those who stood at the levers of control should have a chance to look out for themselves." He too secured the passage of substantial measures of reform—the Federal Reserve Act, the Clayton Anti-trust Act which also strengthened trade unions, lower tariffs, cheap credit for farmers, an eight-hour day for railroad workers, an anti–child labor law, a workmen's compensation act, federal aid to education.

This moderate and democratic reform of the economic system was halted in its tracks, practically snuffed out, by the outbreak of World War I. Wilson foresaw what would happen. In a letter to his Secretary of the Navy, Josephus Daniels, early in 1917 he wrote:

> There are two reasons why I am determined to keep out of war if possible. The first is that I cannot bring myself to send into the terrible struggle the sons of anxious mothers, many of whom would never return home. The second is that if we enter this war, the great interests which control steel, oil, shipping, munitions factories and mines will of necessity become dominant factors, and when the war is over our government will be in their hands. We have been trying, and succeeding to a large extent, to unhorse government by privilege. If we go into the war all we have gained will be lost and neither you nor I will live long enough to see our country wrested from the control of monopoly.

Wilson was right about himself, but Daniels did indeed live long enough to be Franklin Roosevelt's ambassador to Mexico (where I met him in 1936) and to witness another great wave of democratic reform.

In the 1920s, however, American Republicans, British Conservatives, and most other political parties in power pursued economic policies of extreme laissez-faire orthodoxy, returning jubilantly and self-righteously to "normalcy" and the gold standard, sternly suppressing any manifestations of that loathsome heresy "Bolshevism," and allowing Adam Smith's "invisible hand" to work its wonders unvexed and unguided. The experience of the decade demonstrated as conclusively as any macroeconomic exercise ever could that however appropriate laissez-faire may have been to the end of the eighteenth century, it was an unworkable anachronism in the very different economic environment of the early twentieth. Everybody's "fast buck" turned out to be nobody's safe investment. The Wall Street crash of October 1929 reverberated like a crack of doom around the globe. Within less than two years the world economy was prostrate, and breadlines stretched like mortified wounds across the face of every great city.

Before turning to the calamitous 1930s and the origins of World War II, we must look briefly at that revolutionary politico-economic phenomenon which, to the astonishment of all and the outrage of most, had emerged so unexpectedly from the anarchy of Petrograd in November 1917. Even more unexpectedly this movement had survived civil war, foreign invasion, famine, and economic breakdown to constitute itself into a self-proclaimed and "scientifically" validated alternative to the democracy of Thomas Jefferson and the economics of Adam Smith. Only when the Bolshevik armies swept to the Vistula in 1920 and unlikely Communist juntas briefly seized power in Budapest and Munich did the world begin dimly to perceive that the first universal ideological struggle since the Treaty of Westphalia ended the Wars of Religion might be about to break out.

In January 1917 Vladimir Ilich Lenin was in lonely exile in Switzerland, impotent, frustrated, almost unknown, except to his fellow revolutionaries and to the police. By the end of the year he was the government of Russia. Historians have had some difficulty in explaining how a despised little sect of radical revolutionaries, their leader in exile for ten years, were able in so short a time to seize and conquer an empire. There were essentially three factors that account for their success.

Hannah Arendt has written in *On Revolution:* "The outbreak of most revolutions has surprised the revolutionist groups and parties no less than all others, and there exists hardly a revolution whose outbreak could be blamed on their activities. It was usually the other way around; revolution broke out and liberated, as it were, the professional revolutionaries from wherever they happened to be—from jail, or from the coffee house, or from the library." This was certainly true of Lenin and his Bolsheviks. However, Arendt adds in another place: "The revolutionaries are those who know when power is lying in the street and when they can pick it up. Armed uprising by itself has never yet led to a revolution."

In 1917 power was lying in the street in Saint Petersburg, just as it had been in Paris in August 1792. No one was in control, no one had sensed the mood of the people, and hence no one was able to move or mobilize them. Lenin and the Bolsheviks did. Their slogans— "Peace," which almost everyone wanted; "Land to the peasants," which satisfied the ancient demand of the vast majority of the population; "All power to the Soviets," which both offered active participation to the politically energetic among workers and soldiers and consolidated control by the Communists who dominated the Soviets— suited that mood exactly.

The second factor was the genius of Lenin, his instant perceptions of what was required to capture the popular mood, the iron discipline he had imposed on his own party during the previous decade, and the flexibility and realism he displayed under pressure, including his later acceptance of flagrantly unfavorable peace terms with Germany in 1918 and his switch to a semicapitalist New Economic Policy immediately after the civil war. His strategy was based on two components: an inspirational dogma and total pragmatism in its application.

A third factor was of course the fatuousness and ineptitude of the "White" opponents, who sought to restore the old régime very much as it had been. The Russian people were given no choice between these extremes. A contributing element was the ineffective but provocative intervention of the Western powers, including the United States, which made it possible for Lenin to represent the civil struggle as a national patriotic war, as Stalin did resistance to the Germans twenty years later. If there were "laws of history," which there are not, one of them would be: Unless foreign intervention in a civil war is sufficiently massive to be decisive (as was German-Italian intervention in the Spanish civil war), it works to the disadvantage of the faction on whose behalf it occurs.

A claim has been made, in Curzio Malaparte's *Technique of the Coup d'État,* that the mastery of this "technique" by the Bolsheviks, particularly by Trotsky—their sudden seizures of the nerve centers of administration and propaganda in Petrograd in the critical days of November 1917—was a major reason for their success. It was a factor but probably a secondary one. Had there been either an effective government or other parties with internal organization and discipline comparable to the Bolsheviks, their coup would not have succeeded.

In any case, despite war on three or four fronts, economic breakdown, and famine, Lenin, aided by the military genius of Trotsky and the police apparatus of Dzerzhinsky, was able before his death in January 1924 to consolidate the power of the Bolsheviks and to leave his successors in such uncontested command of the new Soviet empire that they could soon begin indulging their inclination not only for iron discipline and dictatorship but for their mirror images, factionalism and fratricide, both outside and inside the Party. Of course these corrupting tendencies had been latent in Marxism from the beginning, and particularly in its Russian manifestations.

As early as 1846 Pierre-Joseph Proudhon, the French libertarian socialist or anarchist (whichever one chooses to call him), fell into heated argument with Marx over the latter's authoritarian tendencies. In that year he wrote to Marx:

> Let us seek together, if you wish, the laws of society, the manner in which these laws are carried out, . . . but, for God's sake, after having demolished all a priori dogmatisms, let's not think in our turn of indoctrinating the people; let's not fall into the contradiction of your compatriot Martin Luther who, after having overthrown Catholic theology, began at once, assisted by excommunications and anathemas, to found a Protestant theology. . . . Let us set the example of a wise and far-sighted tolerance; but, because we are at the head of the movement, let's not make ourselves leaders of a new intolerance, let's not pose as apostles of a new religion. . . . Accept all protests, condemn all exclusions. . . . On this condition, I'll enter with pleasure into your association; otherwise, no!

In a similar vein, but with a specific national application, Alexander Herzen, one of the forefathers of Russian socialism, wrote in 1851: "I believe there is some justification for the fear of Communism which the Russian government begins to feel; Communism is the Russian autocracy turned upside down."

Unfortunately but not surprisingly, the authoritarian tradition established by Marx himself was carried on by Lenin and firmly entrenched in the Russian Social Democratic party in the early years of this century. It is indeed extraordinary that the history of Russia for at least eighty years thereafter, perhaps much longer, and to a lesser extent the history of the rest of the world, has been so profoundly affected by the outcome of seemingly arcane disputes among a handful of Russian exiles. Yet that is undoubtedly the case.

Lenin insisted at that time that the Communist party, as the "vanguard of the proletariat," must exercise the coming "dictatorship" on the latter's behalf, and that the vanguard leadership must be composed of "professional revolutionists" under the tightest discipline, totally obedient to orders from the top. At the Second Party Congress in London in 1903 he prevailed, after a hard battle, over his more democratically inclined opponents, paving the way for the split of the party a few years later into Bolsheviks (majority) and Mensheviks (minority)—and eventually for the dictatorship of Stalin. As Trotsky, who opposed Lenin at that congress, wrote after its close in a remarkably prescient forecast: "Lenin's methods lead to this: the party organization at first substitutes itself for the party as a whole; then the Central Committee substitutes itself for the organization; and finally a single 'dictator' substitutes himself for the Central Committee."

Only six weeks after the November 1917 revolution Maxim Gorki's newspaper *Novaya Zhizn* wrote: "Power has passed to the Soviets only on paper, in fiction, not in reality. . . . Soviet republic? Empty words. In reality it is an oligarchic republic, a republic of a few People's Commissars." Already in December the Cheka or secret police was established under Dzerzhinsky. Elections to a Constituent Assembly held in November had produced an absolute majority for the Right Socialist Revolutionaries and only 25 percent for the Bolsheviks; therefore they dissolved the assembly the day after it convened in January. Lenin was soon demonstrating, as he had no doubt clearly foreseen, that when a small minority seizes power, even in the name of the majority, it can hold it only by very much the same methods used by its deposed predecessors.

Bertrand Russell visited the Soviet Union in May 1920. Ever since the revolution he had been a supporter of the new experiment. Just before the visit he wrote an article for the New York *Liberator* so enthusiastic that it was reprinted under the headline "Bertrand Russell Goes Bolshevik." Immediately after leaving the Soviet Union he wrote his friend Ottoline Morrell from Stockholm:

> Bolshevism is a close tyrannical bureaucracy, with a spy system more elaborate and terrible than the Tsar's, and an aristocracy as insolent and unfeeling. . . . No vestige of liberty remains, in thought or speech or action. I was stifled and oppressed by the weight of the machine as by a cope of lead. Yet I think it the right Government for Russia at this moment. If you ask yourself how Dostoevsky's characters should be governed, you will understand. Yet it is terrible.*

Russell's impressions of Lenin recorded in his journal during the same visit are also interesting:

> He is friendly and apparently simple—entirely without a trace of hauteur, a great contrast to Trotsky. Nothing in his manner or bearing suggests the man who has power. He looks at his visitor very close, and screws up one eye. He laughs a great deal; at first his laugh seems merely friendly and jolly, but gradually one finds it grim. He is dictatorial, calm, incapable of fear, devoid of self-seeking, an embodied theory. The materialist conception of history is his life-blood. . . . I think if I had met him without knowing who he was I should not have guessed that he was a great man but should have thought him an opiniated professor. His strength comes, I imagine, from his honesty, courage and unwavering faith—religious faith in Marxian orthodoxy, which takes the place of the Christian martyr's hopes of Paradise, except that it is less egotistical.

If we pause for a moment to assess the achievements of Lenin in his brief six years of power, so astonishing and so durable on the one hand, yet so flawed and corrupting on the other, it would be well to remind ourselves—and the Soviets—of Marx's astute judgment in *The 18th Brumaire of Louis Napoleon.* "Men make their own history," Marx wrote, "but they do not make it just as they please; they do not make it under circumstances chosen by themselves, but under circumstances directly encountered, given and transmitted from the past. The tradition of all the dead generations weighs like a nightmare on the brain of the living."

*Quoted in *The Life of Bertrand Russell* by Ronald W. Clark.

The Bolsheviks and Lenin inherited two traditions: first, that of Mother Russia, enslaved and retarded since the long Mongol domination, having known little else throughout its history but tyranny, orthodoxy, and intellectual darkness; second, the Bolshevik tradition itself, hammered out by Lenin in the decades before the seizure of power—fanatical, ruthless, disciplined, intolerant of any dissent inside or outside the Party, acting in the name of the proletariat but, like a religious hierarchy, reserving for a small group, even a single man, the sole authority to define and prosecute the "true interests" of the Russian proletariat and of their counterparts throughout the world.

Lenin, one of the towering figures of our century, must be ultimately judged not only by the miracles he accomplished against enormous odds during his brief tenure of power but by the inheritance he left to his successors—a bequest that both validated and facilitated the distortions of ideology and the crimes of execution that they inflicted on the Russian people and the international Communist movement.

To conclude this glance at the salad days of the Soviet Union, I shall quote a few passages from the diary I kept during the three-week visit I paid there with a fellow student in September–October 1929.

We sailed into the harbor of Leningrad on a superb autumn afternoon, all the gilded domes and palaces of Peter's city shining in the sunlight. When we came ashore, however, we saw that the palaces and domes had not been painted in twelve years, were shabby, broken-windowed and desolate. As the crowds of people moved along the Nevsky Prospekt or on the graceful bridges across the canals, clothed warmly but down at heels, silent, unsmiling, it seemed like a city under a spell, condemned to penance for some unforgivable sin.

In the Winter Palace was the tiny room Lenin had occupied during the October days, a small hard bed, a table, a chair. Oddly enough there was also preserved the apartment occupied a century earlier by Nicholas I, almost equally small and simple, crammed with early Victorian bric-a-brac, stiff pictures and prints, mostly military. On a bed, narrow as Lenin's, lay his overcoat and beside a pair of slippers crumbling into dust.

Moscow presented a rather different aspect than Leningrad, less grand and monumental except of course for the Kremlin, yet more lively, vigorous and contemporary. The old buildings were just as shabby and rundown but new ones in ultra-modern style were going up in considerable numbers and the throngs of people, though hardly cheerful in the darkening autumn days, were more animated and purposeful. One got the impression of a city emerging from a chrysalis into a new, unknown but exhilarating life.

The First Five-Year Plan was then only a year old. "Scattered about the streets of the city were huge maps of the Soviet Union with the main centers of planned construction etched out in colored lights. It is new and startling enough so that around each map stands a crowd wide-eyed and open-mouthed."

We saw two memorable plays: Chekhov's *Cherry Orchard* at the Moscow Art Theater, his widow Madam Knipper-Chekhova playing the leading role so superbly that our ignorance of Russian hardly mattered; at the ultramodern Meyerhold Theater a civil war piece called *Two Commanders,* Meyerhold's wife playing the only feminine role and he himself, tall, angular, ungainly, delivering a graceful little tribute to the actors at the end. (Within a few years both of them were to be purged and killed by Stalin.)

Two lovely young ladies from Voks, the tourist organization of the time, escorted us one evening to what they described as a literary and artistic club but which had some of the characteristics of a speakeasy and some of a nightclub. The establishment, a former palace no doubt, was furnished with the most magnificent Empire pieces, had an elaborate billiard room and a library offering magazines from many parts of the capitalist world. The patrons were a voluble and merry lot. We drank vodka, ate superb food, danced with our charming hostesses, and at last were sent properly home alone in a taxi. (We had seen, I suppose, the first stirrings of the "new class.")

This was exceptional. Most people lived drearily on the margins of existence, even though their spirits seemed remarkably high. An American Jew of Russian origin revisiting his native land (thanks to a successful flyer on Wall Street) told us of a little girl saying to her bourgeois grandmother: "I am so glad you are poor now, grandmamma. I don't have to be ashamed of you anymore." The grandmother burst into tears.

I summed up in my diary my impressions at that point: "It appears to me that the success of the present system in Russia depends entirely on whether the people as a whole can maintain that exaltation of spirit which now upholds them until the crucial years have passed. Russia today is like a poor immigrant arriving in America, economizing and denying himself everything for years in order that his children and grandchildren might have an education and the good things of life. Have the Russians to a sufficient extent this love of the unborn?"

Wishing to explore further the vastness of Russia, we took a train for the Caucusus, traveling three days and three nights over a boundless plain, waking each morning to the same interminable, monotonous landscape that had encompassed us at nightfall. It was punctuated only by rare identical villages of thatch-roofed huts, by gleaners bending in the stubbled October fields, by forests of birch and poplar bedecked in gold and russet leaves.

Our compartment was populated by a most jovial and hospitable congerie, laden with hampers of food and drink that they lavishly shared. I recall particularly an attractive young actress from the Moscow Art Theater who laid bare to us, five minutes after we met, the abysmal depths of her unhappiness—with dancing eyes and in tones of the most ebullient cheerfulness. As soon as the news percolated through the train that foreigners were aboard, a rare occurrence in 1929, our compartment became the scene of an almost uninterrupted jamboree, in which we were asked in a hodgepodge of French, German, and Russian every conceivable question about America and in return were regaled with snatches of the lives, hopes, dogmas, and dreams of our interlocutors.

Whenever we came to a station, passengers would tumble onto the platform to fill their teakettles with hot water and to buy fresh-cooked chickens, ducks, eggs, bread, and luscious milk, fruit, and nuts from the red or blue-skirted peasant women. (This was before collectivization had dried up private production and the New Economic Policy still flourished on the farms.)

A conversation with three Red Army officers—young, healthy, jovial—was limited to graphic gestures and a little lingua franca. Amerikanski, we said. Ah! Smiles and interest. Russia *chorosho* (good)? Da, da, *chorosho. Fascisti, Angliski, Franzuski, Amerikanski* would like to shoot Russian leaders, Stalin bing-bing. Stalin *chorosho?* we ask naïvely. *Ah, da! Chorosho!!!* Lenin and Stalin, hands together and shake. One officer is Georgian and knew Stalin, handclasp again, when both were small boys, hand two feet above floor and many smiles. GPU [predecessor of KGB] will protect Stalin against fascists. Are we communists or capitalists? We balance our hands equivocally. There is a chorus: Menshevik, Social Democrat, opportunist. All *schlecht* (bad), much head shaking. One points to the pin with a red star in my companion's lapel, given him by our lovely hostesses in Moscow, and then to his forehead—communism must be in the head as well as on coat. Tovarich, we say. They laugh and nod. Commander (which means officer), one says, czar, he sticks out chest, figuratively pins on medals, twirls large imaginary mustaches and looks arrogant; then, commander, soldat, USSR, tovarichi, good friends. We all laugh and shake hands.

We stopped off at Kislovodsk, a nineteenth-century spa still preserving its leisured, debilitated air, crossed the Caucusus on the fantastic Georgian Military Highway, visited the bazaars of Tbilisi (which I was next to see in 1974), boarded a ship at Batum that cruised along the Black Sea coast—Sukhum, Sochi, Feodosiya, Yalta, Sevastopol—disembarked at Odessa and went on to Kiev.

When we board a last train to the Polish border, we share a compartment with a German engineer who has been installing machinery in Russia for two years and is now going home. Both peasants and workers are badly off, he informs us; a revolt and a bourgeois republic are soon to be expected. I shall never forget the relief and jubilation in his voice as, after we cross in darkness the noman's land between two worlds and tall uniformed figures appear dimly outside the window, he says: *Jetzt komm Polen in Zug* ("Now Poles are coming on board").

"My own feelings as I leave," I wrote, "are mixed and confused. I am half ashamed that, after only three weeks, I feel almost the same relief, the same sense of escape, the German engineer does. Certainly the idealism, the dedication, the determination to build a better world and conviction it will be done, that is communicated by every Russian one meets, except those excluded from the new society by past associations, is tremendously inspiring. Though having on this first visit no means of comparison with the past, it seems to me probable that, however the small upper and middle classes may have suffered, the mass of the people are better off, certainly psychologically and very probably materially, than they were before 1917. Still it is all so drab, dilapidated and woebegone. Who would want to live there?"

So the curtain fell on the 1920s. Two weeks later, on a train climbing through the mountains of Bulgaria, I read in a Berlin newspaper of the Wall Street crash.

≫ 4 ≪

Causes of World War II
1930–1941

Fascism was a consequence of World War I and a cause of World War II, but it was and is much more than that. It is as authentically revolutionary as nationalism or communism, elements of both of which it appropriates and adulterates. It is by no means obsolete. Indeed, it may well prove in the long run to be a revolutionary form to which industrialized societies are much more susceptible than communism.

The term "fascism" is often misapplied. It is not simply any government or movement of the Right, even any extreme or dictatorial movement. On the contrary, it is a very specific contemporary political phenomenon. Fascism is an organized and orchestrated revolt of the middle class against the frustration of its expectations. These expectations are likely to be both economic and national. The revolt will most often be provoked not where expectations have never been met but where they have been met and then thwarted. That was what occurred in Italy in the four years after World War I when economic prosperity, public order, and national ambitions were all disrupted. That was what happened in Germany when, to the national humiliation and inflationary assault on the middle class that followed the war was added the catastrophe of the Great Depression.

Fascism may prove to be a revolutionary phenomenon to which the twenty-first century, even the end of the twentieth, is prone, for two related reasons. First, the great majority of the populations of the industrialized countries, including most of their workers, now considers itself middle class and has become accustomed to a steadily rising middle-class standard of living. Second, a number of economic and political trends already visible suggest that in many places for many reasons, economic systems and governments may not be able to sustain that standard of living at a rising level or even at its present level. If that should prove to be true over an extended period, angry middle classes in some places may again turn from democracy to fascism. Of course in that eventuality it would be a fascism ostensibly unlike that of Germany and Italy between the wars, a fascism with a new and captivating face congenial to its contemporaries. It would probably be racist in one way or another but not necessarily anti-Semitic. Even the possiblity of such a resurrection, however, lends particular interest to the phenomenon of fascism as it has shown itself in the past.

I had personally only brief encounters with it. Visits to Italy gave me the impression that Mussolini's fascism was more a theatrical than a political event. I did not take it very seriously because, it seemed to me, most Italians did not take it very seriously. They were too civilized, too cynical, and too amiable.

On the other hand, when I spent a few weeks in Germany in 1933, Nazism struck me at once as very serious indeed. It seemed even grimmer than Russian Communism because more proficient and more cold-hearted. Heavy-jowled, pot-bellied Brown Shirts and black-jacketed, glassy-eyed SS men roamed every street, clicking heels and exchanging Nazi salutes and "Heil Hitlers." When I heard Goebbels haranguing an enormous throng at the Sportpalast, working himself into a pretended and then into a real frenzy, the atmosphere was certainly theatrical but suggesting theatrics gone mad, cunningly manipulated but ultimately uncontrollable. I photographed Hitler riding slowly through his Chancellory gates, almost unattended. He seemed to be Fallada's "Little Man" ensconced incongruously in a too large official vehicle. But the background music one faintly heard everywhere was both hysterical and sinister, Wagner and the Horst Wessel Lied—"Heute gehört uns Deutschland, morgen die ganze Welt." When I passed through Berlin in 1934 the "Night of the Long Knives" had just taken place—the simultaneous execution of the head of the Brown Shirts, a former head of the Nazi party organization, a former chancellor, and many others. A silence enveloped the city, which was waiting with baited breath for the next blow to fall.

The most promising experiment in democracy in interwar Europe had seemed for a time to be in Germany. It is true that the Weimar Republic was so abused in infancy, both by the Allies and its own nationalists, that by 1925 it had lost the allegiance of half the Germans. Nevertheless, the astonishing outburst of intellectual and artistic activity it generated in its short lifetime testifies both to the persistence of creativity in the German spirit and to the energies and inspirations a democratic revolution can release. Where else in modern times has such a confluence of genius and talent occurred in a mere fourteen years? Gropius and the Bauhaus, which invented much of modern architecture and design; the new theater of Piscator, Reinhardt, Brecht, Zuckmayer, and Kurt Weill; expressionism in art and film, Kandinsky, Kokoschka, Käthe Kollwitz, George Grosz, *The Cabinet of Dr. Caligari,* Fritz Lang, Murnau, Dupont; that scintillating constellation of writers, Thomas and Heinrich Mann, Stefan and Arnold Zweig, Stefan George, and Hermann Hesse.

Yet, while all this intellectual ferment bubbled and sparkled on the surface of society, it lent no strength or legitimacy to the misbegotten republic. At the very outset Weimar lost much of the younger generation. Count Harry Kessler records in his diary, that most intimate and perceptive of interwar albums, a conversation with a young German leftist on February 9, 1919, only three months after the fall of the Kaiser: "The young intellectuals are almost without exception against the Government. It is impossible to exaggerate their bitterness. They say that this Government is worse than the Imperial one, which at least tried to get something done. The present one does nothing and ducks every responsibility. Everything continues on the old pattern. Probably the nation's entire structure will have to be recast. . . . Many of these people say that Germany will have to be defeated a second time before any good will come of it."

A young nationalist might have said much the same thing. The republic went too far to satisfy the old and not far enough to satisfy the young of either Left or Right. The inflation, provoked by the policies of the Allies, radicalized much of the middle class. As the novelist Heinrich Mann wrote of them at the time: "They will become the most dangerous enemies of the Republic, incomparably more dangerous than discharged officers." The onset of the Great Depression, after only five years of artificial prosperity based on foreign loans, threw a substantial proportion of the working class out of work and drove many of them, haphazardly, into the Communist and the Nazi movements. Neither the Socialists nor the Catholic Center, the two main governing parties from 1919 to 1932, could imagine any way of combating hard times except by austerity and deflation, which made everything worse.

In the election of September 1930 the Nazis increased the number of their seats in the Reichstag almost tenfold, from 12 to 107. When in July 1932 President Hindenburg threw out Brüning, the last chancellor representing a traditional party, and installed the political dilettante Von Papen, the professor with whom I was at the time studying German exclaimed: *"Der Alte ist verrückt"* (The old man is mad). He was not so much mad as senile and, more important, manipulated by his foolish entourage and those equally foolish industrialists who imagined Hitler would save them from communism.

Equally at fault, however, were the leaders of the republic who in those critical years had no answer to the question posed in Hans Fallada's best-selling novel, *Kleiner Mann, Was Nun?* (Little Man, What Now?). Indeed it might be said that the failure of leaders to provide a sufficient, even a tolerable answer to this question has provoked most twentieth-century revolutions. In a democracy the "little man" at last has a voice, and, if he is not heeded, is likely to lose patience and self-control.

After the Nazi electoral victory in September 1930, Kessler wrote in his diary: "National Socialism is a delirium of the German lower middle class. The poison of its disease may however bring down ruin on Germany and Europe for decades ahead."

Nazism, despite its rhetoric and pretensions, had no real philosophy or doctrine. Joachim Fest, in his *Face of the Third Reich,* remarks: "National Socialism was propaganda masquerading as ideology, . . . and drew its postulate from the moods and impulses of the masses, in the sensing of which it was abnormally gifted. In view of its capacity for 'mediumistic' communication with the mind of the masses, it seemed not to require any real idea, such as had served to gather and hold together every other mass movement in history."*

German's respect for the military—not peculiar to them alone but

*(Pantheon Books, 1970).

stamped especially heavily on their psyche by their history and education, by Frederick the Great, Bismarck, and generations of despotic,
"patriotic" fathers and schoolteachers—made them prone both to
regimentation and systematic use of force. The uniform, even a brown
or black shirt, tended to legitimize whatever its wearer did. Every
soldier was presumed to partake of the virtues of Siegfried.

Hitler's only real philosophy was his doctrine of the "master race,"
in which he, an undistinguished brunet of Alpine stock, associated
himself with the blond Vikings or primeval Germans who appeared
in Wagner's *Ring*. Hermann Rausching in *Hitler Speaks* quotes him
as saying: "The selection of the new Führer class is what my struggle
for power means. Whoever proclaims his allegiance to me is, by this
very proclamation and by the manner in which it is made, one of the
chosen. This is the great significance of our long, dogged struggle for
power, that in it will be born a new master class, chosen to guide the
fortunes not only of the German people but of the world."

This pronouncement reflects both Hitler's intellectual confusion
and political astuteness, at least as long as he was addressing only
Germans. Apparently the only prerequisite to becoming one of the
"master class" was to proclaim one's allegiance to Hitler. On the other
hand, since only Germans and a few honorary Nordics could do so,
Nazism lost its appeal, indeed became almost an automatic instrument of discrimination and oppression, as soon as it moved across
national boundaries. Napoleon profited in his conquests from the
ideals and visions of the French Revolution, accessible to all people.
Hitler was saddled with the fatal burdens of his own racism. When
Ukrainian peasants came out to greet the Nazis as liberators, they
were bundled into freight cars and shipped off to slave labor.

Actually the representatives of the "master class" grouped around
Hitler, his principal acolytes and lieutenants, were for the most part
a sorry lot. Goebbels himself, near the end of his life, described them
as "this gang of spiteful children." "At best these are average men,"
he said. "Not one of them has the qualities of a mediocre politician,
to say nothing of the calibre of a statesman. They have all remained
the beer-cellar rowdies they always were." Goebbels himself was
probably the smartest of the lot; he and Albert Speer kept the Third
Reich alive during its last two years.

The "beer-cellar rowdies" who ran the party, the police, and the concentration camps seem like monsters out of mythology but were in fact ordinary men. Their sort exists in every society. "One of the lessons of Nazism, and indeed of the other totalitarianisms," says Robert Conquest, who has studied them in depth, "is that a reserve of people suited to the most abhorrent and horrible types of state are in existence in potential, and usable when the time comes." This reserve in Germany, moreover, comprised not only brutal thugs but utterly commonplace paterfamilias, some of whom presided with the utmost conscientiousness over the ovens at Auschwitz and Treblinka.

The quality of Hitler's entourage, and his intolerance of dissent or doubt that might reflect some shards or slivers of the real world, was one of the main causes of his downfall. After Munich in 1938 he was in peaceful command of Europe; after the fall of France in 1940 he was in military command of Europe; at either time, if he had stopped, the Third Reich might have lasted, not for a thousand, but perhaps for a hundred years. He could not stop. He had a dream; he lived in it and acted it out.

In *Inside the Third Reich* Albert Speer wrote:

> In normal circumstances people who turn their backs on reality are soon set straight by the mocking and criticism of those around them, which makes them aware they have lost credibility. In the Third Reich there were no such correctives, expecially for those who belonged to the upper stratum. On the contrary, every self-deception was multiplied as in a hall of distorting mirrors, becoming a repeatedly confirmed picture of a fantastical dream world which no longer bore any relationship to the grim outside world.

Hitler was named chancellor by Hindenburg in January 1933. Even in the elections he held a few weeks later, however, he did not win a popular majority. He consolidated his power by discrete steps. Pastor Martin Niemöller, a hero of World War I and victim of the Nazis, later described the process. "In Germany they came first for the Communists, and I didn't speak up because I wasn't a Communist. Then they came for the Jews, and I didn't speak up because I wasn't a Jew. Then they came for the trade unionists. Then they came for the Catholics, and I didn't speak up because I was a Protestant. Then they came for me—but by that time no one was left to speak up."

Hitler's instruments were terror and propaganda at home and audacity abroad. In 1935 he proclaimed German rearmament; in 1936 his armies reoccupied the Rhineland; in 1937 he intervened overtly in the Spanish civil war; in 1938 he seized Austria and, after intimidating Britain and France at Munich, occupied the Sudetenland; in 1939 he appropriated Bohemia and Memel, astonished the world with his pact with the Bolsheviks, and began World War II with the invasion of Poland.

In *Mein Kampf,* written in prison in 1924, Hitler frankly exposed his intention to unite all the Germans, to dominate and absorb most of Central Europe and the Ukraine, to crush France, and to strike a bargain with the British—whom he like Kaiser Wilhelm admired and envied—to divide the world between them. How could the British and French, who in 1933 were far stronger than he was, have allowed him to rearm, face them down, and subjugate Central Europe under their noses?

Few non-Germans read *Mein Kampf* and even fewer took it seriously. Most West Europeans, including most of their political leaders, were suffering at this time from two complexes, both of which were legitimate but became anachronistic after Hitler's advent to power.

The first was a guilt complex arising from a belated realization that the Versailles settlement was unfair to Germany in many respects, that the war-guilt clause was unjustified, that the right of self-determination, the guiding political principle of Versailles, had not been granted to the millions of Germans outside Germany, that the burden of reparations had been outrageously and unrealistically oppressive, and that Germany had not yet been accorded the full equality with other states that her population, resources, and stature deserved.

Western leaders were therefore inhibited in their own minds and by their public opinion from vigorously opposing German rearmament, from preventing the entry of German troops into the Rhineland, which after all was an integral part of Germany, and from objecting in principle to the incorporation into Germany of Austrians and Sudetenlanders, who in language and culture seemed to be "Germans," just as much as the inhabitants of Alsace-Lorraine were French or of the Corridor Polish.

The second Western complex at this time was antimilitarism. The carnage of World War I, which had come to be understood as irrational, unnecessary, and as ruinous to victors as to vanquished; the flood of books, plays, and movies depicting its horrors and futility; the incontrovertible conclusion that war did not bring a brave new world but one far less comfortable and secure; all these factors produced a public mood in the West, particularly France and Britain, so hostile to war, to military preparedness, or to any other action seen as conducive to militarism, that for some years no political leader, with a few rare exceptions like Churchill, dared contest it.

At Oxford in the 1930s young men took an oath *not* to defend king and country. When Chamberlain and Daladier returned from Munich in 1938, bringing what the former called "peace in our time," they were greeted by crowds as jubilant as those that sent the armies off to war in 1914. Alastair Horne in his account of the first year of World War II, *To Lose a Battle,* documents the degree to which the French in 1940 were still spiritually exhausted from the last war, their morale so brittle it broke at the first onslaught.

In the United States, when Roosevelt denounced the aggressors in his "quarantine" speech in 1937, public reaction was so hostile that he had to back away completely from any measures, pitifully weak in any case, to curb these aggressors. America, still paralyzed internationally by its revulsion against World War I, was able to do even less to avert another world war than the British had been in 1914. Even after war broke out and France fell, Roosevelt was obliged to camouflage the aid to Britain that may have been essential to its survival.

Another grave disability of the democracies was their inability to cope with the Depression, particularly to provide, other than with a pitiful "dole," for the millions of unemployed it generated. Hitler in very short order put everyone to work, paying little attention to the academic credentials of the means by which he did so. The democratic governments, for the most part, persisted with pathetic faith in economic orthodoxy, austerity, balanced budgets, lowered wages, at a time when bold measures of expansion and encouragement were desperately needed. Keynes was not a prophet in his own country. The situation went from bad to worse. No one could understand it. In 1931 Austrian and German banks began to collapse. In Britain a "National Government" was hastily formed to turn the screws even tighter. To its horror it was forced off the gold standard, and to its astonishment England was immediately the better for it. But since everyone was going off gold, the improvement did not last.

On the Continent political systems also began to disintegrate. A single year, 1934, witnessed the storming of the French Assembly by a rightist mob, the bombardment of the Socialist apartment houses in Vienna by the conservative Heimwehr, the murder of the Austrian chancellor by the Nazis, and the assassination of the king of Yugoslavia and the French foreign minister by a Croatian "patriot." The world was once again falling apart.

One event of the 1930s that had repercussions, both martial and social, of great import beyond its immediate scene, was the Spanish civil war. It precipitated and encapsulated at one time and place many of the elements of disruption simmering just beneath the surface of European society.

The fledgling democratic government of Spain (the monarchy and its military administration had been overthrown only in 1931) was based on a wild diversity of parties and ideologies and proved quite incapable in the ensuing five years of reconciling them into coherent, effective, and socially acceptable programs of what would today be called "modernization." The military officer corps refused to accept either rapid changes in traditional standards, the partial breakdown in social order, or their own exclusion from power. Much of the middle class and of the Catholic hierarchy reacted in a similar fashion, taking political shape in the Falange, a movement loosely patterned after the Italian Fascists but with a more religious complexion. The Right feared a "Red revolution," the Left a "fascist" takeover. Both resorted to force and eventually to civil war, which pushed the Republic to the Left and the opposition to the Right, thus realizing the fears of both.

The international repercussions were analogous. Hitler and Mussolini were delighted, for both ideological and strategic reasons, to provide immediate and substantial military help to Franco. Prompt and equally substantial military aid to the Republic by neighboring France might have stamped out the revolt before it took hold, but the new French Popular Front government, divided on the issue, waffled and imposed an arms embargo a few weeks after the war started; the opportunity to nip it in the bud was lost. As the war continued and Italo-German participation became more flagrant, the chief concern of the British and French governments, which disliked and distrusted both Spanish contestants, came to be to ensure that the Spanish war did not escalate into a general European war, which they were not yet either militarily or psychologically prepared to fight. They therefore organized a system of "nonintervention," including an arms embargo, which worked quite well against the Republic and not at all against Franco.

The Soviet Union became the only reliable arms supplier to the Republic; thus the Communists and their Soviet advisers more and more came to dominate the Spanish government. The claim of conservatives outside Spain that its government was "Red" thus became a self-fulfilling prophecy.

The Spanish civil war to a surprising degree agitated and split public opinion in the Western democracies, including the United States. Liberals became zealous, sometimes fanatical, for the Republican cause, organized campaigns in vain attempts to influence their own governments, collected and dispatched food, clothing, and medicines, fought and died in considerable numbers on the Spanish battlefields. Andre Malraux organized and briefly led a patchwork air squadron. Ernest Hemingway and many other writers warned that the bell was tolling for us, the West. On the other hand, conservatives in the democracies, particularly Catholics, were equally zealous and fanatical in their support of the other side. The New Deal administration in Washington was especially torn; its sympathies were with the Republic, but it was inhibited from intervening both by the strong isolationist sentiment still prevailing in the country and by British and French objections to any steps that might expand the war. Indeed, in compliance with the nonintervention policy, a kind of "moral embargo" was applied to the export of American arms to Spain, an embargo that of course weighted almost exclusively against the Republic.

In April 1939 the Republic finally succumbed to these overwhelming odds. However, the Spanish war had significantly hardened public opinion in the West against the fascist dictators and prepared it to end appeasement.

Before coming to the outbreak of World War II, it is necessary to look briefly at what was happening in the 1930s in the Soviet Union, in the Far East, and in the United States.

I have described my impression of the Soviet Union in 1929. I visited the country again in 1934, just before I was married in Warsaw.

The change seemed to me considerable. The First Five-Year Plan had been successfully completed. While hideous stories of the agricultural collectivization and liquidation of the kulaks had reached us in Poland, where I had been a vice-consul, the total reorganization of Soviet agriculture nevertheless seemed to have been successfully carried out. Food in Moscow was not abundant or varied, but it was sufficient. A Party congress had just been held and had responded euphorically to these achievements. There was a more relaxed and hopeful atmosphere among the people, obvious even to the transient observer. It seemed indeed as though the revolution, having achieved its major objectives, might at last be winding down, and its leaders ready to relieve the pressure, distribute a few of the benefits, and grant some modest liberties.

No impression could have been more mistaken. Four months later Kirov, the heir apparent who was reputed to have favored some liberalization, was assassinated, almost certainly at Stalin's behest. His death provided the pretext for the Great Purge during which several million Soviet citizens, including large numbers of the political, military, and technical elite, were murdered. Many of the old Bolshevik leaders—Zinoviev, Kamenev, Rykov, Bukharin, not to mention two leaders of the secret police, Yagoda and Yezhov—were displayed in show trials during which they confessed abjectly to the most implausible crimes and were promptly executed.

Another revolution had begun to devour its children. While Stalin's personal paranoia and lust for power no doubt contributed to the proportions of this massacre, it was in a sense implicit in the Bolshevik party structure and temper we have described earlier. As the dissident Yugoslav communist, Milovan Djilas, later wrote: "It seems to me that Stalin is the most logical, the most natural heir of Lenin. Such a conclusion is not even inconsistent with the hypothesis that Stalin would have liquidated even Lenin himself."

The phenomenon of Stalin, however, is hard to understand except in clinical terms, though the Russian as well as the Bolshevik environment was not irrelevant. A great Russian, Dostoevski, had written in his *House of the Dead:* "Tyranny is a habit; it grows upon us, and in the long run turns into a disease." He probably had in mind Ivan the Terrible, as well as Paul I and Nicholas I. In a more philosophical vein, that remarkable young Frenchwoman, Simone Weil, wrote in *The Need for Roots* during World War II: "Obedience being a necessary food of the soul, whoever is definitely deprived of it is ill. Thus, any body politic governed by a sovereign ruler accountable to nobody is in the hands of a sick man."

Still, one must not let Stalin's monstrous crimes completely overshadow his extraordinary achievements. I shall have occasion to comment on them later in this account, but I might mention here the impression he made on me as I observed him at the Potsdam Conference in 1945. He seemed clearly to possess indomitable will, strictly disciplined passions, delicate sensitivity to the temper of others, an astuteness and guile not easily penetrated, a keen sense of tact and timing, great patience, profound cynicism, untroubled realism, and a comprehensive and meticulous grasp of the vast problems with which he dealt. No inkling of the horrors of which we all knew him guilty, or the boorishness intimates have described, emerged from his courteous and impassive demeanor, his total self-command—unmoved by the prolixity of Churchill or the impatience of Truman—his hooded, penetrating eyes, the dexterous compound of accommodation and implacability with which he did business, graciously conceding inessentials, dismissing with a steely word trespass on his vital interests.

Another witness, William Bullitt, first American ambassador to the Soviet Union, originally a devoted partisan, later an outraged critic, wrote in his first report to President Roosevelt on New Year's Day 1934: "With Lenin one felt at once that one was in the presence of a great man; with Stalin I felt I was talking to a wily Gipsy with roots and emotions beyond my experience. . . . He made the impression on me of a man of great shrewdness and exceptional will (Lenin, you know, said of him that he had enough will to equip the entire Communist Party) but also possessed of a quality of intuition in extraordinary measure."*

After Hitler's advent to power, Stalin sharply altered his foreign policy, joined the League of Nations, promoted Popular Front collaboration among communists, socialists, and other leftist parties in several European countries, and provided arms and advisers to the

---

***For the President* (Houghton Mifflin, 1972).

embattled Spanish Republicans. He invited Britain and France to join
in resisting Hitler's assault on Czechoslovakia but was spurned when
the Western leaders preferred to "compromise" at Munich. Whether
Stalin would actually have fought is an open question. After the shock
of the Nazi seizure of Bohemia in March 1939, conversations were
hastily begun in Moscow among Soviets, British, and French in a
belated effort to organize an alliance or some lesser form of military
cooperation against Hitler. According to the diary of Alexander
Cadogan, Permanent Undersecretary of the British Foreign Office,
Prime Minister Chamberlain on May 20 said that he would rather
resign than sign an alliance with the Soviets; nevertheless, on May 24
he and his cabinet agreed to offer to do exactly that.

These conversations were, however, pursued by the Western Powers in a reluctant and inconclusive fashion. Their intense underlying
hostility to these exponents of "Godless Communism," whom they
viewed as a threat to the political and economic structures and religious beliefs of the West, inhibited alliance. Their repugnance and
suspicions had been magnified by Stalin's purges, including the drastic
purge of his military high command. Another barrier to agreement
was the adamant refusal of the Poles, with whom both British and
French were now allied, to permit Soviet troops to cross Polish territory in case of war. The Poles suspected, rightly as subsequent events
have proven, that Soviet troops once in Poland would never leave. On
the other hand, it was hard to see how the Soviets could play a military
role in a war against Germany if they had no access to the battlefield.

The Soviets, for their part, were at least equally suspicious of the
West and believed, with substantial reason, that the Western leaders
would have been delighted to see Nazi Germany and the Soviet Union
bleed each other white. Hitler had for some time, with complete
disregard for his public anticommunist posture, been secretly seeking
an understanding with the Soviets that would keep them neutral and
permit him to avoid a two-front war. It is not clear exactly at what
point Stalin decided that the Allies were either not serious or would
not offer him sufficient advantages to make alliance worth the risk of
war with Germany. At all events he kept both sides dangling for
several months, until Hitler's insistent demands for immediate decision made further delay impracticable. The Nazi-Soviet pact, in effect
giving Hitler the green light for war on the West in exchange for half

of Poland and a free hand in the Baltic states for Stalin, was announced to a thunderstruck world on August 24, 1939. War began
with Hitler's invasion of Poland eight days later.

The background of the war in East Asia was very different, but the
denouement was much the same. To the outside world the emergence
of Japan as a great power after the Meiji Restoration in 1867 seemed
an almost uninterrupted success story, just as the revival and opulence
of Japan after World War II has seemed. The great zaibatsu or family
trusts built in a few decades an industrial structure only barely less
powerful and productive than those of Europe and the United States.
A fraternity of domesticated feudal warriors was transformed in a
generation into a modern, nationalist officer corps, with an obedient
peasant army and the most up-to-date arms at their disposal. A political structure and body of law imitating European models was superimposed with apparent success on the traditional society. By 1919,
fifty years after the Restoration, Japan had defeated China and
Russia, made an alliance with Great Britain, and participated as an
equal in the victory over the Central Powers.

Such precipitate social transofrmations, however, often prove to be
only skin-deep. As Edwin Reischauer later wrote: "There was no deep
emotional commitment to democratic principles on the part of most
Japanese and many of them viewed with distaste the open clash of
private interests in elections and in the parliamentary processes, preferring the older ideal of a harmonious, unified society, ruled through
consensus by loyal servants of the state." The most "loyal" of these
servants were frequently perceived, by themselves and others, to be
the military. To quote Reischauer again: "Japanese found it easy to
believe that army and navy officers, the salaried military servants of
the state, were more honest and dependable, or as they put it, more
'sincere,' than were rich industrialists and self seeking politicians. And
the military officers themselves, segregated educationally from other
Japanese at a relatively early age and deeply indoctrinated in a proud
military tradition, believed this fully."

So Japanese society in its seeming hour of triumph and equality
with the West after World War I was in fact deeply divided between
two worlds, the thin conspicuous layer of thriving and imitative modernization masking a far more authentic, persistent, and powerful

body of immemorial tradition, religion, conformity, sensitivity, and pride. The mask was Western, the features behind the mask profoundly Japanese.

The composition was not only anomalous but unstable. Just because the western posture was imitative and superficial, it was peculiarly sensitive to shocks from outside and inside. The Asiatic attachment to "face" had not been eradicated. On the contrary, it had been aggravated by exposure to the judgment of those socieites it was imitating. All went well as long as the imported Western theatricals were successful and were applauded; all could quickly turn sour if the stage machinery broke down or the audience began to carp and jeer.

During the war, Japan, after expelling the Germans from China, had occupied substantial territories themselves and imposed twenty-one far-reaching "demands" on the prostrate Chinese. At Versailles the Allies obliged them to give most of these up. They joined with Britain and the United States in negotiating the postwar naval treaties which, though awarding them dominance in the Western Pacific, still fell far short of equality. Infinitely more galling was the "Exclusion Act" adopted by the Congress in 1924 whereby Japanese were singled out as aliens ineligible for citizenship in a great democracy that theoretically opened its doors to all. In a subtle way this piece of Occidental arrogance may have contributed as much to Pearl Harbor as all that followed.

What did follow was, first, the economic depression, which seemed to confirm all that Japanese critics of industrialization and modernization had been warning against. The political as well as the economic system, in Japan as in Italy and Germany, began to buckle and crack. Young army officers provoked a series of incidents in Manchuria which neither their superiors, their government, nor even the emperor were able to check. The occupation of Manchuria followed in 1931, as did a series of brazen assassinations of prime ministers and other leaders, until the civilians in Japanese political life were cowed and neutralized. Thereafter the armed forces moved south from Manchuria, into Shanghai, and finally, in July 1937, seized Peking and began their full-fledged but undeclared war in China.

The response of the West to this creeping aggression was indignant but purely diplomatic and wholly ineffective. A League of Nations Commission demanded that Japan withdraw from Manchuria; Japan thereupon withdrew from the league. The United States proclaimed the Stimson Doctrine of nonrecognition of Japanese conquests, which of course had no effect whatsoever. After 1937, as war intensified in north and central China, the United States, in order that it might continue supplying arms to China, refrained from invoking the arms embargo prescribed for belligerents under the Neutrality Act. On the contrary, it soon commenced to apply a "moral embargo," by exhortation rather than under law, to exports to Japan not only of arms, of which she had enough but of oil and scrap iron, which she needed badly. These pressures were applied with increasing rigor from 1937 to 1941 and culminated in July 1941, in retaliation for the Japanese occupation of Indochina, in the blocking of its financial assets in the United States. This threatened to result in a total interruption of oil supplies required to fuel the Japanese war machine and to impose the "New Order in East Asia" to which Japan had committed itself.

At this point the choice before the Japanese military government seemed to be between evacuating China and Indochina and surrendering the objectives it had been pursuing for the past decade or joining Germany and Italy, with which it was now allied in the so-called Axis, going to war, and assuring itself by the seizure of Southeast Asia of the oil and other supplies it required for conquest and survival. Even a casual student of Japanese character could have predicted what choice would be made.

As a perceptive and sympathetic observer of Japan, Fosco Maraini, has remarked: "Normally, Japanese people manage to maintain their composure. Reactions and emotions are carefully hidden under layers of self-control. Centuries of meditation, zazen and discipline regulate behavior through invisible channels. No public in the world can hold its breath with such utter self-annihilation as a full house at the theatre in Japan. But if a certain point, or mark, or temperature is passed, an explosion may occur. . . . This may happen at work, at play, in sports, in love and sex—or in the lurid light of hatred and war." Such a paroxysm is of course what occurred, and it persisted for four years, through both triumph and disaster.

In the United States, the economic boom of the 1920s had been so sensational, and so widespread in its benefits, that the effect of the crash was correspondingly brutal. It was as much a political and psychological as an economic collapse. Everyone had been gambling on rosy futures, on rags to riches in common stocks. When their expectations evaporated in a week's appalling melodrama, the country fell into a state of shock in which it remained for three and a half years.

In February 1930 I hitchhiked from New York to Florida and back, in July from New York to Colorado. I was not alone. Already four months after the "Black Thursday" in October the highways were strewn with the human jetsam it had wrenched from their moorings. People streamed South or West looking for jobs and met an equal number streaming back because there were no jobs. The only consolation was the companionship of the road. The hitchhiker soon learned that the more dilapidated and overloaded the vehicle that came along, the better chance there was of getting a ride.

Despite the shocking blows they had suffered, the Hoover administration and the business community reacted in much the same fashion as their European counterparts—with belt tightening, budget cutting, tariff raising, whistling in the wind until the operation of "normal economic forces" brought prosperity back again, as it always had before. This time, however, the suffering was too great and too universal. Bankruptcy and foreclosure hit the farmer and the small businessman as hard as joblessness hit the industrial worker. The Okies took to the road, and John Steinbeck wrote their story in *The Grapes of Wrath*. Both progressive and radical politics revived after a decade of eclipse. Bewildered young intellectuals joined communist "cells" or "study groups," for which twenty years later they would be persecuted. The "Revolution" became a respectable subject of conversation not only in shoddy bars but at fashionable cocktail parties. Ambiguous political characters like Huey Long, Father Coughlin, and Upton Sinclair attracted large followings. The "little man" was angry —but he was not revolutionary. He merely wanted the American Dream to work, as his schoolbooks, his newspapers, and his Rotary Club had always promised it would. Now he had lost faith. The iconoclastic mood of the prewar decade returned, but in a more bitter, more impatient, more furious vein.

Hoover was forced into a number of measures that deviated from economic orthodoxy, but they were not enough. By 1932 there were 13 million unemployed, one worker out of four; a quarter of the farmers had lost their farms; hundreds of banks had failed, swallowing up the savings of millions of depositors. In November Franklin Delano Roosevelt was swept into office.

In my adult lifetime there has been no leader in the United States, perhaps in all the Western world, as politically sensitive, astute, and successful as Roosevelt. This was not apparent before he took office. He was not widely known in the country. His campaign in 1932 was murky, straddling orthodoxy and reform. His peers in the eastern establishment thought of him as a "lightweight" until they came to regard him as the devil incarnate. But in his first week in office, with all the banks on "holiday," he assumed command. In his first inaugural address he launched the celebrated slogan: "The only thing we have to fear is fear itself." In his first 100 days he proposed an emergency banking bill, an agricultural recovery program, unemployment relief, federal supervision of the stock market, creation of a Tennessee Valley Authority, prevention of mortgage foreclosures on homes, and an industrial recovery program. By June 1933 Congress had enacted all these proposals into law.

As important as his prompt and comprehensive legislative program was the image Roosevelt projected of a confident and compassionate leader, prepared to do whatever was necessary to override conservative callousness and rescue the little man. His fireside chats over the radio brought him into every home. He became America's father figure. I recall him at White House receptions I attended in the 1930s —tall, imposing, propped buoyantly on his leg irons and cane, handsome head thrown back flashing his famous smile, his handshake firm and warm, radiating assurance and humanity. As one of his Brain Trusters, Rex Tugwell, wrote after his death: "No monarch, I thought, unless it may have been Elizabeth or her magnificent Tudor father, or maybe Alexander or Augustus Caesar, can have given quite that sense of serene presiding, of gathering up into himself, of really representing, a whole people."

To the orthodox business and academic community, however, after the first few months of panic, he came to represent economic heresy, demagogic irresponsibility, subversive doctrine tainted with socialism, dangerously close to "red revolution." To my favorite uncle, a successful businessman in upstate New York, Roosevelt's reelection in 1936 with majorities in all but two states was such a shattering blow that he died of it. Almost the entire press of the country opposed Roosevelt in that election.

What frightened my uncle, the press, and those of their way of thinking was not only the New Deal legislation but its whole tone and philosophy. Pronouncements of Roosevelt and his Brain Trust, which did not actually differ from those of the other Roosevelt and Wilson twenty-five years before, threatened, as they saw it, the very pillars of society: themselves and their established interests, the free enterprise system as they defined it.

In his speech to the San Francisco Commonwealth Club in the 1932 campaign, FDR had said:

> The day of the great promoter or the financial Titan, to whom we granted everything if only he would build, or develop, is over. Our task now is not discovery or exploitation of natural resources, or necessarily producing more goods. It is the soberer, less dramatic business of administering resources and plants already in hand, . . . of meeting the problem of underconsumption, of adjusting production to consumption, of distributing wealth and products more equitably, of adapting existing economic organizations to the service of the people.

In his budget message of 1940, before war interrupted for the second time a surge of American reform, he laid down guidelines for the future which would be subsequently pursued by Harry Truman and Lyndon Johnson. "Private power" he wrote in this message, "is reaching a point at which it is becoming stronger than the democratic state itself. . . . Private enterprise is ceasing to be free enterprise and is becoming a cluster of private collectivisms. . . . Big business collectivism in industry compels an ultimate collectivism of government. . . . The power of the few to manage the economic life of the Nation must be diffused among the many or be transferred to the public and its democratically responsible government."

The New Deal was not, strictly speaking, a revolution. It was better than that. As Robert Frost said: "Revolutions are one thing that should be done by halves," and the New Deal was, in the American tradition, half a revolution, which may have forestalled a more far-reaching one. The United States was not in 1932 in a revolutionary situation. The little parties of the Left were all pitifully weak. However, a malaise and an accumulating anger were feeding the more serious movements of the Right—movements Huey Long, for example, might have pulled together had there been no New Deal. "It can't happen here," Sinclair Lewis wrote of fascism, meaning that perhaps it could have.

When Roosevelt took office, Keynes had not yet published his *General Theory of Employment, Interest and Money,* the modern revision of Adam Smith, but its doctrine was in the air. Roosevelt grasped its essence before it was systematically formulated. Economic depressions were sustained and aggravated, if not caused, by shrinkage of effective demand, the absence of sufficient consumer buying power to keep the system running at full steam. The cure was not to restrict demand further but to pump in more purchasing power either by enlarging private investment or, if a breakdown of confidence made that impossible, making the government the employer of last resort. That was what Roosevelt instinctively did, and what Keynes and a new wave of economists, which soon became the mainstream, later legitimized.

As many people were saying in those days, the free enterprise system had solved the problem of production but not the problem of distribution, either in terms of stability or of equity. Roosevelt was not a theoretician, but he saw that central deficiency clearly and would not accept it, most of all in a time of crisis but not even in better times. He wanted the system to work better all the time, more consistently and more humanely, and he thought it could. He kept on saying that right up to the end. As Robert Sherwood, the playwright who was in the wartime White House, later wrote in *Roosevelt and Hopkins*: "Although crippled physically and prey to various infections, he was spiritually the healthiest man I have ever known. He was gloriously and happily free of the various forms of psychic maladjustment which are called by such names as inhibition, complex, phobia. His mind, if not always orderly, bore no traces of paralysis and neither did his emotional constitution; and his heart was certainly in the right place."

The business establishment at the time charged that the New Deal was introducing state socialism. Subsequent left-wing critics have complained that it bolstered the old order and prevented "significant" reform. As a matter of fact, it was a typically American compromise, leagues short of socialism but carrying vigorously forward the American tradition of progressive reform. The historian Charles Beard, who later became an enemy of Roosevelt because of differences over foreign policy, wrote in 1938: "Whatever else may happen, it seems safe to say that President Roosevelt has made a more profound impression upon the political, social and economic thought of America than any or all of his predecessors." Forty years later that seems extravagant praise. Sixty or seventy years later yet it may not.

During the latter part of the turbulent prewar years I was, by chance, a minor participant close to the eye of the storm.

At the end of 1930 I had passed the examinations for the Foreign Service and been assigned as vice-consul at Alexandria, Egypt. After fifteen months in Egypt I was brought back for further training in the State Department. While in Washington in 1932 I witnessed General Douglas MacArthur's first conspicuous military operation—driving the angry, bedraggled "bonus marchers" from their discomforting proximity to the Capitol—and heard over the radio the Democratic Convention in Chicago rather surprisingly nominate that "lightweight dilettante," Franklin Roosevelt, for the Presidency of the United States.

In August 1932 I was sent as vice-consul to Warsaw. Since as a consequence of this assignment I married a lovely Polish woman and thus initiated a lifelong association with Eastern Europe, it seems worthwhile to say a few words about Poland between the two world wars.

Poland was, with Hungary, one of the two most persistently feudal countries in Europe. It was governed by Marshal Pilsudski, an earthy, crotchety, and beloved national hero, and his less beloved "colonels," but social arrangements had changed very little over the past two hundred years, despite partition by Russia, Prussia, and Austria, subjection for a century and a half, liberation, and establishment of a republic in 1918.

The great landowners—Radziwills, Potockis, Czartoryskis—and countless smaller "nobility" owned most of the land and enjoyed a pleasant life divided between unscientific agriculture and genteel debauch. The great mass of the people were peasants living in the direst poverty, sometimes even lacking matches and salt. When the landlords strolled or rode about their estates, as I often witnessed as a weekend guest, the peasants bowed and scraped and kissed their hands. The Catholic Church, because of its role in preserving Polish nationalism during the long eclipse, was immensely popular and powerful.

The middle class was small and a substantial part of it Jewish, which generated covert and sometimes overt anti-Semitism. Nearly half the population was made up of non-Polish minorities: there were 6 million Jews and a million Germans and, east of the so-called Curzon Line, 90 percent of the peasantry was Ukrainian, White Russian, and Lithuanian.

Notwithstanding this anachronistic social and national structure, the Poles themselves, from highest to lowest, could not have been more delightful, hospitable, warm, and witty. Whether spending a night on the town floating merrily on vodka and champagne, or entertaining a guest on their estates with gargantuan feasts and horseback rides through endless forests, they were the most charming of companions.

Incidentally, I have run across a little note recalling that, excluding a very modest rent allowance for my comfortable Warsaw flat, my salary for 1932, on which I lived very well indeed, was $2,536 and my taxes $61.44.

However, I enjoyed this sybaritic life only for a little more than a year and then, rather quixotically, cut it off by resigning from the Foreign Service. I did so for several reasons. I was bored stiff by most of the consular work I had to perform; I was exasperated because the State Department had, on purely bureaucratic grounds, turned down requests by both our Cairo and Warsaw embassies that I be shifted from the consulates to them; I had two books simmering in my mind, a novel and a study of contemporary political movements, which I very much wanted to write; and finally, after Roosevelt took office in March 1933 and the kinetic excitement of the New Deal began to crackle across the intervening spaces, I could not bear to be missing those exhilarating moments in my country's history. So I took the plunge, hardly dreaming that within two dozen months I should be back in the State Department's paternal embrace and should remain there for thirty-five years.

In the meantime I spent two months on the Polish seacoast writing my novel. On a weekend cruise to Stockholm I encountered my future bride as we stepped expectantly out of contiguous staterooms. I asked if she spoke English. She said "yes," which turned out to be the only word she knew, but it was enough.

I tarried in half a dozen capitals collecting material for my book on politics. In Berlin, then in its first Nazi year, I was able to make contact with an underground socialist movement called "New Beginning," which had been struggling to invigorate the Socialist party. Its two leaders, Karl Frank and Richard Lowenthal (who were risking their lives each hour of day and night), I met clandestinely there; I was later to meet Frank in Washington in wartime, where I came to his assistance at some cost to myself. Lowenthal I was not to encounter again until long after the war, when he had become a distinguished professor at the Free University of Berlin and then, irony of ironies, in the late 1960s had been driven from his classroom as a "reactionary" by the radical students of that day.

In December 1933 I returned to New York to complete and try to market my novel. I lived in bohemian austerity in Greenwich Village. In the summer of 1934 I returned to Poland and, love conquering all in the best romantic traditions, married my beautiful bride and carried her triumphantly across the seas. Soon learning, however, the truth of the old maxim that two cannot live as cheaply as one, particularly when each of the two has been accustomed to living rather well, we soon joined the hegira of young intellectuals to Washington in search of a job and the brave new world.

> Bliss was it in that dawn to be alive,
> But to be young was very Heaven.

I first found temporary asylum in the WPA (Works Progress Administration). I recall its chief, Harry Hopkins, speaking to a meeting of his senior staff, perched on the edge of a table, his suit crumpled, tie pulled loose, and collar half open, lock of uncombed hair falling over his forehead, an ugly, nondescript man evoking images of Carl Sandburg's poems—"the people, yes."

I recall the long evenings of passionate talk among the young New Dealers and their girls, the dragons slaughtered, the utopias devised. I recall the square dances recapturing a vanishing America, the skating parties on the frozen pool under the Lincoln Memorial in starlight, the weekend excursions to the Blue Ridge Mountains and hikes along the Appalachian Trail, though there were still rattlesnakes then in this Garden of Eden. I recall my young bride running joyously down Massachusetts Avenue to meet me as I came home late from work.

For I did before long find a job in Rex Tugwell's new Resettlement Administration. My division was intended to plan and build decent low-cost housing in the decayed outskirts of a hundred cities. With greatest care and objectivity we selected the cities that needed such housing most. Alas for the vanity of human purposes, a battle of the giants above our heads—Tugwell and Ickes for public works, Hopkins for work projects to absorb the maximum number of unemployed—resulted in victory for the latter, and after only four months I lost my job.

Fortune was, however, with me. Just at that moment, the summer of 1935, Congress, impressed by the then popular thesis that "the merchants of death" had pressed a naïve and innocent Uncle Sam into the First World War, passed a "Neutrality Act" designed to keep him out of another by controlling all exports of "arms, ammunition and implements of war" and embargoing their export to belligerents. A new division was set up in the State Department to administer this act; one of my professors at Princeton, Joseph Green, was made its chief; to my astonishment he invited me to be his deputy. Since I was jobless and the work promised, in the uproarious circumstances of 1935, to be fascinating, I accepted with alacrity. So I commenced my second career in the State Department, where I was destined to remain this time many years, to experience three wars, attend four celebrated international conferences, hold ten foreign posts, including five as chief of mission, and serve the last of these years at the United Nations, first as deputy to Adlai Stevenson and Arthur Goldberg and eventually as Principal U.S. Representative.

As it turned out, my new post proved to be in the very eye of the storm that the dictators in Europe and Asia were conjuring up in 1935. Within a month we found ourselves, miracle of miracles, cooperating as best we could with the unspeakable League of Nations in sanctions against Mussolini's Italy during its invasion of Ethiopia and sharing in the general disillusion when these sanctions collapsed. Like the Walrus and the Carpenter I agonized over our discouragement of the export of arms to Spain, which meant chiefly the Republic for which I felt profound sympathy, but accepted Roosevelt's reluctant acquiescence in the warnings of the ill-prepared British and French.

I joined enthusiastically in administering the "moral embargo" against exports to Japan essential to its operations in China, though not unaware that this embargo on oil and iron must, if effective, lead to a showdown between us. In the spring of 1941, by which time we were in fact, through our office and others, conducting economic warfare against the Axis, I was sent to the Philippines to close loopholes there on Japanese purchases of copper, iron ore, vegetable oils, and hemp. I recall vividly being visited by a grim-faced Japanese consul general who informed me icily that his government would be profoundly disturbed by these discriminating measures. I replied in similar tones that we were profoundly disturbed by his government's behavior.

The Filipinos were at that moment clearly prepared for the outbreak of war at any moment, as was Hong Kong, through which I passed on my return. However, no similar readiness was apparent in Hawaii, where I also paused briefly. The general impression there seemed to be that, while war might well come, it would come to other people. It came of course to all of us four months later.

After the wrong lessons had been learned in World War I and the wrong remedies applied in the five years thereafter; after the subsequent breathing spell had been cut short by preposterous economic speculation and *its* dire effects aggravated by even worse remedies; after the Nazis and the Japanese military had come to power, there was very little hope of avoiding World War II. In theory of course it could have been done.

The French and British, if they had read *Mein Kampf* attentively and believed it, might have followed Marshal Pilsudski's advice to march into Berlin and throw Hitler out as soon as he became chancellor in 1933. Or they could have prevented the military reoccupation of the Rhineland in 1936 and inflicted a humiliating and perhaps decisive defeat on Hitler before he was ready. Or they could have stated flatly in 1938 that an attack on Czechoslovakia would mean European war, spurned the offer of Munich, and allied themselves with the Soviet Union. Such steps might have deterred even Hitler. The United States might even, in theory, have joined in some of these acts of will.

In fact, however, none of them was psychologically or politically feasible in the climate of the time. Public opinion in all the great powers had been too deeply conditioned by the conclusions they had drawn from their experience of the past two decades. The fact that many of these conclusions were inapplicable to the circumstances of the 1930s, so different from those before 1914 or even of the 1920s, was not recognized until too late.

The phenomenon of Nazism was so novel, so unprecedented, so inherently barbaric and hence so anachronistic in twentieth-century Europe, that it seemed quite incredible to his neighbors that Hitler meant what he said or that, even if he had, he would not soon be sobered by the "responsibilities of power." Nazi Machiavellianism was at the same time so much more extreme and so much more candid than the traditional Machiavellianism of the old chancellories of Europe that they simply did not believe the evidence of their eyes and ears—until 1939, and then it was too late.

Before leaving the causes of World War II, however, it would be right to note that not all observers of that sinister period have been ready to lay all the blame on Hitler and the Nazis. Evelyn Waugh, who fought in the war and subsequently wrote three novels about it, had a Jewess in Tito's Yugoslavia in the last of these novels, *Unconditional Surrender,* express a more catholic judgment, which probably reflected his own views.

"Is there any place that is free from evil?" Waugh's character asked. "It is too simple to say that only the Nazis wanted war. These communists wanted it too. It was the only way in which they could come to power. Many of my people wanted it, to be revenged on the Germans, to hasten the creation of the national state. It seems to me there was a will to war, a death wish, everywhere."

⪼ 5 ⪻

Course and Consequences of World War II

1941-1945

The Second World War differed in several significant respects from the first.

It was more universal. Combat in the first war had been confined almost entirely to Europe and its approaches, with minor clashes in the German colonies and the Middle East. Combat in the second took place almost everywhere—from the Pyrenees to the Caucusus, from the deserts of Libya to the jungles of Burma, from New Guinea to the Aleutian Islands, from Chungking to the North Cape. In nearly every occupied country resistance continued until liberation. There were few neutrals.

The first war took by surprise every government on both sides. It was not premeditated. The generals had war plans which, in the initial confusion and panic, were allowed to determine the political decisions —the Russian general mobilization which provoked the German declaration of war; the execution of the Schlieffen Plan through Belgium which assured the involvement of Britain.

The second war, on the contrary, was calculated by one side and improvised by the other. Therefore, those taking the offensive won initially an almost unbroken series of victories: in Europe from the partition of Poland in September 1939 through the occupation of France in 1940 to the drive to Stalingrad and to Cairo in 1942 (inter-

rupted only by German repulses in the Battle of Britain in 1940 and
before Moscow in 1941); in the Pacific similarly, the dazzling advance
of the Japanese from the Philippines through Singapore and Java
almost to Australia, until halted by the battles of the Coral Sea and
Midway.

The second war, in contrast to the first, was a war of mobility and
maneuver, not of position and stalemate. It was a war of grand strategy in which Winston Churchill could atone for the failure of Gal-
lipoli by a triumphant assault on the "soft underbelly" of Europe. It
was brand-new Blitzkrieg in which von Rundstedt, von Manstein, and
Guderian sliced across France from the Ardennes to the sea in ten
days and across Russia from the Bug River to the outskirts of Moscow
in twenty weeks, in which Rommel flung armies of tanks across
leagues of desert, in which Patton dashed from Brittany to the German frontier in seven weeks, in which, most astonishing of all, the
Japanese captured the Pacific empires of Britain, Holland, and the
United States in four months.

It was a war in which naval task forces roamed the vast reaches of
the Pacific and fought great battles invisible to each other, in which
the armies of MacArthur clambered up the chain of islands from
Guadalcanal to Okinawa, in which wolf packs of Nazi submarines
lurked off the coast of Florida and decisive battles of supply were
fought on the approaches to the Arctic Sea.

It was the glorious heyday of war in the air, of which Douhet and
Billy Mitchell had dreamed, of Stukas and Zeros, of Spitfires and
Flying Fortresses, of Göring and Dowding, Doolittle and LeMay, of
"the few to whom the many owed so much."

The other side of these glittering martial triumphs was that, thanks
to the airplane and blitzkrieg, there were no more noncombatants.
Everyone, at least in Europe and the Pacific, was at the front. Not
since the Hundred Years and Thirty Years wars had women and
children suffered so much and died in such numbers. Frantic streams
of refugees were harried down the highways and byways of Europe
and Asia and slaughtered as they ran. The laws of war, as of peace,
were suspended. Civilian resisters in the vast occupied areas were
tortured, executed, carted off in hundreds of thousands to slave labor
and concentration camps. Six million Jewish men, women, and children were exterminated with the coldest calculation. Poles, Russians,

and Chinese fared little better. It was a very nasty war indeed.

The slaughter of noncombatants was by no means all on one side. In response to the air bombardment of Warsaw, Rotterdam, London, and Coventry, and as the only feasible means for the Anglo-Americans to carry war to the Nazi homeland from 1940 to 1944, most major German cities were demolished from the air with enormous civilian losses resulting. A number impossible to establish precisely but believed to be more than 100,000 were killed in a quite unnecessary raid on Dresden when the war was almost won. Before the atomic bomb was used, most Japanese cities were destroyed. About 80,000 people were incinerated in a single fire raid on Tokyo in March 1945.

Devastation in World War I was limited almost entirely to the battlefields. In World War II the cities of Europe, China, and Japan became the battlefield, and none that "military necessity" made targetworthy escaped. As I saw them at the end of the war or shortly after, Berlin, Warsaw, Manila had suffered in a moment a magnitude of ruin that twenty centuries had not been able to inflict on Rome or Athens.

After the burning of several ancient monuments in Paris during the Commune in 1871, Swiss historian Jacob Burckhardt wrote: "Part of one died with the Louvre. One dies gradually in parts. . . . Such events will occur again and again on this hollowed out ground we stand upon." Events surpassed even his melancholy vision. What would Burckhardt have thought of the almost total destruction of Dresden, that irreplaceable jewel of baroque architecture and civilization. Few of our contemporaries, however, "died in parts." After two world wars one gets thickskinned.

Another marked contrast between the two wars was the public mood with which they were greeted. We noted earlier the jubilation and radiant optimism with which the outbreak of the First War was welcomed in all the capitals involved. The popular mood at the commencement of the Second, even in Germany which began it, was quite different—somber, resigned, caught up helplessly in a train of events beyond control, acutely conscious of the horrors ahead but perceiving no alternative. No doubt there was enthusiasm and arrogant assurance among dedicated Nazis and Japanese military men, but these sentiments were not shared by the general public. The "phony war" from the fall of 1939 to the spring of 1940 deepened the sense of futility and unreality.

On the other hand, once the shattering presence of war was brought home by aerial bombardment, as in Britain and Germany, by brutal occupation, as in the Soviet Union, Poland, and Yugoslavia, or by both as in China, the people's resolution, fortitude, and dedication were magnified a hundredfold. The war became visibly a struggle for national survival. Everyone fought. The battles of war production and transportation to far-off, dangerous places were an indispensable component of battles fought with the weapons produced and transported. Women stood shoulder to shoulder with men and were needed as badly. Ironically, "total war" played a role in the liberation of the "gentler sex."

The posture and impact of propaganda was also different, at least on the Allied side, more discriminating, less simplistic, much more benign in its ultimate effects. That master of the Big Lie, Joseph Goebbels, was as outrageous as his forebears but proved less credible, even to the Germans, in war than in peace, until the aerial devastation of cities gave him and them a common cause. The Allies for the most part drew a distinction between the German and Japanese people and their Nazi and military leaders who had corrupted them, though it was difficult for the inhabitants of occupied countries, scenes of both calculated and spontaneous cruelties, to share this forbearance. Yet it was of the utmost importance, for it diluted the popular demand among the victors for indiscriminate postwar punishment, which had proven so fatal an indulgence after World War I, and permitted instead the reconciliation that so soon after 1945 welcomed Germans and Japanese not only into the community of nations but into alliance with their conquerors.

The war aims of Clemenceau and Lloyd George, on the one hand, and of Woodrow Wilson, on the other, had differed radically, and this difference had been responsible for the errors of Versailles and, to some degree, the rejection of the peace settlement by the American people. The contrasts among the war aims of Churchill, Stalin, and Roosevelt were of course even more fundamental, reflecting the vast differences between their social systems, national interests, personalities, and experiences.

Churchill's aim was to destroy Nazism and Fascism root and branch but otherwise to restore as much of the status quo ante as possible. He was realist enough to recognize that after the massive loss of blood and treasure in two world wars, Britain could not again monopolize the map or rule the waves as she had once done. Her powers could never again be equal to those of the United States or the Soviet Union.

On the other hand, he was not about to give up one iota more than he had to. He announced that he "had not become His Majesty's First Minister in order to preside over the liquidation of the British Empire." He saw no good reason why the overseas empires of all the victorious nations should not be preserved. In Europe he was quite prepared to base the peace on the balance of power, to divide the Continent into spheres of influence in which the Russians would manipulate governments in some countries and the British and Americans in others. He was torn between detesting the Soviet system and recognizing the need to come to some accommodation with it to avoid another war.

Stalin was the most enigmatic and yet the most single-minded of the war leaders. I have described in the previous chapter my impressions of him at Potsdam. He was a man of extraordinary ability and even more extraordinary vices. Averell Harriman, the American who knew him best, has written:

> It is hard to reconcile the courtesy and consideration that he showed me personally with the ghastly cruelty of his wholesale liquidations. Others, who did not know him personally, saw only the tyrant in Stalin. I saw the other side as well—his high intelligence, that fantastic grasp of detail, his shrewdness and the surprising human sensitivity that he was capable of showing, at least in the war years. I found him better informed than Roosevelt, more realistic than Churchill, in some ways the most effective of the war leaders.

Stalin's war aims combined tenacity and opportunism. His minimum aim was certainly to establish along Russia's western boundaries an extensive bulwark against a resurgent Germany or any other potential invader, a bulwark to be created in part by annexing territories to the Soviet Union and in part by controlling neighboring countries through communist parties firmly under Soviet control. It was a cordon sanitaire in reverse. This was not in principle incompatible with Churchill's conception of spheres of influence, but that compatibility depended on how far the Soviet sphere was to extend and how exclusive and impervious it was to be.

There is some evidence that Stalin's original intention was to dominate totally only Poland and Rumania, which were nearest his borders. As the animosities and fears of the Cold War accumulated, he presumably decided to play it safe by moving his glacis westward to the Elbe and the Adriatic. Elsewhere his aims were elastic and tailored to circumstances. His negotiations with the Nazis during the period of their alliance (1939–41) made clear that he also had substantial ambitions to reach southward toward the Mediterranean and the Persian Gulf. These ambitions were manifested in 1945 by encouragement of civil war in Greece and pressure on Turkey and Iran. These probes, however, being secondary and not vital, were abandoned without major confrontation when the Western Allies firmly resisted.

Roosevelt was conditioned by his experience in World War I and in the years of his Presidency. He immediately perceived the incompatibility of powerful Nazi and Japanese empires, under megalomaniac and barbaric leaders, with the security not only of their neighbors but of the United States. He no doubt foresaw that unless they could be defeated by their neighbors, the United States would at some point be involved in the war. This perception induced him to arm the neighbors and to commence rearmament at home. At the same time he was keenly aware of the strength of American isolationist sentiment and felt obliged to emphasize, as Wilson had in 1916, his determination to keep the country out of war if he could. This political and moral dilemma necessitated a display of deviousness on his part which was unjustifiably magnified, with at least equal disingenuousness, by contemporary critics and, subsequently, by revisionist historians.

Other World War I experiences influenced him powerfully—and demonstrated again the perils of applying indiscriminately the lessons of one historical period to the incongruent events of another. Because German nationalists had claimed they were not really defeated by the Allies in World War I but were "stabbed in the back" by revolution at home, Roosevelt insisted at the Casablanca Conference on demanding "unconditional surrender." This formula had the additional advantage of reducing the persistent apprehension of both Soviet and

Western Allies that the other would make a separate peace. Both Stalin and Churchill, whose peoples had suffered cruelly from the Germans, were temperamentally disposed to it. Nevertheless, by seeming to bind the fate of the German people to that of their Nazi leaders, it may have prolonged the war for several months, and in so doing profoundly affected the shape of postwar Europe.

Another of Roosevelt's idiosyncracies, which Churchill and Stalin did *not* share, was his determination to separate the military conduct of the war from its political aims and to adjourn discussion of the latter until victory was assured. One reason for this procrastination was simple prudence. Given the wide divergence in political aims among the Soviet Union, Britain, and the United States, any discussion was bound to be divisive, as acerbic debate over the future of Poland repeatedly showed, and thus to interfere with prosecution of the war. The Western Allies, particularly the Americans, had a guilty conscience because they were repeatedly promising, and repeatedly adjourning, the Second Front Stalin demanded and thus obliging the Russians to bear the main weight of the war.

Other considerations in Roosevelt's mind were probably the mischievous intrusion of domestic politics into military operations in some of America's earlier wars, and more particularly, American revulsion at the discovery that the Allies in World War I had been secretly dividing enemy real estate among themselves while proclaiming the purity and nobility of their war aims. A further incidental factor was that Roosevelt, while obliged to retain Cordell Hull as his Secretary of State because of Hull's prestige with Congress, found him personally uncongenial, unhelpful, and tedious, and so excluded him systematically from high-level meetings.

One can understand and sympathize with Roosevelt's concerns on all these points, particularly that only cohesion and success of the military alliance could consummate any political aims. Nevertheless, there is a cogent argument to be made that had he been willing to look more acutely and boldly beyond victory to the future of Europe, Roosevelt should have joined Churchill in pressing Stalin for firm postwar commitments at an early date when the Soviets were locked in desperate battle and might have been prepared to settle for much less than they later obtained. Edgar Snow quotes Maxim Litvinov, former Soviet foreign minister, as asking him in June 1945: "Why did you Americans wait till right now to begin opposing us in the Balkans and Eastern Europe? You should have done this three years ago. Now it's too late, and your complaints only arouse suspicions here."

Roosevelt's calculated separation of military strategy from political purpose in World War II has led me to the conclusion, contrary to prevailing opinion, that he was a greater peacetime than wartime leader. By carrying through a program of effective and moderate domestic reform at a time when the country had lost heart and nerve, he did even more for its long-term security than he did in organizing resistance to the Germans and Japanese. The war was won but, with more attention to political goals, it might have been better and more durably won.

Still another far-reaching consequence of the artificial separation of military and political planning was that military commanders were allowed, indeed expected, to make supposedly military but in fact political decisions without consultation with civilian authority. While I was with Stettinius in San Francisco in late April 1945, a message for him from Washington reported that Stalin had asked Eisenhower, whose troops had entered Czechoslovakia and were moving rapidly without opposition toward Prague, to pull them back to Pilsen; Eisenhower proposed to comply with this request in order to avoid possible clashes with the Russians. I hastily organized a meeting of senior officers with Stettinius who, on their advice, sent an urgent message to Eisenhower recommending he disregard Stalin's plea, which was based on political grounds, and move at once into Prague. Unfortunately Stettinius's message arrived too late; Eisenhower had already agreed to Stalin's request. When I was assigned to the American embassy in Prague two years later, I found that both Soviets and Czech communists had been spreading the word throughout the population that at Yalta Czechoslovakia had been placed in the "Soviet sphere" and were stating as evidence the fact that Eisenhower had refrained from entering and liberating Prague when he could easily have done so. No such decision had been taken at Yalta, but the belief of many Czechs that it had, taken together with their recollection of Munich, significantly reduced their willingness to resist Soviet domination.

Other notable examples of "military" decisions with profound political and human content, taken without apparent attention to the

latter, were the bombing of Dresden and the fire bombing of Tokyo
in early 1945, each of which wiped out some 75,000 civilian lives. A
civilian judgment as to whether each of these holocausts was so essential to victory as to justify this slaughter might have been appropriate.

Relevant to this point is a passage from a memorandum that Talley-
rand submitted to Napoleon nearly a century and a half before: "Sire,
three centuries of civilization have bequeathed to Europe a law of
nations for which, in the words of a famous writer, human nature will
never be grateful enough. This law is founded upon the principle that
nations should in time of peace do each other the most possible good,
and in time of war the least possible harm. . . .

"This law, the child of civilization, has furthered the growth of its
parent. To it Europe owes the preservation and the increase of her
prosperity, even at the height of the frequent wars which have divided
her."

This "law of nations," always, alas, more honored in the breach
than in the observance, was tacitly repealed in World War I and
totally forgotten in World War II.

To Roosevelt's eternal credit, however, must be laid his clear recognition and his repeated public endorsement of the necessity, after the
war, both of disarmament and of an international organization to
maintain peace. These necessities had come painfully to be understood
by the end of World War I, but the American people had rebelled
against them and so opened the way to the second war. Roosevelt was
determined that the error not be repeated.

In his Four Freedoms message to Congress in January 1941, almost
a year before the United States was bombed into the war, he spoke
of "a worldwide reduction of armaments to such a point and in such
a thorough fashion that no nation will be in a position to commit an
act of physical aggression against any neighbor." In the Atlantic
Charter that Roosevelt and Churchill proclaimed at their meeting off
Newfoundland in August 1941, they declared that "they hope to see
established a peace which will afford to all nations the means of
dwelling in safety within their own boundaries" and called for "the
abandonment of the use of force" and, "pending the establishment of
a wider and permanent system of general security," the disarmament
of nations threatening aggression.

In his fireside chat the day after Pearl Harbor Roosevelt said: "We must begin the great task that is before us by abandoning once and for all the illusion that we can ever again isolate ourselves from the rest of humanity. . . . We are now in the midst of a war, not for conquest, not for vengeance, but for a world in which this nation and all that this nation represents will be safe for our children."

The phrase "United Nations" was first used, at Roosevelt's initiative, in the joint declaration he and Churchill prepared in Washington in December 1941. All the nations fighting the Axis subscribed to it, and it was signed in the White House on New Year's Day, 1942.

In *Roosevelt and Hopkins* Sherwood quotes Harry Hopkins as saying to him the day after Roosevelt signed the Lend-Lease Bill in March 1941:

> You and I are for Roosevelt because he's a great spiritual figure, because he's an idealist, like Wilson, and he's got the guts to drive through any opposition to realize those ideals. Oh, he sometimes tries to appear tough and cynical and flippant, but that's an act he likes to put on, especially at press conferences. He wants to make the boys think he's hard-boiled. Maybe he fools some of them, now and then— but don't ever let him fool you, or you won't be any use to him. You can see the real Roosevelt when he comes out with something like the Four Freedoms. And don't get the idea that those are any catch phrases. *He believes them!* He believes they can be practically attained.

Despite Roosevelt's best efforts to ignore political war aims, other than those of the most general and noncontroversial character such as the Four Freedoms, politics intruded into all the wartime summit meetings between East and West. Where the main issues were international organization, as during Hull's visit to Moscow in 1943 or during the drafting of the United Nations Charter at Dumbarton Oaks in 1944, differences were overcome or muted. But where the treatment of liberated territories, particularly those adjacent to the Soviet Union, was concerned, the acute differences of perception, interest, and ideology that were shortly to bring on the Cold War emerged more and more intractably.

Some historians, astigmatized by subsequent history, have charged that at the most celebrated of these meetings, Yalta, in February 1945, a sick, "appeasing" Roosevelt surrendered Eastern Europe and China to a cunning, insatiable Stalin. The role at this meeting of Churchill, later the darling of the hardliners, is conveniently ignored.

I recall personally that when the American delegation returned from Yalta, its tough-minded State Department members, "Doc" Matthews and "Chip" Bohlen, were both astonished and jubilant that Stalin had accepted, almost without amendment, an American draft of a "Declaration on Liberated Territories" and had approved a compromise on the political settlement in Poland. Had these documents been implemented as written, as at that point still seemed possible though unlikely, free elections would have been carried out in the Eastern European countries, including Poland, and the character of these governments would have been very different from those that ultimately emerged.

To no one's intense surprise, they were not implemented, at least not as the Western authors understood and intended them. It very soon became clear, within days of the Yalta meeting in regard to Rumania, within a few weeks in regard to Poland, that the Soviets had a quite different understanding of the meaning of the exalted language used in the Declaration—they would guarantee the outcome of "free elections" by first installing governments under their control. Roosevelt's indignation at this delinquency was expressed in several of his last telegrams to Stalin and Churchill. Truman, in one of his first acts as President, lectured Molotov scathingly on the subject when the latter passed through Washington on his way to the U.N. Conference at San Francisco. Neither protest had the slightest effect. It is probable that Stalin agreed so casually to the declaration because he considered it mere window dressing, needed by the Western governments to satisfy their public opinion but not affecting the informal division of "responsibilities" which he had made with Churchill the previous autumn or the facts of life mandated by overwhelming military forces on the ground.

Nevertheless, the condemnation of Yalta is, for the most part, unfounded. Bohlen, who attended most of the wartime and postwar summit meetings, later wrote: "The map of Europe would look exactly the same as it does today if there had never been a Yalta Conference." That judgment is difficult to dispute. What determined the fate of Eastern Europe was the presence of Soviet military forces which had poured into these countries in the process of defeating the German armies. Stalin is quoted by Djilas, who met with him on several occasions during the war, as saying: "Everyone imposes his own system as far as his army can reach. It cannot be otherwise."

It is conceivable that had the demand for unconditional surrender not been maintained, had the Nazis been overthrown by an internal coup and an armistice concluded sometime in 1944 before the Russian armies had penetrated much beyond their 1939 frontiers, a more independent and democratic Eastern Europe might have been preserved. Even that is, however, unlikely. Stalin would almost certainly have taken advantage of the defeat of Germany, under whatever circumstances, to insist on and impose, at least in Poland and Rumania, the "friendly governments" which he considered, in light of Russian historical experience, indispensable to the security of the Soviet Union.

When Arthur Bliss Lane, ambassador-designate to Warsaw, called on Roosevelt in March 1945 before departing for his post and protested events in Poland, Roosevelt replied: "Do you want me to go to war with the Soviet Union?" That was probably the only way a free Poland could have been restored at that time. Hungary and Czechoslovakia may have initially fallen in a different category in Stalin's mind. He did permit indisputably free elections in both countries in 1945 and 1946. It was only when the Cold War began to heat up in 1947, and thereby to fuel his paranoia about Soviet security, that he moved to extend his domination to Budapest and Prague.

Another charge subsequently leveled at Roosevelt was that he surrendered at Yalta parts of Japan—southern Sakhalin and the Kuril Islands—and parts of China—Port Arthur and joint operation with the Chinese of the Manchurian railroads. The reason he did so was of course to ensure the prompt entry of the Soviet Union into the war in the Pacific, which all his military advisers assured him was absolutely essential if the American invasion of the Japanese main islands, planned for the coming November, were to succeed, and to save the scores of thousands of American lives that might be lost if the Japanese armies in Manchuria were moved back for defense of the homeland. This expectation turned out to be an egregious and fateful example of faulty intelligence. The Japanese armies, Japanese shipping, and Japanese industry had already been so mortally damaged that even had the atomic bombs not been dropped on Hiroshima and Nagasaki, surrender could almost certainly have been brought about without invasion. Soviet entry into the Pacific war was quite unnecessary to achieve victory. The mistake, however, was not made at Yalta but in previous deliberations of the Joint Chiefs of Staff.

The war in Europe was finished by the end of April, but two more important Allied conferences were held before the conclusion of the war in the Pacific. The San Francisco conference in May and June, which I attended as an assistant to its chairman, Secretary of State Stettinius, completed the drafting of the United Nations Charter and secured its approval by the fifty-one founding members. Roosevelt's posthumous triumph was confirmed when the charter was ratified by the United States Senate by the astonishing majority of eighty-nine to two.

The final wartime meeting, which I attended as secretary general of the American delegation, was held at Potsdam near Berlin in July and August. While not as widely misinterpreted as Yalta, elaborate fantasies have been woven about Potsdam as well.

In a book on the subject published several years ago, Charles Mee wrote: "The conference exhibits three men who were intent upon increasing the power of their countries and of themselves and who perceived that they could enhance their power more certainly in a world of discord than of tranquility. . . . We see three men who took the stuff of historical forces, of international conflict, of differing political and economic needs, and shaped them into the stuff of casus belli."

This judgment is grossly mistaken in almost every respect. The three leaders were obviously trying to protect and promote what they saw as the national interests of their countries, which all three were keenly aware were in some instances in fundamental conflict. Nevertheless, each just as clearly perceived those interests would be best preserved by an effort to maintain as much of their wartime cooperation, in Europe and prospectively in the Far East where the war still continued, as was possible without sacrificing other basic interests.

In a message to Stalin a month before Potsdam, Churchill had written: "There is not much comfort in looking into a future where you and the countries you dominate, plus the Communist parties in many other states, are all drawn up on one side and those who rally to the English-speaking nations and their associates and dominions are on the other side. It is quite obvious that their quarrel would tear the world to pieces and that all of us leading men on either side who had anything to do with that would be shamed before history."

Far from desiring to shape "the stuff of historical forces" into "the stuff of casus belli," all three were still in the summer of 1945 at great pains to moderate and accommodate, to the point they felt they safely could, the emerging conflicts between them, lest these conflicts should "tear the world to pieces" and "shame before history . . . all of us leading men on either side."

Nor is there the slightest ground for claiming that any one of these three "perceived that they could enhance their power more certainly in a world of discord than of tranquility." No one who studies the career of Harry Truman objectively could imagine that he had an appetite for personal power. At Potsdam he was angry at what he believed to be Soviet violations of the Yalta agreements, but far and away his chief concern was to end the Pacific war as quickly and at as little cost in American lives as possible, and for this purpose to maintain the Soviet alliance insofar as it was possible to do so without what he would consider indefensible moral compromise. He was certainly as aware as Roosevelt had been that the American people, after having just fought one great war around the globe, would have no inclination whatsoever for seeking a "casus belli" for another. On the contrary, his conduct of relations with the Soviet Union during the next year and a half offers convincing proof of his determination to go as far as he thought he could in seeking accommodation rather than provoking conflict.

Churchill was of course unceremoniously and unexpectedly removed from office in the midst of the Potsdam Conference. There is no shred of evidence, however, that either he or his mild successor, Clement Attlee (whom Churchill described as "a modest man who has much to be modest about"), were seeking "to enhance their power in a world of discord" or to shape conflict into a "casus belli." The behavior of an obviously exhausted Churchill during his days at Potsdam clearly demonstrated a desire to compose conflicts, not enhance them. The overwhelming victory of the Labor party in the June elections brought home to both British leaders the will of their war-weary people to concentrate henceforth on domestic reform rather than imperial ambition or even the preservation of empire. Indeed within three years British dominion in India, which had lasted for two centuries, was abandoned without a shot being fired.

As to Stalin, while his ambitions on his own western marches, and in Germany as well, were clear enough, it was equally clear that he had every reason to pursue them, to the extent he could, by accommodation rather than conflict. Indeed subsequent experience repeatedly showed that while Stalin would push his advantages in Eastern Europe as far as he thought he safely could, he would also, when confronted by an Allied firmness ready to risk war, back down with unruffled aplomb. His fundamental prudence was demonstrated in Berlin, in Greece, and in Austria, not to mention Yugoslavia, where in 1948 one of his own satellites single-handedly defied him.

As to his personal power at home, that needed no enhancement. It was never in question. It is true that when Averell Harriman at Potsdam said to him: "It must give you great satisfaction after all the Soviet Union has been through to be here in Germany," Stalin grumbled: "Czar Alexander got to Paris." It is probable that, in his hours of paranoia, he would have liked to exercise over wider territories the uninhibited personal power he enjoyed in the Soviet Union and Eastern Europe; but, in his overriding hours of sobriety and realism, he had a keen appreciation, as his whole career so strikingly demonstrated, of what was possible and what was not.

The two issues that in fact occupied the center of the stage at Potsdam were German reparations and Poland's western frontier. After the appalling devastation wrought by the Nazis in the Soviet Union, the Russians were determined to extract as substantial reparations as possible, preferably in the form of equipment to rebuild their industries, and therefore most of all from the Ruhr where Germany industry was still mainly centered, despite the bombing. The Americans and British, who felt a responsibility for the health and welfare of the western zones they occupied, were unwilling to let the Soviets bleed the baby they were trying to nourish and hence indirectly bleed them. Moreover, they saw political dangers in giving the Russians access to the Ruhr.

As to Poland, Stalin insisted in compensating the Poles, that is, *his* Poles, for the loss of their eastern provinces to the Soviet Union by ceding them Silesia and Stettin in the west, which had been German for centuries. Churchill protested that a German irredenta would be created and might cause future wars. Stalin was unmoved, and Truman prepared to bargain. In the final compromise, which permitted the conference to adjourn on a harmonious note, the Western states accepted the Polish frontier proposed by Stalin, who agreed to appropriate his reparations primarily from his own zone of Germany.

One more momentous event, pregnant with unforeseen and unexamined consequences, occurred before the end of the war—the explosion of the first atomic bombs on Hiroshima and Nagasaki, the loosing of the genie from the bottle.

Truman's purpose was to end the war without having to invade the Japanese main islands, which his military advisers had warned might cost half a million American casualties. Had this been the inescapable alternative, it would be hard to contest the decision. There is grave doubt, however, whether these were the only possible choices. By the beginning of August the Americans had a much clearer appreciation than they had had at Yalta of the depth of Japan's exhaustion and the probable imminence of its collapse. The response of the Japanese to the proclamation issued at Potsdam had not been unequivocal, but it had given sufficient evidence of a will stretched almost to the breaking point to have warranted further parley. The invasion was not scheduled until November, three months away. There would have been ample time to have pressed further the attack by air and sea, which would probably have been conclusive. Had it not been, there was always the other alternative, proposed in June by some of the deeply troubled scientists who had made the bomb—dropping one for demonstration on an uninhabited or lightly inhabited spot. At the very least there was not the slightest excuse for dropping the second bomb at Nagasaki, three days after Hiroshima, before sufficient time had elapsed to determine whether the first alone would bring about surrender.

Charles Mee, in the book quoted above, argues that the bomb was dropped on Japan in order to impress and intimidate the Russians. There is no contemporary evidence whatsoever that Truman had this in mind. Mee himself quotes the President as saying later: "I regarded the bomb as a military weapon and never had any doubt that it should be used." He mentioned casually to Stalin at Potsdam, after the Alamogardo test, that the United States "had a new weapon of unusual destructive force." Stalin said he was glad to hear it and hoped the Americans would make "good use of it against the Japanese." Whether he had been briefed about the nature of the bomb from the reports of the spy Klaus Fuchs at Los Alamos is not certain but is probable. In fact he had no desire to see the war against Japan end before he came into it and could seize, perhaps increase, his spoils. He could have expedited the peace parleys, in which the Japanese had unwisely chosen him as an intermediary, but was careful not to do so. In any case he was not then or later intimidated by the bomb.

Americans are an impatient people, and Truman was a particularly impatient man. This was patently visible at Potsdam. America had been at war for nearly four years, and its losses had been heavy. The President felt it to be his duty to end it as soon as possible without sacrificing one more American life than necessary. The atomic bomb was a weapon "of unusual destructive force," but it was in his eyes just another weapon. His military chiefs all advised using it, indeed assumed it would be used, probably for much the same reason as the President, though the itch to try out a phenomenal new arm may not have been absent.

To suppose that in dropping the atomic bomb in August 1945 the Americans had its effect on the Russians primarily in mind is an unwarranted extrapolation backward from a Cold War that had not yet begun.

Contemporary reactions, even from sophisticated military men, were quite different. Two days after Hiroshima, Douglas MacArthur said to Teddy White in Manila: "White, do you know what this means? Men like me are obsolete. There will be no more wars, White, no more wars." Unfortunately, this did not turn out to be the case. Perhaps the most decisive result of the demonstrations at Hiroshima and Nagasaki was to intimidate *both* superpowers so that in the subsequent thirty-five years neither has ventured to use an atomic weapon. Had they not witnessed this dramatic and unambiguous display, one or the other might subsequently have yielded to the temptation to try out a nuclear weapon in circumstances far more likely to produce a holocaust than was its use at the end of another kind of war. So possibly the 150,000 who were wiped out at Hiroshima and Nagasaki did not, like the soldiers at Verdun and the Somme, die in vain.

What were the consequences of the war, over and above the total defeat of the Axis? To what extent was World War II and its immediate aftermath the cause of the Cold War and the little wars that clustered around it, in the same sense as World War I and its aftermath had been a primary cause of World War II? Could the subsequent confrontation that, as Churchill warned, would "tear the world apart," have been avoided?

There can be no doubt that, wholly apart from the intentions or the initial behavior of the chief protagonists, the physical outcome of the war in Europe made confrontation extremely likely. By the movement of the Soviet armies to the Elbe, by the partition of Germany, by the absorption of half a dozen East European states into the Soviet empire, territorial buffers that had existed for centuries between two dissimilar "European" civilizations, for the last three decades between two barely compatible social systems, were demolished overnight. The heirs of Ivan the Terrible and Thomas Jefferson, of Karl Marx and Adam Smith, suddenly found themselves cheek by jowl along newly established and for the most part artificial boundaries, in the durability of which neither had much confidence.

The West, having seen the Soviets advance in four years from the Pripet marshes to the heart of the Holy Roman Empire, feared this might be but a step in a march to the Atlantic. The Soviets, having by the accident of war achieved the territorial and political gains they had dreamed of but been denied after 1917, were acutely aware of the vulnerability of these gains.

The Iron Curtain, much as Churchill might deplore it as a violation of the cultural community of historic Europe, was an almost spontaneous immunizing reaction by both sides to this sudden juxtaposition of two societies, each regarding the other as unhealthy and corrupting.

We have suggested earlier that each great war is likely to be a principal cause of the next one, because the victors impose exorbitant humiliations and the vanquished inevitably respond with demands for "justice" and revenge. Through a peculiar and happy combination of circumstances, this syndrome was for the most part absent after World War II. Partly because some of the lessons of World War I had been learned by the United States, Britain, and France, but much more because the collaboration of Germany and Japan proved essential to contain the Soviets, the two principal defeated states were soon welcomed into close alliance with the Western victors. Far from being punished, once their guilty governments had been purged, they were indulged and pampered. Each has, it is true, its irredenta, but these lost territories are for the most part in the hands of the Soviets and are retrievable only by war, which in a nuclear age is enormously hazardous, or by an accommodation with the Soviets, the costs of which are too high. World War II has, therefore, not created incentives for new wars by the vanquished comparable to those created by the Franco-Prussian War of 1870 or World War I.

The threats to peace that almost immediately emerged from World War II arose from profound differences among the victors. The question that has troubled historians has been whether the Cold War, first in Europe and then worldwide, could have been avoided by wiser and more prudent policies by both sides during the critical years from 1944 to 1947. The short answer is that, given the deeply engrained national and ideological predispositions on both sides, the circumstances of victory recalled above, and, to a lesser degree, the personalities of the protagonists, a Cold War could not have been prevented. The confrontation might have been mitigated, but it could hardly have been avoided.

How might it have been mitigated? Possibly, though only possibly, in various ways. An earlier concentration by Western leaders, particularly Roosevelt, on the distribution of power in Europe *after* the war might have led them to conclude that, while the overthrow of Hitler and the Nazis was essential, the total defeat of Germany was less important than ending the war before Soviet armies had occupied almost half of Europe. If this premise had been faced and accepted, there would have been no insistence on unconditional surrender. Instead the Germans would have been invited to overthrow Hitler and make peace at the earliest possible moment.

There might have been earlier opening of a second front in Northern Europe, which Stalin repeatedly demanded, which the Americans wanted but Churchill resisted because he was determined not to suffer again the enormous losses of manpower Britain had incurred in World War I. Had an earlier D-day in France been undertaken and succeeded, the Western armies might have met the Soviets on the Oder, or even the Vistula, instead of the Elbe.

Germany was divided into separate zones of occupation, largely at the insistence of the American and British military who considered tripartite administration cumbersome, and, more important, did not want the Soviets messing around in western Germany, including the Ruhr. However, had the gamble of a unified occupation been taken, Western armies would have been present with the Soviets throughout the whole of Germany. The German people, overwhelmingly anti-Soviet, would almost certainly have rallied to the West rather than the East, and the final outcome might have been a united Germany, as all the Allies originally envisaged, which was democratic in the Western sense, even though neutral, and might have played in Central Europe the role of buffer between East and West that Austria now plays in its very limited area.

There might have been at an early stage a more candid and realistic acceptance of Churchill's proposals for spheres of influence, rather than the naïve American revulsion at this revival of World War I wickedness. If the Soviets had been freely conceded a predominant influence in the contiguous border states of Poland, Rumania, and Bulgaria, as it was conceded in Finland, their security concerns might have eased and they might have been content, as their intention seemed to be until the Cold War began, to leave a substantial measure of independence to Hungary and Czechoslovakia and to refrain from pressing the civil war in a Greece conceded to the West. Such a division of Europe, if Roosevelt had been willing to bargain for it in 1942, might have been codified in more or less binding agreements while the Soviets were still fighting deep in their own territories, rather than being proposed when they were already overrunning their old frontiers in the winter of 1944–45.

Finally, it is arguable that the most serious mistake the Americans made immediately after the war was to fail to grant to the Soviets the substantial credits they so desperately needed for the reconstruction of their devastated country. They requested $6 billion in January 1945 and never received a straight answer. An alternative or a supplement to credits might have been provision of more considerable reparations from western Germany. Stalin probably interpreted the long procrastination and ultimate refusal of credits as a deliberate decision to keep Russia weak and subject to Western pressure. The refusal was not in fact so clearly calculated, but it did reflect the political differences and waning confidence between West and East that had already emerged by 1945. It is possible, however, that, had a generous program of loans or credits by the United States been adopted and implemented gradually over a period of years, the Soviet Union would have acquired a strong vested interest in maintaining reasonably cooperative relations with the West. This could conceivably have become a far more effective means of restraint—implicit and collaborative rather than explicit and threatening—than the Truman Doctrine, NATO, and the whole panoply of the Cold War proved to be.

It is probable that, given the political and psychological impediments on both sides to the realization of any of these might-have-beens, none could have been achieved, even had one or more been seriously pursued. Still, the fact that none of them was pursued, indeed even considered comprehensively and in depth, recalls a simple, unequivocal lesson of history to which we have already alluded several times. Clausewitz was right in saying that war is the pursuit of politics by other means, that war should be conducted in accordance with clearly determined political aims and its strategy adapted to the achievement of these aims as much as to immediate military victory. The fact that this maxim is so rarely observed in the heat of battle, even in immediate postwar settlements, is the chief reason why so many soldiers, and nowadays civilians, die in vain, why so many wars are lost so quickly after they have been won, and why one war so often leads to another.

Before moving on from World War II, it seems once again relevant to set forth a few of my personal experiences and impressions during those years from Pearl Harbor to Potsdam.

Three weeks after the war in Europe broke out in 1939, Roosevelt asked Congress to repeal the arms embargo provisions of the Neutrality Act which my division in the State Department had been administering. In November the embargo was lifted, American arms began to flow in quantity to Britain and France, and my division evolved, slowly at first, rapidly after the fall of France, from an enforcer of neutrality into an instrument of economic warfare. From then on we worked in close collaboration with the British Embassy to restrict the flow to the Axis powers of any supplies of military value, not only from the United States but from neutrals.

A few evenings after the attack on Pearl Harbor I stood in a small crowd in the chill December darkness on the lawn behind the White

House and heard Winston Churchill, his stocky figure solid as a rock beside Roosevelt in the dim light of the portico, speaking movingly of his American mother, his heritage from two English-speaking nations, and his unshaken confidence that they would triumph together.

I shared this confidence, and, despite the appalling series of disasters that followed for us and our allies during the next six months, I never for a moment doubted that we would win. In my diary on January 4, 1942, I noted that American entry in the war made this outcome certain. I also remarked that it might be easier to beat Germany than Japan, because Germany was easier to get at; I thought that we should be able to knock out Germany by the winter of 1943–44 and Japan a year later.

Incidentally, I was astonished throughout the war by the alternating complacency and panic of military intelligence, with some of whose officers we were in frequent touch. They expected the Polish army to hold out longer than it did; they were totally surprised by the fall of France but thereafter almost unanimously certain that Britain would fall very shortly; they thought the Russians would be beaten in a matter of weeks; they never imagined there would be an attack on Pearl Harbor, but when it came and was followed by a series of disasters, were convinced Alaska would be occupied by March or April; after the tide turned they had no doubt that victory in Europe would be achieved by the autumn of 1944; on the other hand, they were persuaded until the last minute that the war against Japan could not be ended until late in 1946. Fortunately, in most of these cases, Roosevelt and Churchill had more perspicacity and more sangfroid.

In the early fall of 1941 most of the responsibilities for economic warfare were shifted from the State Department to a new agency under Vice President Wallace, first called the Economic Defense Board, later the Board of Economic Warfare. I was at first placed in an office under Assistant Secretary Dean Acheson charged with liaison with the new agency but very shortly, when Undersecretary Sumner Welles judged that this office was insufficiently protective of his beloved Latin Americans, it too was abolished. Acheson rather sheepishly informed me that when he saw an express train roaring toward him (a reference to Welles's notable combination of impetuosity and inflexibility), he thought it only prudent to step off the track.

At this point I had a brief assignment with a new division charged by Cordell Hull, even at this early date, with postwar planning. It was headed by a short, roly-poly, twinkly-eyed, extremely sharp and guileful gentleman of Russian-Jewish extraction named Leo Pasvolsky. He had been Hull's longtime and trusted adviser on economic matters but was henceforth until after the San Francisco conference to engage exclusively in postwar planning, to which he devoted himself with the deepest dedication, pragmatism, and adroitness.

I recall that one of my responsibilities was to serve as secretary of a newly created committee of experts on postwar security, of which Norman Davis was chairman, Hamilton Fish Armstrong (to become my very close friend) an articulate member, and Grayson Kirk, later president of Columbia University and of the Council on Foreign Relations, first my assistant and later my successor.

However, postwar planning, except planning for the military occupation of liberated territories, enjoyed little prestige outside, or even inside, the State Department in 1942. My diary at the time reports a conversation with William Castle, Undersecretary of State under Hoover, noting a conversation *he* had with Charles Evans Hughes, former Chief Justice of the Supreme Court and Secretary of State. Hughes remarked that it was useless to do any postwar planning for Eastern Europe and the Balkans since "the Russians would decide all that." In my diary comment I was doubtful of this prediction unless "the British abdicate completely and leave a howling vacuum." Unfortunately, as earlier portions of this chapter make clear, it was American rather than British "abdication," but most of all the implacable torrent of Soviet armies, which decided the fate of Eastern Europe and the Balkans.

With the Allied invasion of North Africa in November 1942, I was shifted to an Office of Foreign Territories charged with representing the State Department in interagency direction of civil operations in the liberated areas. Working in this office strained my diplomatic abilities to the utmost, since it was headed by a very odd couple in reluctant and uneasy association: Ray Atherton, an extremely able but ultraconservative professional, whose object was to restore the status quo ante in the liberated territories, and Paul Appleby, a transplanted New Dealer, whose object was to upset the status quo ante.

My sympathies were with Appleby, but since Hull's were with Atherton, he usually won.

An additional ace in Atherton's hand was that he was zealously carrying out the policy of Roosevelt and Hull (which he and Admiral Leahy, our ambassador in Vichy, had inspired) of denigrating de Gaulle and the so-called Free French and supporting more expedient but less noble characters, such as Darlan and Giraud. Appleby leaned to the Free French and was vocally hostile to anyone linked to Vichy. I was already convinced at the time that de Gaulle, while a stiff, inflexible, and uncongenial character from the Anglo-Saxon point of view, would prove to be a hero to the people of France and that we would do far better to accept him early than late. However, Roosevelt and Hull, for reasons I could never quite fathom, had acquired a passionate dislike for this all too Gallic champion. Atherton imposed their policy with an iron hand, and before long Appleby sank without a trace.

As a consequence of the outcome of this bureaucratic hassle, Atherton, who was interested only in confounding de Gaulle, let responsibility for economic operations in liberated territories return to Dean Acheson, from whom he had originally filched it. Acheson put in charge of these operations a close friend, Tom Finletter, who was later to become Secretary of the Air Force under Truman and a power in New York liberal politics with Eleanor Roosevelt. Finletter, to whom I was now assigned, soon found himself as deeply mired in bureaucratic politics as Appleby had been, but he handled them, at least for a time, much more adroitly. Among the more jealous and pretentious of the numerous nabobs with whom he, and occasionally I, had to cope were Harry Dexter White, Henry Morgenthau's right-hand man, later father of the Bretton Woods agreements, still later a suicide under suspicion of being a communist agent; and Herbert Lehman, just retired as Governor of New York and now heading a new agency for overseas relief, ultimately to evolve into the United Nations Relief and Rehabilitation Agency.

At this point the Allied armies invaded Sicily and southern Italy, and it became necessary, since the Italians after twenty years of Fascism were not judged fit to run their own affairs, to set up an Allied civil administration. Every agency in Washington dashed forward to share the spoils and glory. Acheson and Finletter were able to grab the ball on the economic side, and a team was quickly organized under another former New Dealer, "Beany" Baldwin, to proceed to Naples.

By this time I had become extremely restless watching the war from Washington and had determined to seize the first opportunity to get closer to the action. This seemed a golden one. I applied for a place on the team, passed inspection by Baldwin, and was accepted. Came September and we were ready to take off. I had all my gear—uniform, helmet, olive-drab blankets, mosquito netting, first-aid kit—had practically kissed my reluctant wife and son good-bye, and was to take off at any moment.

Alas, Acheson and Finletter, while seeming prudently to have covered the bureaucratic waterfront, had forgotten the White House. This was a not unnatural omission in those benighted days before minions of that establishment had taken on plenipotentiary powers, but it proved to be a fatal one. Suddenly, without warning anyone but no doubt with secret zest and amusement, Roosevelt created out of thin air a wholly new "Foreign Economic Administration" under a hitherto unknown gentleman named Patrick Crowley and attached to it all the functions we in the State Department had been preparing to perform. I was left high and dry, just when almost airborne.

Fortunately for me, though my disappointment at losing my Italian province was very keen indeed, the needs of the day were so great that I was soon reemployed. Adolph Berle, Assistant Secretary of State, one of Roosevelt's original Brain Trusters, needed a temporary assistant, and I was named.

Berle, a boy wonder who had graduated from Harvard at eighteen and whose *Modern Corporation and Private Property* is still a relevant classic, was a small, intense, impatient, pyrotechnical man, contemptuous of those of lesser intellectual prowess (almost everyone) and little inclined to conceal that scorn. He compulsively involved himself in feuds with most of the other senior officers of the department. On the other hand, he was uniformly courteous and benevolent to subordinates. The last time I saw him, many years later and shortly before his death, was when he kindly appeared with me on a radio program to publicize one of my books, *The Insecurity of Nations.*

Berle's duties, and hence mine, were diverse, mysterious, and, for most Americans in those days, glamorously novel. They involved political supervision of the various clandestine activities into which the war had almost for the first time drawn us. We sat on the Joint Intelligence Committee of the Joint Chiefs of Staff and did liaison with Bill Donovan's Office of Strategic Services, the forefather of the CIA.

The main OSS issue at the time was the relative amount of aid to be afforded to Tito or to Mihajlovic, protagonist in the field of the Royal Yugoslav Government in exile. Berle, despite or perhaps because of having been a longtime liberal, was strongly pro-Mihajlovic. Indeed he was ahead of his time in opposing substantial aid to communist-dominated Resistance movements anywhere in Europe outside the Soviet Union and, like Charles Evans Hughes, in expressing the greatest apprehensions, as early as 1943, that they might take over much of the Continent. It was, however, ironic that the chief target of his ire was Tito, who was within four years to inflict on Stalin the unkindest cut of all.

My most time-consuming duty, however, was to go over each morning two or three fat loose-leaf books, each containing as many as 100 hectographed pages. This was only the political part of the previous night's "take" of "Magic," our interception and code-breaking of enemy and neutral messages at which we had become highly adept, which should have enabled us to forestall Pearl Harbor and did help us win the battle of Midway. My job each morning was to run through this vast compendia and mark the dozen or so messages I thought would be of most interest to the six or seven senior officers of the department authorized to see this material, indeed the only ones there who knew of its existence.

Many of these insights into enemy assessments and intentions were of great usefulness to us, and I assume the military messages, which I did not see, were even more helpful. I did not have serious doubts about the utility of this exercise in wartime, but even at that time I find the following comment in my diary: "A person with an excellent first-hand knowledge of Europe, for example, can from his reading of the newspapers predict developments practically as well as one with access to the most secret sources."

I have never been certain since, during the many years I have read thousands of such intercepted messages at home and abroad, that the continuance of this practice in peacetime, and its astronomical multiplication, is worth the vast expenditure of time, energy, and funds it requires. It may well have become only one more of those vast "boon-doggles" that persist unnecessarily but have become sacrosanct under the label of national security. I can recall extremely few intercepts that contained information I had not already learned, deduced, or guessed from more conventional sources. Yet the process, once started, like so many others in human society, rolls on like an avalanche, accumulating more and more useless debris. After all, there is a fascination in reading other people's mail, no matter how trivial.

I might mention one further sidelight on this exotic activity that came to my attention two years later. At one point in San Francisco when the Soviets were being particularly unpleasant and inscrutable, I asked Stettinius whether we should not be intercepting their messages. He replied that this had several times been proposed, but Roosevelt had rejected it as disloyal. I respected the President's scruples but doubted they were being reciprocated on the other side.

As I have said, my assignment to Berle was temporary, and I was at the beginning of 1944 shifted to another that had a considerable impact on my career.

Edward R. Stettinius, Jr., former chairman of the U.S. Steel Corporation and Lend-Lease administrator, was named Undersecretary of State in September 1943, replacing Sumner Welles, who had quarreled irreconcilably with Cordell Hull. Stettinius was soon appalled by the disorganization and the vendettas in the Department, whereby an array of rival fiefdoms reported independently to the Secretary and Undersecretary without coordination, even little knowledge of what the others were doing. The clashes of personalities, between Berle and Acheson, between James Dunn representing Europe and Wallace Murray representing the Near East, between Herbert Feis and Leo Pasvolsky battling for control of economic policy and the Secretary's ear, between Stanley Hornbeck, jealously monopolizing his Far Eastern turf, and everyone else with an interest in it, were monumental and distracting.

Stettinius created a Policy Committee of senior officials which met at first once a week, later three times a week, to consider matters of common concern and, in theory, to hammer out common policies. I was selected in January 1944 as executive secretary of this committee, to prepare its agenda and follow up execution of its decisions, and performed these functions for a year and a half. At first the senior officials fought with Stettinius and me to prevent "their" issues being placed on the agenda and, if they were, fought with each other as to how they should be disposed of. Eventually Stettinius, particularly after he became Secretary of State, got them accustomed to peaceful coexistence.

Stettinius has been much denigrated both by contemporaries and historians on the grounds that he had neither the training nor the experience to fill in those critical times the office of Secretary of State, to which Roosevelt appointed him in December 1944, allegedly because the President and Harry Hopkins wished to direct foreign policy without interference from the civilians. While it is quite true that Stettinius was neither a statesman nor a philosopher, he was a superb administrator and morale builder in his own organization. He was a great conciliator who never would admit that a difference was irreconcilable nor a problem insoluble. He had many friends and few enemies. He had done a magnificent job of sending an enormous volume of Lend-Lease supplies to Allies around the world. He reformed fundamentally the administration of the antique and sclerotic State Department. Many of his reforms have survived the countless reorganizations of the succeeding three and a half decades—which testifies to their soundness.

The caliber of the men he gathered around him as Secretary is further evidence of his flair and effectiveness: Joseph Grew, former ambassador to Japan, as Undersecretary, who was to play such a significant part, by insistently advocating retention of the emperor, in bringing about the Japanese surrender; Will Clayton, one of the ablest public servants I have known, as Assistant Secretary for Economic Affairs; Dean Acheson, reincarnated in charge of congressional relations, in which capacity he obtained almost unanimous Senate consent to the U.N. Charter and the Bretton Woods agreements; Nelson Rockefeller as Assistant Secretary for Latin American Affairs; Archibald MacLeish as Assistant Secretary for public relations, aided incidentally by a young man who then emerged for the first time in the public eye—Adlai Stevenson.

It is true that Stettinius was not always notable for his discretion. I recall his once telling the British ambassador in my presence, just after Roosevelt had been nominated for his fourth term with Harry Truman as candidate for Vice-President, of a "general feeling" in

Washington that if anything should happen to Roosevelt, Truman would have to be "poisoned." This facetious remark reflects the low repute in which an undistinguished product of the Kansas City "Pendergast machine" was held in Washington at that time. Yet only ten months later Truman was to fire Stettinius and to go on to become one of our outstanding Presidents in this century.

One of my early assignments with Stettinius was to attend the Dumbarton Oaks Conference in 1944 at a lovely, Old World estate in the heart of Washington, where American, British, and Soviet delegations drew up the first draft of the United Nations Charter and where I began an association of more than a quarter-century with that institution. I served as secretary of what turned out to be the most important committee of the conference, dealing with the security and enforcement powers of the organization. The committee met in a little upstairs room under the roof and, day after day sweltering without air conditioning in the August and September heat, hammered out the brave new compact "to save succeeding generations from the scourge of war."

By far the smartest characters on this committee were two "Russians"—Leo Pasvolsky of our delegation and Arkady Sobolev of the Soviet. Most of its debates were a duel between them, and they were jointly the authors of most of this part of the charter. On the other hand, the head of the entire Soviet delegation was their ambassador to Washington, a solemn, humorless young man who looked as though he were sucking a lemon, Andrei Gromyko. One was not sure whether the extremely laconic character of his contribution was due to lack of wit or lack of instructions.

Of course some of the basic principles were as good as settled before the conference even met. For example, the United States and the Soviets were equally insistent on the right of veto for permanent members of the Security Council, at least insofar as substantive matters were concerned. I attended U.S. meetings preparatory to the conference at which members of the Senate and the House and generals and admirals representing the Pentagon were adamant in insisting that American "boys" must not be sent into foreign wars, as the charter would provide under certain circumstances, without the explicit consent of our government, which required our right to exercise a veto if necessary. The argument on this point at Dumbarton Oaks, and subsequently at Yalta and San Francisco, revolved not about the veto per se but about subsidiary issues: whether the veto should apply to procedural matters, whether there should be freedom of debate in the Security Council, not subject to veto, and whether in particular a permanent member who was party to a dispute should be able to veto discussion of and action on that dispute. Ultimately, after hot arguments at Yalta and during a visit to Moscow for the purpose by the mortally ill Harry Hopkins, the liberal view, which the United States espoused, prevailed on all these three points. Stalin had other fish to fry.

One rather odd incident at this conference involving Alger Hiss has always stuck in my mind. After having worked through most of the war with Stanley Hornbeck on the Far East, Hiss had come to head a new division concerned with postwar planning. He had particularly become an authority on the embryonic United Nations. In this capacity he had been named Secretary General of the Dumbarton Oaks Conference, been taken by Stettinius to Yalta, and became subsequently Secretary General of the San Francisco Conference. At the time of Dumbarton Oaks he was considered to be one of the two or three most brilliant young men in the department, certain of a distinguished career.

It was therefore with the utmost amazement that, in a relaxed moment at the conference, I heard him make an inexplicable remark. The conferees used to take their lunch on the terrace in the shade of great oaks and elms, overlooking the glorious gardens. At one such lunch I was sitting at a small table with Hiss and one or two others. I do not recall the context of the conversation or the precise words he used, but I do vividly remember that he said in effect that he sometimes wished that he was dead.

Those of us at the table were struck quite dumb. As I say, I could not at the time conceivably imagine why a young man of such promise should make such a despairing remark. As I reflected years later, it occurred to me that it was precisely for this reason that he made it. Whatever may have been the nature of clandestine involvements that later brought about his ruin, he may already in 1944 have acutely and daily felt the intolerable weight, the ever-present danger, they imposed on his peace of mind and all his brilliant prospects.

Soon after taking over as secretary of the Policy Committee, I acquired another and even more fascinating duty with Stettinius. Like Roosevelt but even more so, he had an intense dislike for reading any document longer than a single page. He was not a scholarly or contemplative type and acquired his information through his ears and his nose.

At the same time, there was coming into the department daily a vast flood of papers, telegrams, dispatches, messages from Allied authorities, reports from military commanders, interdepartmental memoranda, "Magic" intercepts, of which the Secretary and Undersecretary must have at least some awareness. I was therefore told to scan all this torrent of material and to brief Stettinius about its highlights —at odd moments between appointments in his office, in his apartment at the Shoreham (where I once had tea with John Maynard Keynes and his Russian ballerina wife), in his bedroom while he was being massaged, in his car going from home to office or elsewhere, slightly breathless at his side as he strode across to the White House at his usual impetuous clip. In consequence, I was probably during the last year of the war one of the best informed individuals in Washington, except about purely military planning.

Other harried executives in and out of the department began to voice the same need as Stettinius for help in keeping abreast of the spinning kaleidoscope of events. Secretary of the Treasury Henry Morgenthau had played a considerable part in the conduct of foreign policy before we entered the war, but subsequently, to his exasperation, he was elbowed aside. He complained to Stettinius that no one told him anything. To mollify his ire, I was asked to brief him once a week, under the injunction from Stettinius "to tell him something but not too much." Subjected to Morgenthau's sharp questioning each week in his stately chambers in the Treasury Building, I found observance of this injunction required considerable ingenuity, but we eventually parted friends. The last time I saw him, fifteen years later, he called at my office in the embassy in Morocco, an old man, a little unsteady on his feet, but still both courteous and inquisitive.

Incidentally, his principal difference with the State Department in 1943–44 had been about Germany, which he wished to divide into several states limited largely to innocent pastoral pursuits. Oddly enough this view was shared by Sumner Welles. However, the prevalent opinion in the department, with which I agreed and which ultimately prevailed, was that such division would merely exacerbate German nationalism and provide it with a perennial irredentist goal: moreover, "pastoralization" was totally impractical in the twentieth century. I even argued that dividing Germany into "zones of occupation," an exercise then being planned by the European Advisory Committee in London, was likely to break up the country more lastingly and disturbingly than was then imagined. However, the thought of a joint threepower occupation of the whole of Germany gave our military shivers of horror, as I have said.

It may be relevant that at about this time, March 1944, I noted in my diary: "I fear that most of the difficulties of the post war world will arise from the immaturity of the American and Russian peoples, neither of which is ready for the position of world leadership which is being thrust upon them." A little later, in May of that year, I wrote that in postwar planning then under way, "altogether too much attention is being paid to the disposition of the enemy states. The really central problem of the next 50 years will be what might be called the intellectual modernization of Russia and China."

On the afternoon of April 12, 1945, Washington was suddenly pervaded by mysterious and dreadful rumors. An uncanny hush descended upon the busy bureaucracy. Stettinius was called to the White House and after a time returned to inform us that the President was dead. This was not entirely unexpected. During the 1944 campaign his speech, as we heard it on the radio, had often been slurred. His photographs in recent months had revealed alarming deterioration. The last time I had seen him, at his fourth inaugural in January on the back portico of the White House, his head was held proudly and his voice was firm, but he was clearly a sick and weary man.

Still, the shock was terrible. We had lived under his strong and benevolent arm for twelve years. The war was still on and was already giving birth to a host of intractable problems. Truman was an almost totally unknown quantity. How would we survive?

Oddly enough, I received a posthumous note from President Roosevelt. After my Italian plans fell through, I had decided to apply for reinstatement in the Foreign Service, with a view to breaking out of Washington after so many years and going to a post abroad as soon as possible. The mills of the bureaucracy had ground slowly, my application had at last been accepted, and a brief memorandum requesting presidential approval had been sent to the White House. There it totally and mysteriously disappeared for many months. Some days after Roosevelt's death Chip Bohlen, who was handling liaison with Harry Hopkins, saw on Hopkin's desk a batch of mail that had trickled back from Warm Springs. On top was the memo requesting my reinstatement, and on it was scribbled in a shaky, almost illegible hand, perhaps on his very last morning, "OK FDR."

I was not, however, destined to return to foreign service until I had in 1945 attended two famous conferences, at San Francisco and at Potsdam.

At San Francisco my first duty was to draft each evening a report from the Secretary to the President on what had occurred during the day. (Incidentally, had Secretary Byrnes followed this practice during his official peregrinations, he might well have prolonged his tenure of office.) My second duty was to continue and to expand my briefing of Stettinius, since the conference absorbed most of his time, about the whole melodrama of events around the world in what we know now, but did not know then, were the closing weeks of the war.

Two sad little incidents stand out in my memory. The first was a visit with Stettinius to a military hospital to which severely wounded from the battle of Okinawa had just been flown. I recall the long rows of maimed and mangled men, some surviving only in a hobgoblined world of their own, others fumbling awkwardly to muster some response to the strange civilian "brass" at their bedsides.

The second was the last meal in the penthouse of the Fairmont Hotel with a stricken Stettinius, who had just learned what others had long known—on his return to Washington next day he would be required to resign his great office. At the pinnacle of his success, just after the conference he had shepherded had been triumphantly concluded and the United Nations Charter signed with pomp and ceremony, his own future lay in ruins at his feet. Four of us ate quietly at the shrunken table and, looking out the high French windows at the beautiful city, talked of casual, inconsequent things.

Within a few days I was off to Potsdam as Secretary General of the U.S. delegation. Jimmy Byrnes, who had barely been sworn in as Secretary of State, had accepted Stettinius's nominations for the delegation almost intact, adding only three or four of his own people including, somewhat incongruously, Ben Cohen, one of the chief architects of the New Deal; Admiral Leahy, former Chief of Naval Operations and ambassador to Vichy, and Joseph Davies, husband of Marjorie Merriwether Post, prewar ambassador to Moscow, and apologist for Stalin. Actually none of these three, nor indeed Averell Harriman, Robert Murphy, or most of Stettinius's nominees played much part in the substantive decisions of the conference. Perhaps Will Clayton and Ed Pauley, because of their involvement with the reparations question, which was Truman's and Byrnes's main concern, were the most influential.

I have commented in the historical section of this chapter on the issues debated, resolved, or unresolved at Potsdam. Let me conclude with half a dozen vignettes plucked from fading memories.

Before the conference opened, our delegation toured what was once Berlin, saw the desolation of tumbled brick and twisted steel stretching as far as the eye could see, smelled the stench of burning, corruption, and dust. At one end of the Unter den Linden a black-market bazaar was in lively progress, Berliners, mostly women, some in rags, some still displaying faded elegance, bartering watches, jewelry, priceless antiques, for food or cigarettes proffered by callow Red Army soldiers. Refugees from the East streamed along the main highways, pulling their few pitiful rescued possessions in little carts, a sleeping child often sprawled on top. In Hitler's massive marbled Reichschancellory everything of value had been wrenched from floor and walls; only one room was ankle-deep in third-class military medals, no longer of interest to anyone. In the dark, dank, gutted cellars where Hitler and Goebbels had died, the stink, the murk, and the silence were almost unbearable. We got out as fast as we could.

The American and British delegations were housed in Neu Babelsberg, a gracious colony of villas, untouched by war, inhabited until a few days before our arrival by producers, directors, and actors from the nearby UFA film studios, a little Hollywood on the Wannsee. Behind the elegant villa where the American "mess" was installed there was a fresh grave in which was buried, we were cheerfully informed by our mess sergeant, the owner of the villa who had been ousted without warning by the Russians and had imprudently sought to return under cover of darkness to retrieve some of her property.

I recall a great reception given by the British in a pompous Victorian palace built by Kaiser Wilhelm. Having been asked by a junior

member of the British delegation to help entertain one of his princi-
pals, I was introduced to a bald little man figuratively sucking his
thumb in a corner of the vast hall, totally ignored by all the bemed-
aled, beribboned personages chattering there. He was Clement Attlee,
within a fortnight to become Prime Minister of Britain. When I
dropped in at British headquarters the evening after the election
returns came in, the gloom could have been cut with a knife. Both
civilian and military Oxbridge types thought the end of the world had
come. Yet the most impressive Britisher taking part in the conference
was Ernie Bevin, the enormously corpulent, indefatigably combative,
instinctively incredulous trade-union leader, now Foreign Secretary.

The conference itself was held in the Cecilienhof Palace, which had
belonged to the Hohenzollern Crown Prince and Princess. The
American delegation met in what had been their heterogeneous library, which included a number of volumes on naval affairs bearing
the nameplate of the Prince's father, a would-be "naval person" in his
own time. We noticed one day that Admiral Leahy was examining
these volumes with deep interest, and the next that several had disappeared. Before the conference ended, there were yawning gaps on the
library shelves. Many of us had followed the Admiral's impeccable
example, on the theory that any volumes we did not "liberate" the
Russians after our departure would.

I have given earlier my impressions of Stalin, Churchill, and Truman at the conference. Stalin certainly overshadowed the other two
in confidence, competence, and cunning. He also completely dominated, indeed presumably though not visibly terrified, his own subordinates. Molotov, who met in the mornings with the other Foreign
Ministers and reported in the afternoons to the Big Three, was repeatedly reproached for having been too adamant and uncompromising
with "our friends," overruled on nonessentials, and supported ada-
mantly on the things that mattered. While Churchill rambled on
about history, justice, and future generations, Stalin leaned back in his
chair and watched the smoke of his cigarette curling lazily to the
ceiling. He was never angry or impatient, as Truman and Bevin
sometimes were. He rose only twice from his chair during the sessions:
once to show the President a map of Stettin and its environs, which
he proposed be ceded to Poland in further compensation for what it
had "lost in the East," a second time warmly to greet Field Marshal

Alexander, the conqueror of Italy, who had been called in to make a point by Churchill.

I recall old Henry Stimson, a little late for an appointment with Stalin, shuffling down a long carpeted corridor with half a dozen Russian underlings circling anxiously about him and chivying him on.

I recall the last night of the conference, almost midnight, the three great men tired but jovial, their work almost complete, in a few minutes tying up the loose ends, offhandedly confirming the fate of populations and principalities.

After our return to Washington I had been slated to be assigned to our Prague embassy. However, thanks to the unexpected Japanese surrender and other accidents, I found myself in September en route to the headquarters of Lord Louis Mountbatten's Southeast Asia Command in Kandy, Ceylon, and, after a few weeks there and in Delhi, on to Bangkok to reopen as chargé d'affaires our legation there. At thirty-eight I had my first independent post.

❧ 6 ❦

Military Effects
of World War II
1945-1979

No axiom has been more conclusively demonstrated than that wars breed wars. During the entire twentieth century so far, from the Boer War to the Afghan war, "great powers" have been almost continuously engaged, singly or jointly, in some kind of armed conflict, most of which have led to another or to several others.

Thanks most of all to the inhibitions imposed by nuclear weapons, there has not been for more than a third of a century a war in which two major military powers fought each other. That is an historical anomaly which cannot be relied on to last. As Hiroshima and Nagasaki come to be seen by present and future generations more as an outlandish aberration in bygone history than as an authentic and contemporary human experience, they may, as Santayana warned, be more easily repeated. The Chinese have a habit of saying that war between the two superpowers is inevitable but not imminent. I should rather say that, as long as nuclear weapons are deployed on hair-triggers and brandished as threats, war is imminent but not inevitable.

Potential causes of World War III are lying about the global landscape in rich profusion. It will be the purpose of this chapter to examine those potential causes, to try to determine whether they are manageable and avoidable or whether, as always before in human history, they will sooner or later overtake and overwhelm us, though this time, thanks again to nuclear weapons, more conclusively than in the past.

There has been a growing paradox in human affairs ever since Columbus and Vasco da Gama knit Europe with the two Indies at the end of the fifteenth century. Particularly in the present era of aircraft, telephones, and communications satellites, of Western motors turning on Eastern oil and the masses of the East undergoing sudden metamorphosis through Western technology, there has developed an interdependence among nations and peoples that quickly transmits information and misinformation, appetites and expectations, turmoil and conflict, from one end of the earth to the other. To paraphrase Churchill, never in history have so many owed so much to so many.

The paradox is that, while gradually since the fifteenth century the older nations have learned to manage their own internal affairs more or less satisfactorily—with some recent glaring exceptions—no community or hierarchy of nations has yet learned to manage even passably their interdependence. The leading European nations of the sixteenth and seventeenth centuries wasted their talents and energies trying to impose their theologies on each other. The eighteenth century canonized the balance of power but could never keep it steady for more than a decade or two. The Holy Alliance after the Congress of Vienna tried in vain to halt history in its tracks and to seal off their populations from new and dangerous thoughts. The Europeans of the eighteenth and nineteenth centuries claimed a "civilizing mission" excused their appropriating half the globe. Britain, France, Germany, Russia, and Austria so mismanaged even their own interdependence and that of their empires in the present century as to provoke and succumb to two world holocausts. The international law-making and peacekeeping institution conceived after World War I by Lord Grey and Woodrow Wilson was stillborn.

It is not surprising therefore that neither of the two "superpowers," which alone were left with substantial economic and military resources after World War II, nor the somewhat more ecumenical international institution they established, have been able to avoid conflict or to reconcile and regulate a world physically more unified but spiritually more ruptured. Indeed it would be hard to imagine an odder couple to charge with rebuilding world society harmoniously.

Every nation is a product of its own history. The history of Russia comprises a catalogue of catastrophes and traumas that only the toughest and most resilient of peoples could have survived. Yet, in triumphing over every obstacle and every expectation, they were politically retarded and psychologically maimed. Two and a half centuries of enslavement to an Oriental despotism that by turns oppressed, corrupted, and neglected them; a despotism of their own, equally brutal, capricious, and absolute; repeated invasions not only from the East but from Poles, Swedes, Germans, and even French; an Iron Curtain separating them for centuries from the civilization of Europe, from Renaissance, Reformation, and Enlightenment; an aborted revolution in 1917, frozen after only nine months into a mold as rigid, as sequestered, and as dogmatic as that of the Czar: it is little wonder that the Russians, though they look like other Europeans, do not think or act like them.

As early as the 1770s, when Diderot was a guest of Catherine the Great, who paid little attention to his "enlightened" advice, he wrote: "In Russia there is a nuance of panic terror in the attitude of people. . . . They always seem to be existing just before an earthquake or just after it, and they have the appearance of trying to find out if the ground is really firm under their feet." Two hundred years later, after three calamitous invasions, a totalitarian revolution, decimation of the more diligent peasantry, and the purging of millions of innocent officials and intellectuals, they *know* the ground is not firm under their feet.

It may be safely said that never in their long history have the Russian people enjoyed good government. Madame de Stael described the system in her day, alluding to the palace coup that eliminated the mad Czar Paul, as "despotism mitigated by strangulation." A modern British writer, Ronald Hingley, has summed it up in the following terms: "A force overwhelming and arbitrarily imposed, commanding total obedience except on the occasions when deceit and trickery allow loop-holes for evasion, a force feared but not respected—such has been authority to the Russian throughout the ages."

It is hardly surprising that such a system, arising from unique circumstances, is ill adapted either for export or for sharing responsibly in the management of world affairs. Nonetheless, it has had and continues to have pretensions to do so. The Russians have not yet adopted the Western phrase "civilizing mission," but, like other peoples, many of them have believed throughout their history that they have been chosen by God to lead the benighted out of spiritual darkness into some mystical orthodox paradise of sweetness and light. Two writers of genius from quite different eras, Dostoevski and Solzhenitsyn, have shared this dream.

A similar dream, in modern Marxist but no less extravagant form, has inspired the Soviet régime and its elaborate apparatus of Comintern, Cominform, peoples' democracies, and "wars of national liberation." Additional legitimacy and zeal have been conferred on this national enterprise by the supposition that it is based on a "scientific" doctrine destined inevitably to triumph. The fact that it has so far triumphed only in three countries outside the area dominated by Russian armies—China, Cuba, and Vietnam—and that the greatest of these has since fallen prey to heresy, may have shaken but has not shattered the convictions of the faithful. One reason why it has not triumphed more widely is that Soviet Russians, like earlier Russians brought up under the despotisms and with delusions of grandeur, are usually ill fitted to propagate the faith abroad. Constitutionally intolerant of dissent, unwilling to sacrifice dogma to pragmatism, as arrogant to "lesser breeds without the law" as the haughtiest of British colonials, their excursions into the outer world end up more often in expulsion than in the dictatorship of the proletariat.

The other superpower, the United States, though it has fared much better than its rival in its three decades of paramountcy, was also ill prepared for the world responsibilities that it had firmly rejected in 1920 but could not shirk twenty-five years later.

For three-quarters of a century, from the Monroe Doctrine in 1823 until the battle of Manila Bay, it remained politically and psychologically secluded in its hemisphere, preoccupied and shaped, as Frederick Jackson Turner pointed out, with the acquisition, occupation, and development of its vast continental empire or, as some of the empire builders described it, with the accomplishment of its "manifest destiny." Though divided among a multiplicity of religious sects, it had a single political creed, democracy, to which it was passionately attached but which, during this period, it sought to propagate outside its own territory by example and by missionary endeavor rather than by military power. As John Quincy Adams wisely put it: "We should be friend of civil liberties around the world but not a guarantor of those liberties."

However, as the last continental frontier was reached about 1890, manifest destiny, democratic zeal, and Christian evangelism began to fuse into transoceanic ambitions that bore a striking resemblance to the wicked imperialisms of the Old World. In 1898 William McKinley appropriated Hawaii, liberated Cuba, and, after a night of agonized prayer, concluded that it was his duty to retain and civilize the Philippines on the other side of the Pacific. Andrew Carnegie, captain of industry, philanthropist, and crusader for peace, exultantly looked forward to the day when in his country "five hundred millions, every one an American, and all boasting common citizenship, will dominate the world—for the world's good."

This was the mood, exemplified also by Theodore Roosevelt, which in the decade and a half before World War I curiously paralleled the most progressive era in American domestic politics since the Jacksonian revolution. Both culminated under the aegis of Woodrow Wilson in his admirable domestic achievements and in the crusade "to make the world safe for democracy." Disillusionment with the meager results of that crusade; resentment at having been wrenched from the comfortable cultivation of their continent and embroiled in the quarrels of Europe; relief at the prospect of a return to a "normalcy" (shorthand for private acquisition and enjoyment)—these sentiments created the mood of isolationism that dominated the next two decades. Nevertheless, all the earlier strains of "manifest destiny," patriotic, commercial, evangelical, remained firmly implanted just below the surface, ready to bloom again as soon as the climate was propitious.

So the second superpower that unexpectedly found itself saddled with global responsibilities after World War II was also historically and psychologically conditioned to confront them in ways ill adapted to many of the obstinate realities it would encounter. Its advantages over the other superpower were considerable: an immunity from the ravages of war that had so cruelly devastated both its rival and its allies; a much more productive, even though not consistently reliable, economic system; a remarkably successful form of government which, although less exportable than Americans supposed, was congenial to

Western Europe and respected in principle, if not usually in practice, in much of the rest of the world. These were only relative advantages, however, more easily enjoyed at home than in a diverse and unaccommodating world. They did not equip the United States either for imposing and managing a global Pax Americana or for dealing effectively with the potential causes of World War III—which appeared even before the guns of World War II were silent.

By far the gravest of these potential causes was the almost immediate confrontation of the two victorious superpowers, first in Europe, then in East Asia, shortly over most of the globe, together with the multiplication of their armed forces and weapons, of which the most unprecedented and monstrous were nuclear weapons. Since the appearance of this most extraordinary of human inventions at Alamogordo and Hiroshima has dominated military and international affairs ever since, and for the first time in human history has created a real possibility of race suicide, it deserves prior consideration among all the imaginable causes and consequences of World War III.

Weapons do not cause war, but they do create continuous anxiety and tension among nations fearful of what their rivals will do with them; they facilitate abrupt resort to war and its rapid escalation, whenever anxiety and tension reach a pitch that overcomes judgment and reason. These "side effects" are no less characteristic of nuclear than of other arms.

When Churchill was informed by Truman at Potsdam of the first successful explosion at Alamogordo, he called it "the second coming in wrath." Addressing the Council of Churches in August 1945, just after Hiroshima and Nagasaki, John Foster Dulles, then a private citizen, said: "If we, a professedly Christian nation, feel free to use atomic energy in that way . . . the stage will be set for the sudden and final destruction of mankind." When Bernard Baruch presented to the United Nations in 1946 the American plan for controlling the atom, he declared: "We are met here to judge between the quick and the dead." In a minority annex to a report of the General Advisory Committee to the U.S. Atomic Energy Commission in 1950, opposing construction of the thermonuclear or "hydrogen" bomb, Enrico Fermi and Isidor Rabi, two of the distinguished scientists who had contributed to the wartime bomb, wrote: "The fact that no limits exist to the destructiveness of this weapon makes its very existence and the knowledge of its construction a danger to humanity as a whole. For these reasons . . . we think it wrong on fundamental ethical principles to initiate the development of such a weapon."

Some years later, after Stalin had died, Nikita Khrushchev expressed the view that if nuclear war occurred, "the living would envy the dead." At a meeting with Kruschev, with the British Prime Minister Harold Macmillan remarked that nuclear war must be avoided because there would be few survivors. "Khrushchev replied, with obvious distaste," Macmillan reported later, "that on the contrary there would be many survivors, yellow and black people, that the whites would be fools to permit such an eventuality and that the Russians are after all Europeans."

Despite these solemn scientific, ethical, and racist warnings, fears of what "the other side" was doing led Americans, Russians, and British, later joined by French and Chinese, to proceed, as soon as the knowhow and the economic resources were available to them, to develop nuclear weapons.

At the last cabinet meeting he attended, on September 21, 1945, Henry Stimson, elder statesman, former Secretary of State, since 1940 Secretary of War, advocated presenting to the Soviet Union a proposal to control and limit immediately use of the bomb, with a view to stopping all work on military application of atomic energy if Russia and Britain would agree. This proposal took shape next year in the Baruch Plan, which failed of adoption essentially because of the already insuperable mistrust between the two superpowers, so recently allies. The United States insisted that the plan go into effect by stages, during which this country would continue to be sole possessor of the bomb, and that it be accompanied by an inspection system not subject to Security Council veto. While these safeguards seemed eminently reasonable to Americans, they were no doubt perceived by Stalin in the emerging Cold War atmosphere as intolerable instruments of U.S. political pressure on the Soviet Union. He preferred to proceed with his own nuclear weapon, which would ultimately give him commensurate power, the military "parity" finally achieved after colossal effort on both sides nearly thirty years later.

So the attempt to put the genie back into the bottle failed almost immediately. Thereafter the competition between the superpowers in nuclear and other weapons escalated almost continuously. It is futile to apportion blame for a mutually burdensome and potentially disastrous process to which both contributed prodigiously. While the Americans from time to time mistakenly perceived a "bomber gap," a "missile gap," and other supposed Soviet ascendencies, in fact the United States was almost always the forerunner in the production of new and more lethal weapons systems. This was not due to any peculiar wickedness but simply to American technological superiority. In the gathering momentum of the arms race, what President Eisenhower so aptly called "the military-industrial complex" was assembled—a very large number of able, energetic, ambitious, highly trained technologists, both military and civilian, who over many years concentrated all their abilities and energies on meeting what they considered to be their patriotic responsibilities by producing the finest, most sophisticated, and most effective weapons they could conceive, design, and manufacture. "The root of the problem has not been maliciousness," Herbert York, a former director of research at the Pentagon, has written, "but rather a sort of technological exuberance that has overwhelmed other factors." In the absence of any form of arms control, the momentum of technology, in military as in other fields, was irresistible. The unwritten rule was that if a new weapon more effective than an old could be produced, it should be, for otherwise the adversary might produce it first. No doubt the same considerations prevailed on the Soviet side, though lesser technological and economic resources caused them to lag behind until the 1970s.

The process was well described by Robert McNamara, who as Secretary of Defense under Kennedy and Johnson presided over the most considerable buildup of U.S. strategic forces. "We didn't plan to have," McNamara later wrote, "the numerical advantage that we had in 1966 or 1967 vis-a-vis the Soviets. We didn't need it. The reason we had it was the range of uncertainty that one must guard against, and there's no other way to guard against it than by assuming the worst, and acting accordingly. Then, when the worst doesn't happen, you've got more than you need, and that's bad enough. But worse than that they see you have it and they react, and then you've got to do it again. And that's exactly what happened. That's what causes escalation; that's what makes it so dangerous."

An admission in a similar vein was made a few years later by Henry Kissinger who said that had he foreseen the consequences at the time, he would have opposed deployment of MIRVs (multiple warheads in a single missile) and would have proposed placing a ban upon them in the SALT I agreement. Their deployment by the Americans spurred the Soviets to follow suit by packing MIRVs into their very heavy missiles. American "worst case" crystal-ball gazers thereupon predicted that having copied this American invention, the Soviets would be able in the early 1980s to knock out most American land-based missiles in a first strike. If this were true, it would certainly be a case of being hoist by one's own petard.

The outcome of the process described by McNamara, conducted over a period of twenty years, was that by 1979 the United States had deployed, in land-based and sea-based missiles and bombers, nearly 10,000 strategic warheads targeted on the Soviet Union, capable of delivering over 6,000 megatons of nuclear explosives. The Soviets had at that time a somewhat smaller number of warheads (with a larger megatonnage) but were rapidly catching up as they installed MIRVs on their missiles. Both sides therefore had the capacity to destroy within minutes all the large cities and major industries of the other and to wipe out, by blast, fire, radiation, and a multiplication of aftereffects, as much as half the other's population, some 200 million human beings. These statistics do not include casualties from the several thousand nuclear weapons deployed in and around Europe, designated as "tactical" because they are not targeted on the territory of either of the two superpowers. If used, these would wipe out additional tens of millions of Europeans, together with much of the artistic heritage of mankind created there during two and a half millennia. Recent deployment by the Soviets, and projected deployment by NATO, of intermediate range ballistic and cruise missiles with nuclear warheads multiplies these "capabilities."

The theory of course is that these hideous weapons will never be used because they will "deter" either side from commencing a nuclear war. Yet each is continuously conjuring up elaborate scenarios in which the other might see some decisive advantage in doing precisely that. The authors of these scenarios therefore insist it is necessary to build still more ingenious and destructive weapons systems, which are in turn quickly reproduced by the other side. Deterrence is therefore conceived to be constantly threatened and inherently precarious, as indeed it is. Gross miscalculation by a paranoid political leader, accident to which all human inventions are prone, unintended escalation of a conventional war through what is supposed to be "limited" use of tactical nuclear weapons—any of these could, as quickly and unexpectedly as occurred at the outbreak of World War I, plunge the planet into Armageddon.

Another paradoxical consequence of this extravagant and fundamentally nonsensical militarization of the planet has been noted by Hannah Arendt. "Under modern circumstances," she writes, "this appearance or reappearance of total war . . . contradicts the basic assumption upon which the relationship between the military and the civilian branches of government rests: it is the function of the army to protect and defend the civilian population. In contrast, the history of warfare in our century could almost be told as the story of the growing incapacity of the army to fulfill this basic assumption, until today the strategy of deterrence has openly changed the role of the military from that of a protector into that of a belated and essentially futile avenger."

It is impossible to refute Arendt's conclusion that if by design or accident deterrence fails and war breaks out, soldiers, sailors, and airmen will be wholly unable to protect civilians from enormous, incalculable casualties and therefore will necessarily fail in what in modern times at least has been supposed to be their primary mission. It may even be, in view of the fantastic elaboration of battlefield weapons now taking place, that they will be almost equally unable, even in a so-called conventional war, to protect themselves or to sustain combat for long. Combat with arms now on the drawing board, perhaps even with those now being tested, may prove to be more than the human psyche can withstand without regression or collapse. The British military historian John Keegan has recently written: "It remains for armies to admit that the battles of the future will be fought in never-never land. . . . The suspicion grows that battle has already abolished itself." It is entirely possible, therefore, that soldiers, abetted or driven by technology, may be rapidly condemning themselves to obsolescence.

While soldiers of all nations insist, no doubt sincerely, that their principal object is to deter war, their conception of their patriotic and professional duty is first of all to ensure that, if war comes, their nation will not be defeated. This then becomes, often unconsciously, their real object, in pursuit of which they are impelled constantly to insist that they never have enough of the tools of their trade; for no matter how stupendously armed they are, they can always conceive of situations in which their arms might, if their adversary proceeds as they fear he might, be outnumbered or outclassed. Their adversaries have the same perceptions and anxieties and react in the same way. Soldiers and sailors are in fact the most cloistered of all our professions, the most immured in the cocoon of their own professional preoccupations, the most out of touch with life in all its other aspects, the least able objectively to assign to military security its appropriate place in a national agenda where "security," in order to embrace modern realities, must have a far broader definition.

Lord Salisbury, British Prime Minister at the end of the last century, once told a colleague: "You listen too much to the soldiers . . . you should never trust the experts. If you believe the doctors, nothing is wholesome; if you believe the theologians, nothing is innocent; if you believe the soldiers, nothing is safe."

The fact is that the two superpowers have together maneuvered themselves into a position which, to a simple mind, makes absolutely no sense. They have translated the military doctrines and behavior of more primitive times into a qualitatively different modern context which assures that the application of that doctrine and behavior would result in their mutual destruction. Neither intends so to behave, neither is so irrational as not to know what the consequence of such behavior would be; but each irrationally fears that the other would be that irrational. The result is an irrationality on both sides that keeps both, contrary to their most vital interests, continuously poised on the brink of common suicide. They are playing Russian roulette with live ammunition in all chambers of their guns.

It may be useful at this point to quote the testimony of several distinguished witnesses who in recent years have commented upon what seems to them the real significance of military confrontation under modern circumstances.

In his annual report for the year 1968, the Secretary General of the United Nations U Thant wrote:

> The only reason which could induce the Soviet Union and its allies, or the Western Powers, to attack the other would be a pervading fear by

one side of a preemptive strike by the other. This fear is fed by, and grows proportionately with, the increase in the offensive military power of the two superstates. It is clearly the buildup of excessive military power beyond any reasonable demands of defense which has become the most ominous threat to world peace.

McGeorge Bundy, for five years National Security Adviser to Presidents Kennedy and Johnson, has written: "The neglected truth about the present strategic arms race between the United States and the Soviet Union is that in terms of international political behavior that race has now become almost completely irrelevant. The new weapons systems which are being developed by each of the two great powers will provide neither protection nor opportunity in any serious political sense."

George Kennan, originator of the doctrine of "containment," ambassador to the Soviet Union who was declared persona non grata by Stalin, has in his subsequent writings frequently illuminated the Alice in Wonderland character of the U.S.-Soviet military competition. In an article in *Foreign Policy* in 1972, he wrote: "Today the military rivalry, in naval power as in nuclear weaponry, is simply riding along on its own momentum, like an object in space. It has no foundation in real interests . . . no foundation, in fact, but in fear, and in an essentially irrational fear at that. It is carried not by any reason to believe that the other side *would,* but only by an hypnotic fascination with the fact that it *could.* It is simply an institutionalized force of habit."

Thirteen years earlier in an article in *Foreign Affairs* Kennan had already written: "The ideal military posture is simply the enemy of every political detente or compromise; and whoever is not prepared to make sacrifices and to accept risks in the military field should not lay claim to any serious desire to see world problems settled by any means short of war."

Finally let me quote three relevant comments made by Henry Kissinger during his last month as Secretary of State in January 1977: (1) "Seldom before has foreign policy had to be conducted against the background of such vast ideological divisions; never before has it been conducted in the knowledge that miscalculation could mean the end of civilized life." (2) "Those who are talking as if in the strategic field we could still talk about a meaningful conduct of military operations are not doing this country a service and they are not doing mankind a service." (3) "I believe that to achieve a *usable* military superiority in the field of strategic nuclear weapons is extremely unlikely and relatively easy to prevent, and the obsession with it distracts us."

It is reasonable to conclude that the two imperial competitors are, at great pains and enormous expense, escalating a political and ideological conflict of interests into a game of life and death for their respective populations. This escalation, together with the fears and traumas it generates, constitutes both the primary potential cause of World War III and the element which, if such a war did occur, could make it fatal for much of mankind.

A second major potential cause is the presence across the midriff of Europe, from the Arctic Circle to the Mediterranean, of a vast array of military forces, massively armed with conventional and tactical nuclear weapons, who have settled in this ancient and thickly populated heartland of Europe for more than a third of a century. This is an abnormal and unnatural situation. Not since the Thirty Years War three hundred years ago have armies in hostile confrontation so long occupied, even with the consent of their hosts, such vast territories outside their national boundaries.

It is not only abnormal; it is a source of constant danger. Neither side is or ever can be certain that the other does not intend to launch at any moment the great offensive of which it is capable, or that, if it did, it would not prove stronger and prevail. Each is therefore perpetually preoccupied with building up and modernizing its own forces, purportedly in order to strengthen their defensive capabilities but, to no one's surprise, always provoking similar counteraction on the other side. No week passes that some official statement or some "background" commentary from a source in NATO or the Warsaw Pact does not appear, alleging provocative behavior or ominous preparations on the other side.

As a matter of fact, it is extremely unlikely that either would launch a major attack, because their leaders must be wholly aware of what the repercussions would be. Any serious battle between the forces of the two alliances in Europe would very probably touch off World War III. Moreover, given the proliferation of tactical nuclear weapons of all sizes and shapes integrated into the weaponry of both forces and strewn across the battlefield, it would be almost equally certain that a war in Europe lasting more than a week or two would provoke the use of these weapons. Whichever side suffered reverses at the outset, and hence feared defeat, would be almost irresistibly tempted to resort to "limited" use of "small" nuclear weapons to "stabilize" the situation, which would of course elicit an equivalent "stabilization" from the other side. The only question at that point would be whether the nuclear escalation could be limited to the European battlefield or would soon lead to strategic exchanges—that is, to full-scale nuclear war. Certainly a creeping extension of the employment of tactical weapons against "lines of communications," against airfields, against reserves or reenforcements on their way to battle, some of which would fall within the borders, for example, of the Soviet Union or of France and Britain, would soon blur the distinction between tactical and strategic and be likely to escalate shortly from the former to the latter.

The obvious probability of a rapid and fatal expansion of hostilities along these lines makes it unlikely that the leaders of either side would intentionally initiate a major offensive and hence a major war. The conceivable gains—occupation of a devastated and bitterly hostile Western Europe if a Soviet offensive succeeded, "liberation" of an equally devastated Eastern Europe if the West succeeded—are so grossly incommensurate to the physical and political losses to the aggressor almost certain to result from almost certain escalation that no rational leader on either side would be likely to light the fuse.

The real danger, and a potential cause of World War III, flows from the continuously present possibility of an incident or accident, unsought and unprovoked by the authorities of either side, arising from the carelessness or bravado of some subordinate officer, in turn misinterpreted and answered in kind by his immediate adversaries, which thereupon acts upon tempers, fears, and machismo to elicit support at higher and expanding levels of command—until great armies respond to what a corporal's guard began, and a shot fired in error or in hazard becomes the shot heard round the world. As the prologue to World War I demonstrates, such seemingly implausible scenarios can, in the presence of two armed camps, be set off by an insignificant spark and within a few days become a roaring conflagration.

A third potential cause of World War III arises from the fact that the military, political, and ideological competition between the two superpowers has since 1945 expanded from Europe over the entire globe. Confrontation therefore can occur, and often has occurred, anywhere on land or sea or in the air, even in outer space. There are absolutely no limits, geographic or conceptual, to the alleged interests of these two presumptuous giants. They have arrogated to themselves the right anywhere in the world, in a famous phrase, "to destroy a village in order to save it," that is, to save it from the other side, a fate assumed to be worse than death or destruction.

It is hardly necessary to document this statement, since the catalogue of superpower exercises, adventures, and confrontations, first in Europe but soon thereafter in expanding circles around the world, is so well known. Still, a few of the most striking examples may be identified to illustrate the point.

One might say that approximately sixteen years were needed after the Nazi surrender to establish even the precarious equilibrium in Europe described above. Before World War II had ended there was a civil war in progress in Greece between Communist and anti-Communist resistance movements, each armed and abetted by its respective godparent. This conflict was, more than anything else, the origin of the Truman Doctrine in 1947; it lasted until 1949, when the Yugoslav defection cut off the main channel for supplies to the Greek Communists, and Stalin wisely decided the game was too risky to pursue further. A result in any case was the entry of Greece and Turkey into NATO and the extension of the "North Atlantic" alliance eastward to the Caucusus. By its abortive adventure in Greece, therefore, the Soviet Union contributed decisively to the "encirclement" on its southern borders of which it later so bitterly complained.

The most painful neuralgic point in Europe during these thirteen postwar years was of course Berlin. The Berlin blockade of 1948 played a major role both in splitting Germany into two hostile states and in heating up the Cold War. As late as 1961 a Berlin crisis provoked by Khrushchev caused many in the West to believe that war was imminent. Actually the withdrawal even of the impetuous Khrushchev, when the West stood firm at Berlin, corroborates the thesis put forward above that neither side's leaders will intentionally initiate a major war in Europe. It is true that the erection of the wall in that year, by reducing to a trickle the hemorrhage of trained manpower from East Berlin, removed perhaps the most acute reason for Khrushchev's anxiety and bluster. The Berlin question has since 1961 subsided into placid obscurity. It is perhaps fair to speculate, however, that his humiliating setback in Berlin probably contributed to Khrushchev's decision to proceed with his Cuban gamble the next year.

Further illustrations of the sometimes brutal exertions employed to establish the present balance in Europe are the Communist coup d'état in Czechoslovakia in March 1948, which also played a major part in stimulating in the West fear of unlimited Soviet ambitions; the astonishing defection of Tito from the Soviet fold and Stalin's almost equally astonishing, though prudent, refusal to use force to bring him to heel; the savage and total suppression in 1956 of the Hungarian effort to achieve similar autonomy; and the joint Warsaw Pact military invasion of Czechoslovakia in 1968 to stamp out even the milder ideological deviations of the Prague Spring. The lines between East and West in Europe had actually solidified by 1948—with Yugoslavia remarkably poised in no-man's land—but even twenty years later, probably still today, neither side is wholly confident that even its own camp is absolutely firm. "Deviationists" and "Eurocommunists" continue to plague policy planners and decision makers on both sides.

Long before this the confrontation had moved beyond Europe into other arenas, first of all the Middle East. It was only reluctantly and under well-advertised pressure that the Soviets withdrew from their wartime occupation of northern Iran. Thereafter there was created a cordon sanitaire or zone of containment along the Soviet Union's southern flank from Greece through Turkey and Iran to Pakistan. The Arab-Israeli conflict, Western commitment to Israel, and the Franco-British attack on Egypt in 1956 offered the Soviets an opportunity to leapfrog this uncomfortable barrier, first by supplying arms to the Arabs and eventually by much more intimate arrangements with some of them. American support of Israel and Soviet support of the Arabs during the Arab-Israeli wars of 1967 and 1973 evoked threatening gestures and heightened tension between the two superpowers, leading both to the sober conclusion that they might be maneuvered against their will into confrontation and even war by their reckless Middle Eastern clients and that it therefore behooved them to join in finding a peaceful settlement to the Arab-Israeli conflict. Unfortunately these clients, some of whom moved with surprising agility from one camp to another, proved as unmanageable as ever, the respective formulas of the superpowers for reconciling them drifted apart along lines of divergent interests, and by 1980 the likelihood of superpower confrontation in the region had increased exponentially.

Undiminished Western dependence on the oil of the Persian Gulf made unrestricted access to the area an absolute necessity for the West. At the same time there began to emerge a requirement of the Soviet bloc for imported oil, which made the acquisition of significant leverage in the region a more and more tempting gambit for the East. The xenophobic but politically ambivalent revolution in Iran brought that country to the verge of anarchy, which gave its ethnic minorities encouragement to revolt and its neighbors encouragement to intervene. The detention of American hostages for many months in Teheran obliged the United States and its allies, against their will, to impose sanctions on Iran, which destabilized the area further and offered new opportunities to the Kremlin. Soviet imposition of a Communist government in Afghanistan in 1978 and, when the tenure of that regime fell into dire jeopardy from nationalist rebels, Soviet invasion with their own forces at the end of 1979, reawakened long-standing fears of a Russian drive to warm-water ports.

Whatever Soviet intentions may have been, there could be no doubt that they had for the first time projected their own armies outside the Warsaw Pact area into a nonaligned country, that the invasion brought them into close military juxtaposition with two notably unstable countries, Pakistan and Iran, and that it added still another ominous link to the chain of Eastern bloc military penetrations of the approaches to the Persian Gulf—Ethiopia, South Yemen, and now Afghanistan.

This constellation of provocations, as the West perceived it, caused the United States to deploy strong naval forces in the Arabian Sea and to apply a formidable array of economic and other sanctions against the Soviet Union. Most of the hard-won gains of détente during the preceeding eight years were wiped out in the short span of a few months, revealing starkly how vulnerable and precarious those gains had been. It more and more began to seem again, as it had for a time in the 1950s and 1960s, that the Middle East might be coming to play the fatally inflammatory role between great powers that the Balkans had played before World War I.

Great-power rivalry and confrontation in the Far East after World War II were complicated and exacerbated by several facts: first, fighting on a substantial scale continued there, that is, in China, Korea, and Vietnam, almost uninterruptedly for nearly nine years after the Japanese surrender; second, one of the consequences of this fighting was the triumph in the most populous country in the world of a communism presumed throughout this period to be identical and monolithic with the Soviet variety; and third, there occurred in 1950 and thereafter a very rapid reversal of the original American decision after World War II to withdraw militarily from the mainland of Asia. To explain these developments it is necessary to return for a few moments to the concluding war years.

From the point of view of Roosevelt and Churchill, conducting a global war against Germany and Japan, the Chinese front in World War II was a backwater, remote from the main theaters of combat, extremely difficult to supply, and worth supporting only to the minimum extent necessary to keep it alive, to detain Japanese forces deployed there, and to provide one of several springboards for the final assault on Japan. Moreover, what arms and supplies the Chinese did receive were not for the most part used against the Japanese but either drained away in corruption and in manipulation of internal forces or reserved for the eventual showdown with the Communists, which was Chiang Kai-shek's main objective.

Chiang himself and his artful wife were at first the hope and then the despair of the legion of American advisers, civilian and military, who, as inexpensive substitutes for the arms that could not be provided, were dispatched to comfort, stiffen, and reform the Chinese Nationalists. Naturally, since Chiang's aims were Chinese and theirs American, they did not succeed and, like General Stilwell and the State Department China hands, grew ever more angry and contemptuous.

Teddy White, who was in Chungking first as an employee of the Chinese government and later as a correspondent for *Time,* subsequently wrote of Chiang: "He was a man I learned first to respect and admire, then to pity, then to despise." White also wrote, however: "No government in Asia, or anywhere else for that matter, was ever so completely penetrated by 'Americanists' as was the Republican government in Chungking. And no government, except perhaps that of the Republic of South Vietnam, was so completely ruined by American ideas, aid and advice."

This is an excessive judgment. Chiang was ruined much more by his own faults and frailties, and by the opaque and formidable situation he confronted, than by American advice, which he systematically disregarded. It is true, however, that Americans for at least half a century, intoxicated by their missionary dreams and commercial fantasies, had had a peculiarly exalted and chimerical conception of China and their role there. In a speech to the Senate as early as 1900 Albert Beveridge, a progressive follower of Theodore Roosevelt, had declared: "The Philippines are ours forever. . . . And just beyond the Philippines are China's illimitable markets. We will not retreat from either. . . . We will not renounce our part in the mission of our race, trustees under God, of the civilization of the world. And we will move forward to our work . . . with gratitude for a task worthy of our strength and thanksgiving to Almighty God that He has marked us as his chosen people, henceforth to lead in the regeneration of the world." This heady philosophy did not differ essentially from that enunciated in the 1940s by Henry Luce, editor in chief of *Time,* chief promoter of the "American Century" and the China Lobby.

Roosevelt's policy during the war was more realistic, though in the long rather than the short run. A student of maps and of history, he foresaw that China, as the most populous and one of the most civilized countries in the world, was certain eventually to be one of its great powers. He tried therefore to preempt for China a position in postwar councils commensurate with its inherent resources, by meeting with Chiang in Cairo in 1943, by attempting to ensure an accommodation between him and Stalin, and by securing for China a seat as one of the five permanent members of the United Nations Security Council. Truman pursued a similar policy in three ways: (1) by assisting Chiang's army to occupy immediately after the Japanese surrender as much as possible of the Chinese territories evacuated by their forces, including Peking and the principal cities of Manchuria; (2) by extending massive military and economic aid to the Nationalists throughout the ensuing civil war; and (3) by attempting to mediate and end that war through the strenuous efforts of the Marshall and Wedemeyer missions.

All these endeavors proved to be vain. Within four years after the Japanese surrender, the Nationalists, who in 1937 controlled the whole of China except the northeastern provinces occupied by Japan and a small pocket of Communists in the northwest, had been driven bag and baggage from the mainland to the island of Taiwan where, since the Communists have never had amphibious military capabilities, they still remain.

How could such a debacle occur so quickly and so utterly? The Republican Party—having a longstanding emotional commitment to China, frustrated and resentful at their long exclusion from political power, spurred by the passionate preaching of Henry Luce and his media empire—blamed the Democrats for "losing China." They also denounced the State Department's China hands—John Davies, John Service, John Carter Vincent, and others—for being the messengers of disaster. These men had reported during and after the war that the Nationalist government was rotten, corrupt, politically blind, and militarily incompetent and was certain to lose out to the Communists unless it rapidly and radically reformed itself.

In response to these Republican charges, the State Department in the summer of 1949, at the direction of President Truman and Secretary Acheson, prepared and published a so-called China White Paper of documents refuting these claims, describing in detail the enormous volume of aid extended to the Nationalists, demonstrating that nothing further could have been done short of sending large American military forces (which not even the Republicans advocated), and that, as always in such cases, China was "lost"—and won—by Chinese.

The China White Paper was prepared under the direction of Ambassador-at-Large Philip Jessup who, incidentally, was for many years thereafter the target of totally unfounded right-wing attacks for having done so. I was an assistant to Jessup at the time and participated in drafting the letter that transmitted the paper to Truman and summarized its conclusions. A few quotations from that letter follow.

Of the situation in the latter years of World War II, the letter said:

> The mass of the Chinese people were coming more and more to lose confidence in the government. It was evident to us that only a rejuvenated and progressive Chinese government which could recapture the

enthusiastic loyalty of the people could and would wage an effective war against Japan. American officials repeatedly brought their concern with the situation to the attention of the Generalissimo and he repeatedly assured them that it would be corrected. He made, however, little or no effective effort to correct it and tended to shut himself off from Chinese officials who gave unpalatable advice.

Of the situation after the war the letter reported:

The National Government had in 1945, and maintained until the early fall of 1948, a marked superiority in manpower and armaments over their rivals. . . . Since V-J Day, the United States Government has authorized aid to Nationalist China in the form of grants and credits totalling approximately 2 billion dollars. . . . In addition to these grants and credits, the United States Government has sold the Chinese Government large quantities of military and civilian surplus property with a total procurement cost of over 1 billion dollars. . . . A large proportion of the military supplies furnished the Chinese armies by the United States since V-J Day has, however, fallen into the hands of the Chinese Communists through the military ineptitude of the Nationalist leaders, their defections and surrenders, and the absence among their forces of the will to fight.

The central conclusion of the letter and the White Paper, which I thirty years later see no reason to revise, was:

The unfortunate but inescapable fact is that the ominous result of the civil war in China was beyond the control of the government of the United States. Nothing that this country did or could have done within the reasonable limits of its capabilities could have changed that result; nothing that was left undone by this country has contributed to it. It was the product of internal Chinese forces, forces which this country tried to influence but could not. A decision was arrived at within China, if only a decision by default.

The history of U.S.-China relations from 1937 to 1949 and of the subsequent domestic political debate in the United States clearly illustrates the dangers of overestimating what any nation, no matter how powerful and how dedicated, can achieve or can prevent inside another nation, particularly if their societies are so different that the two are incapable of understanding each other.

It has also been charged that the U.S. government should have realized that the Chinese Communists were certain eventually to prevail, given their own political skills and the ineptitude and decrepitude of their rivals. The Americans should therefore, this argument goes, have more substantially responded to Mao's and Chou's offers of cooperation during and after the war and should have recognized them as the government of China as soon as the civil war was won.

In theory this argument is plausible, but it ignores political realities of the time. The longstanding emotional attachment of Americans to "traditional," "democratic," and potentially Christian China, which they believed the Nationalist régime embodied, made it politically impossible to abandon the Nationalists during the civil war, even after they had lost it. Similarly, the mounting passions of the Cold War, which associated the Chinese Communists undiscriminatingly with the Soviets, made anything more than the most arms-length relationship with them, even before the Korean War, in the highest degree hazardous in terms of domestic politics.

Even the White Paper letter of transmittal displayed these preconceptions by remarking: "However ruthlessly a major portion of this great people [the Chinese] may be exploited by a party in the interest of a foreign imperialism . . . [American policy] will necessarily be influenced by the degree to which the Chinese people come to recognize that the Communist regime serves not their interests but those of Soviet Russia and the manner in which, having become aware of the facts, they react to this foreign domination."

In one of those ironic reversals with which the Muse of History delights in astonishing and confounding her acolytes, it was, ten years later, the Chinese Communists themselves who, "having become aware of the facts," reacted against "this foreign domination," or the "hegemony of the polar bear" as they later came to call it.

The major consequence of World War II in East Asia, and of the ensuing civil war in China which the United States so substantially misjudged, was unnecessarily to estrange for three decades two of the world's greatest nations. This alienation and mutual misconception of character and intentions contributed significantly to two subsequent wars—Korea in 1950 to 1953 and Vietnam from 1965 to 1975—each of which in turn had profoundly pernicious consequences both globally and domestically. A more glaring example of the self-destructive effects of passions and misperceptions conjured up by war would be hard to imagine.

Not only Americans suffered from miscalculation. The initiation of the Korean War was disastrous for the Soviets. Khrushchev in his memoirs attributes this initiative to Kim Il Sung, who, in seeking Stalin's support during a visit to Moscow late in 1949, claimed that the South Korean population would enthusiastically welcome the North Korean invaders and that victory would be easy. Stalin rather casually approved the enterprise, believing that a war of internal unification or "national liberation," as Khrushchev called it, would not invite foreign intervention. He was, nevertheless, careful to reject proposals that Soviet troops or "advisers" participate. Mao's approval was also sought and obtained.

Judging in retrospect, it is very probable that Stalin's and Mao's aims were limited to Korea, which seemed to be easy pickings, falling outside America's recently announced "defense perimeter," and that the attack was in no sense intended to be an opening gun in any general Communist offensive. Insofar as it had a geopolitical aim outside the peninsula, the attack may have been designed to balance, indeed to destabilize, the exclusive Western control of Japan which had stuck in Stalin's throat ever since 1945.

As became apparent within hours of the attack, however, its repercussions were far to exceed Stalin's, Mao's, and Kim's complacent expectations. I vividly recall being awakened, as Director of the State Department's Office of Eastern European Affairs, in the early morning hours of June 25, 1950, by a telephone call from Dean Rusk, then Assistant Secretary for the Far East, informing me of this totally unexpected attack. Later I remembered having read a Pyongyang broadcast of two or three weeks before in which the North Koreans boldly claimed they would celebrate the national holiday that August in Seoul, a claim casually dismissed in Washington as routine propaganda.

American reaction to the actual attack, however, was immediate and unequivocal. I attended two meetings in the State Department later that same day, in the second of which the secretaries of State and Defense, Acheson and Pace, participated. Opinion was unanimous that unless there was an immediate American political *and* military response, Stalin, whose adventures in aggrandizement since V-J Day had hitherto not involved the use of overt military force, would feel emboldened by success in Korea to resort to force elsewhere, particularly in Europe. That was certainly my opinion, which I voiced at both meetings. It is questionable, in retrospect, whether this judgment was correct, whether the cautious Stalin who had suffered a serious setback in the Berlin blockade only the year before would have risked war with an atomically armed America by a military adventure in Europe. Such, however, was undoubtedly the perception and the apprehension in Washington in the light of Soviet expansion since 1945 and the Communist victory in China.

In any case I continue to believe that, even if we greatly overestimated Stalin's aims, the original American response was correct, including certainly the decision to use the United Nations, as its Charter provided, as the chief instrument for resisting aggression. Otherwise South Korea would certainly have been overrun and annexed to the North, thereby both tipping the strategic balance in East Asia to our disfavor and further aggravating the domestic paranoia in the United States. What was *not* necessary at that time, yet was already initiated by the U.S. government in August of that year, was the rearmament of Germany, an enterprise which introduced serious strains into the Western alliance during the next five years and could have been much more painlessly managed had it followed rather than preceded economic and political movement toward European unity.

A further miscalculation by both East and West that soon emerged in Korea was the Chinese involvement. General MacArthur's brilliant success in expelling the North Koreans from the South by the Inchon landing so exalted his stature and confirmed his infallibility in Washington that no one dared question his conviction that he could move his forces northward to the Chinese border without provoking a Chinese military response of any consequence. Explicit Chinese warnings through third parties that they would not tolerate such an advance by the Americans, presumably because they feared we would not halt at the Yalu but would march on into their main industrial complex in Manchuria, were ignored. Within five months of the outbreak of the war, therefore, the Americans and the Chinese, without either having intended or wished to do so, found themselves fighting each other on a large scale, which they continued to do for two and a half years. One was reminded, in miniature, of the outbreak of World War I.

Thus the Korean War so confirmed and deepened the hostility between the United States and Maoist China that a wall was built between them that endured for twenty years, and there was awakened in America an extravagant and unwarranted expectation of Chinese invasion of Indochina. This fear in turn produced the ill-conceived and unnecessary American intervention in Vietnam, Laos, and Cambodia. A second consequence of Korea, as noted above, was to redouble fears of Soviet-inspired military attacks elsewhere and hence further to mobilize in exorbitant battle array the rival faiths and fanaticisms on the two sides of the Iron Curtain.

A third consequence, and not the least fateful, was to exaggerate egregiously, under the malign necromancy of Senator Joseph McCarthy, Americans' paranoia about the supposed threat to their values and survival posed by atheistic communism. It is one of the most amazing phenomena of American history that an obscure, oafish, and unscrupulous freshman Senator should have for five years so dominated American political life as to intimidate the soldier President Dwight Eisenhower and his entire administration, to drive from office and their professions on the flimsiest charges officials, writers, and actors, and to maim the American psyche so deeply that two decades later it had not fully recovered. Indeed it may be argued that it was McCarthy's all-too-popular persecution of those he claimed "lost" China that drove John Foster Dulles, John F. Kennedy, and Lyndon Johnson into the morass of Vietnam, lest they be politically damned for "losing" another country that was never theirs.

There was at least one other momentous consequence of World War II and its aftermath and of the Korean War, which leads us directly into an examination of the quarter-century that followed Korea. Though the United States had been through much of its history a violent nation, because of the frontier where combat and lawlessness were givens and each man was armed; though it had fought numerous wars and annexed vast territories; though it loved military heroes and elected at least half a dozen of them President, it had never been a militaristic nation in the sense of having a standing army exercising a continuing and powerful influence on politics. After each war it demobilized rapidly down to bare bones. American armed forces numbered 166,000 in 1914, rose to 4,300,000 in 1918, and declined to 240,000 by 1933. At the end of World War II they amounted to 12 million, but by 1948 they had already shrunk to 1,400,000. With the Korean War, they rose to 3,700,000, remained at about this level during Vietnam and, even after abolition of the draft, remained above 2 million in 1979. As President Eisenhower pointed out with considerable concern when he left office in 1961, the "military-industrial complex" had been born. Once grown to manhood, it became almost indestructible. It conditioned American society as never before in peacetime.

The traditional American martial spirit and posture, reflected in the past in occasional paroxysms of "manifest destiny" or crusade, were transformed under the pressures created by World War II and its aftermath into a sustained hypersensitivity to both real and imagined threats to American security, and into a formidable, permanently mobilized military force designed to deal with those threats. The fact, moreover, that World War II vastly diminished the military and economic power of Europe and Japan and vacated their empires, created a global vacuum into which American anxieties and energies impulsively and irresistibly flowed. For the short space of twenty-five years, until Vietnam demonstrated its limitations, Henry Luce's "American century" seemed to have arrived. A critical corner in American history had been turned.

Let us return, however, to a review of military developments in the Far East after Korea. With the French defeat and withdrawal from Indochina in 1954, this peninsula, so remote and alien to both superpowers, became illogically a main focus of their competition. The North Korean attack and the subsequent Chinese intervention had convinced the United States and its allies that both the Soviet Union and China might now be prepared to undertake military expansion around their borders and that only armed "containment," which was extrapolated from George Kennan's much more modest doctrine into an array of bilateral and multilateral alliances around the peripheries of the two communist great powers, could hold them in check. This premise was embodied in 1954 in the Southeast Asia Treaty Organization, of which the United States was really the only effective military participant, and in a strong and growing U.S. political, economic, and military presence in each of the three Indochinese states—Vietnam, Laos, and Cambodia.

Our policy in Southeast Asia was motivated not only by this perception of impending Chinese expansion but by two other notions: the "domino theory" that if one Southeast Asian nation was "lost" to the Communists, the others would inevitably topple one after the other, all the way down to Indonesia; and that any limited war fought in Vietnam would be more or less like the Korean War, a battle between two armies facing each other on a single military front. It was for such a war that the South Vietnamese army was trained by the Americans.

All three of these American perceptions were misperceptions. While the Chinese were quite prepared to provide modest assistance to "liberation movements" in Indochina and elsewhere, they were far too preoccupied with overwhelming economic and political problems at home to engage in substantial military operations outside their borders, unless they supposed, as they did in Korea, that their own territory was in danger of being invaded. Their subsequent unwillingness to become involved in Vietnam, even when the United States was fighting a major war there and bombing close to their borders, supports this judgment. Moreover, given the ancient animosity between Vietnam and China, which has since erupted into a small-scale war, better-informed Americans should have known that the Vietnamese were much more likely to behave like Yugoslavs than like Bulgarians.

The second misperception was that if the Communists took over the Indochinese states, the capitulation of neighboring states would necessarily follow. Events have proved the contrary. The nearest neighbor, Thailand, is no more and no less likely to "go Communist" than it was before the Vietnam war. Its political orientation and destiny will depend primarily on how well or badly present and future Thai governments perform in coping with Thailand's domestic problems.

The third misperception was equally flagrant and fatal. The Vietnam War, as it soon developed, was as different from the Korean War as the Chinese civil war had been from the American one. Unlike South Korea, South Vietnam had for years been profusely sown with Viet Cong, who had been fighting the French and their Vietnamese "collaborators," and continued in the same dogged guerrilla fashion, with massive aid from the North, to fight the Americans and *their* "collaborators," neither of whom were trained for or understood this type of war. Extending the war to Laos and Cambodia was equally unproductive, merely extending the area of devastation and of eventual Communist victory. The belief of some American military officers that they could have "won" the war if they had been "unleashed," that is, if they had been permitted to bomb anywhere at any time and to use atomic weapons if they chose to, is another delusion. They could have magnified the devastation; they could have brought the United States to the brink of World War III; but they could not have thus pacified either Vietnam or American public opinion.

Ironically, Indochina today is principally an arena of rivalry not between East and West but between the two communist great powers. That does not mean that it is of no concern to the rest of the world. It remains an area of instability and conflict and as such could all too easily, so long as balance-of-power politics determines the behavior of governments, again draw into its vortex misguided warriors from far away.

The most traumatic case of superpower collision in the latest interwar period was of course the Cuban missile crisis. Installing nuclear armed missiles next door to the United States was an act of unmitigated folly on the part of Khrushchev and the Politburo, not because it lacked an American precedent but because it ignored the predictable furious American reaction. In *Khrushchev Remembers* the Soviet leader assumes full responsibility and attempts to justify what he did. He asserts that his action was necessary to protect Cuba from an American invasion, which he was convinced would eventually occur in response to the humiliating American defeat at the Bay of Pigs. He feared, moreover, that the overthrow of Castro would jeopardize prospects of further Communist successes in Latin America. Second, he claims he was copying and countering American missiles in Turkey and Italy targeted on the Soviet Union. "Now they would learn," he wrote, "just what it feels like to have enemy missiles pointing at you; we'd be doing nothing more than giving them a little of their own medicine." Actually both sides already had intercontinental missiles "pointing" at each other, but the United States had more and was in 1962 forging even farther ahead. A third, perhaps the major, Soviet motive may have been a desire to catch up quickly in a nuclear arms race by installing some of their existing medium-range missiles close to the United States. A final, unavowed motive may have been, as suggested above, a hankering on Khrushchev's part to revenge his humiliation at Berlin the year before.

Installation of the missiles in Cuba was an act of folly, first because it represented such an abysmal misunderstanding of American psychology and, second, because it exposed Soviet nuclear weapons, hitherto carefully confined to home territory, to being seized or destroyed by American conventional forces, without Soviet conventional forces having any capability whatsoever to defend them. All the Soviets could have done would have been to start a nuclear war. For a few days during the crisis, even though President Kennedy wisely chose less provocative means than armed attack for eliminating the missiles, there was the gravest apprehension in the United States that war would occur. I did not share in this apprehension, any more than I had expected war over Berlin the previous year. I did not think, even with the mercurial Khrushchev in power, that the Soviet leadership would commence a nuclear war, or a war likely to become nuclear, as long as massive retaliation against their own country was certain or even probable. I have not changed my view.

In any case it was a famous victory for the United States and another humiliation for the Soviet Union. Like most such victories and humiliations it had to be paid for. It is clear that shortly after these conspicuous defeats, the Soviet political and military leadership, determined that they must never again be faced with such a threat in a position of military inferiority, began the enormous buildup of intercontinental missiles, "outreach" navy, and "modernized" forces in Europe, which has in recent years been creating such profound apprehensions in the West. Khrushchev grossly miscalculated both the immediate and the long-term effects on the Americans of having enemy missiles "pointing" at them from close at hand, just as the Americans miscalculated the effects on the Soviets of the missiles in Turkey and Italy and of the vast expansion of American strategic forces in the 1960s. All these "defensive" deployments of nuclear weapons on both sides contributed in the end to the insecurity of both.

The final area of the so-called Third World in which the superpowers have been competing is Africa. Soviet efforts to exercise an influence there in the early 1960s did not meet with much success. They were squeezed out of the Congo by the United States, working through the United Nations in a more subtle variation of the Korean operation. Of the African leaders on whom they wagered at this time —Nasser of Egypt, Nkrumah of Ghana, Ben Bella of Algeria, Modiba Keita of Mali, and Sekou Touré of Guinea—one died, three were ousted from power, and the fifth drifted away from them. For a time thereafter Africa was treated to "benign neglect" by both superpowers. In the Nigerian civil war both actually supported the same side.

This truce or era of indifference ended in 1975, by which time the Soviet Union had acquired the military capabilities in the strategic and "outreach" categories to which it had been devoting large resources since the Cuban crisis. Ironically it was also able to employ Cuban military forces as its surrogates in Angola and Ethiopia. In light of past history, it is not at all certain that Soviet successes in these two countries will prove any more durable than those in Egypt and Ghana. Either coups d'état might overthrow their friends, or the friends themselves, as passionately attached to their sovereignty and independence as most Third World leaders, might come to resent an alien presence no longer necessary to maintain them in power or to defeat intrusive neighbors.

Nevertheless, the process of installing Soviet and Cuban presences in Southern Africa and the Horn, coinciding with escalation of guerrilla warfare in Rhodesia and Namibia, with the installation of pro-Soviet governments in Southern Yemen and Afghanistan, and with turbulence in Iran, again stimulated acute apprehensions on the Western side. There was, on the one hand, fear that the Soviet-Cuban military presence in Angola and Mozambique and support of Rhodesian and Namibian "liberation movements" might lead to involvement in black-white warfare in Southern Africa and to the installation of Communist-dominated régimes there. Even more, the West feared that a creeping Soviet encirclement and penetration of the Persian-Arabian Gulf area could reduce or jeopardize the outward flow of oil so essential to the economic health, political stability, and military strength of the Western world.

These areas of superpower competition in the Middle East and Africa, some old, some new, clearly involved what would be perceived in the West at least as vital political and strategic interests. If the Soviets, tempted or misled by their new military capabilities and by their discovery of the usefulness of the Cubans, should seek to press these advantages too far in these critical areas, they could quickly provoke superpower confrontations prone to escalation to perilous levels.

Indeed, as a recent study by Richard Smoke cogently points out, the chances of escalation in situations of this kind are considerable. "There is an inherent upward tendency in warfare," Smoke writes. "Escalation is not a mere possibility—something that may happen or not, like a rainstorm over a battlefield. It is an ever-present 'pressure' or temptation or likelihood, something that requires more deliberate action to stop and reverse than to start. . . . As escalation proceeds, a double gap is likely to open up between the two sides. Each finds it cognitively more dissonant to make a significant new offer, and cognitively more difficult to 'hear' any hints of a new offer from the other—which the other is also finding it cognitively more difficult to make. As the escalation sequence goes on, this double gap will widen. As time passes and events become more threatening, each side may, so to speak, gradually retreat into its own universe."*

As one reviews objectively, however, the record of superpower competition outside Europe during the thirty years since World War II, it may be puzzling to Americans, who see themselves as "pacific" and the Soviets as "aggressive," to note that during this period it has been the United States that has engaged in two considerable wars, in Korea and in Vietnam, has maintained "military advisory groups" in literally dozens of countries, and has continuously deployed powerful naval task forces in most oceans around the globe. As Mao Tse-tung picturesquely remarked: "Both the Americans and the Soviets are hegemonists, but the Americans don't understand this business. They try to catch ten fleas with their ten fingers."

Until very recently, on the other hand, the Soviets, though they have twice by military action suppressed revolts or "deviations" among their allies, have neither fought a war, sent more than a handful of military personnel outside the Warsaw Pact area, or deployed navies far from their home waters. Alas, as Soviet capabilities have grown, they have likewise yielded to the temptation to display and use them. Afghanistan is a recent example. Global military deployments by the two superpowers, while not yet symmetrical, are tending to

War: Controlling Escalation (Harvard University Press, 1977).

become more so. No one should be surprised. The history of the interwar period demonstrates that neither will accept any position of inferiority vis-á-vis the other any longer than it has to. The long immunity of the United States to serious military competition in Third World areas not close to the Soviet or Chinese periphery is fading fast.

It is quite another question whether either side profits by this competition. The original American justification for it was "containment" of perceived Communist "expansionism," provoked by the Soviet occupation of Eastern Europe, by the attack in Korea, by military aid to states in the Middle East, and by Soviet support of "wars of national liberation," which sometimes were genuine wars of independence against colonial powers but equally often were wars of Communist factions seeking to overthrow indigenous national governments. A corresponding Soviet justification has been to break out of or leapfrog over the "encirclement" they have perceived as threatening them, for years along their western and southern boundaries, since their quarrel with China along that immense frontier as well. *Both* superpowers now claim the need and right to help anywhere they can "friendly" governments who ask for assistance and allege they are threatened, externally or internally.

Another factor behind these global deployments and interventions is often ignored. A number of years ago a distinguished American Senator, Richard Russell, chairman of the Senate Armed Forces Committee, remarked: "If it is easy for us to go anywhere and do anything, we will always be going somewhere and doing something." His remark was frequently recalled during discussion in late 1979 and early 1980 of the "quick strike" or "rapid deployment" force, which President Carter proposed in the wake of the seizure of American hostages in Iran. It is difficult to imagine how such a force could have rescued the hostages in Iran, or indeed how its use in most Third World conflicts could be more productive than counterproductive.

Nevertheless, the existence of a capability creates a standing temptation to use it. Denmark, though it may have a more vital need for Persian Gulf oil than the United States, is not tempted to send a naval task force there to assure its supply, because it does not have one. The United States, having several, may, in case of crisis in the gulf, be compelled to "do something" by sending one, even if there is nothing a naval task force or any American military force could do to control the crisis, even if the threat of American intervention would be more likely to exacerbate anti-Americanism and play into Soviet hands. Now that the Soviets are beginning to acquire similar naval outreach capabilities, they will be subject to the same temptations and will no doubt from time to time succumb to them.

The exorbitant lengths to which such military interventions can be carried, and depths into which they can precipitate the intervenor, are of course best illustrated by U.S. involvement in Vietnam. From modest military and economic aid designed to shore up weak anti-Communist Vietnamese, Laotian, and Cambodian governments after French withdrawal, American involvement gradually burgeoned over more than a decade into a military presence of half a million soldiers and an aerial bombardment of Vietnam that loosed on that small country more tons of explosive than were dropped on Germany throughout World War II.

Among the consequences were a distortion of the American economy and demoralization of American politics from which the country has not at this writing fully recovered. All this expenditure of lives, treasure, and moral credit was later shown to be unnecessary; a victorious Communist Vietnam soon demonstrated not subservience but intransigent animosity to China, and the Southeast Asian "dominoes" outside Indochina showed no signs of toppling.

The United States encountered great difficulty in detaching itself, emotionally and physically, from Vietnam. President Johnson was wrong to escalate massively in 1965; Richard Nixon and Henry Kissinger were wrong not to withdraw much more rapidly in 1969–70. As De Tocqueville wrote long ago: "There are two things which a democratic people will always find very difficult—to begin a war and to end it."

Nevertheless, some of the lessons of Vietnam were rather quickly absorbed. Kissinger said somewhat belatedly in January 1977: "As the decade drew to a close we began to learn that we cannot legislate our own moral preferences upon the world at a time when we no longer enjoy physical predominance. We came to see that abstract principles are not self-fulfilling; they can lead to an overinvolvement as pernicious as our earlier isolation."

As a matter of fact, the lesson was even more penetrating and farreaching than Kissinger suggests. An immense physical predominance over North Vietnam did not enable the United States, for a variety of reasons foreign and domestic, to legislate or impose its "moral preferences" on Indochina. Those preferences are shared in Western Europe and do not need to be "legislated" there. Elsewhere in the world they are only partially and occasionally shared. To the extent they are not, they cannot be imposed more than briefly and precariously by military force or legislated by "human rights" campaigns even when accompanied by economic benefits or embargoes. Much of the successful American foreign policy during the 1970s under Nixon, Ford, and Carter—détente and SALT agreements with the Soviet Union, normalization of relations with China, withdrawal from Indochina, more evenhanded peacemaking endeavors in the Middle East and Southern Africa, opening of a more constructive dialogue with Third World countries on common economic problems —has been largely a process of painful redressment of some of the errors of the previous twenty years.

Unfortunately, one can already perceive, as uncomfortable memories fade and uncongenial lessons are forgotten, a tendency to slip back into some of the old postures and mistakes, to widen rather than narrow the traditional gaps in détente, to mute conciliation and stress "leverage" in the economic dialogue with less-developed countries, to enlarge, brandish, and even employ military might as a substitute for diplomacy and negotiation in Third World conflicts. This ominous tendency is in several senses unavoidable. It still seems easy for us to go anywhere and do anything, easier for us to do it militarily, as we have obvious military capabilities, whereas our ventures in diplomacy so often encounter the puzzling recalcitrance of those we are trying to help. Equally relevant is the new factor of an emerging Soviet corresponding capability to intervene, a capability enhanced by the availability of Cuban surrogates whose presence on Third World battlefields is more acceptable than that of Americans, Russians, or other Europeans. So the prospect is not so remote as it recently seemed that, despite the lessons of Vietnam and, for the Soviets, of Egypt, Indonesia, Ghana, and so on, both superpowers may soon find themselves in a series of unplanned confrontations around the globe.

This prospect is greatly enhanced by the near-certainty of the spread of turbulence in the Third World. Here we find more than 100 countries moving at dizzy speeds from the seventeenth, eighteenth, or nineteenth centuries, as the case may be, into the late twentieth. Modernization, transported so rapidly over the air lanes and the air waves, devalues and disrupts ancient and precious aspects of culture and threatens the vital interests of those who hold them dear or profit from them. Under these circumstances no régime in a developing country, old or new, is secure, and coup d'état or civil war is almost always impending. Iran is certainly not a universal paradigm, but it is likely to prove to be a more than an occasional one.

Moreover, the boundaries of new countries, drawn artificially by careless imperialisms, cutting across tribes, natural resources, and common sense, give rise among many of these countries to irredenta, militant minorities, aggressive ambitions, and chronic, nerve-racking insecurity. From all these unsettling factors, internal and external, areas of turbulence and conflict in and among Third World countries are certain to grow rather than diminish. In addition to the areas of conflict we have considered, the Middle East, East Asia, Southern Africa, others are likely to explode with equally sudden violence. Local wars, and wars giving rise to international chain reactions, will be a perennial source both of temptation and of peril for great powers during the rest of this century.

Another new factor aggravates the dangers of this globalization of Third World-superpower competition and conflict: the proliferation of nuclear energy, of plutonium production, and potentially of nuclear weapons. The efforts of the Carter administration to restrict this proliferation have encountered the stubborn obstacles of national sovereignty and economic need on the part of both sellers and buyers of this protean technology. If the outcome is that a much larger number of countries than the present six or seven possess nuclear weapons and that an even larger number have at hand small quantities of weapons-grade plutonium, the world, with or without superpower competition, will be a much more dangerous place to live in.

Nations less experienced in the handling of nuclear weapons and nuclear reactors, less able or willing to enforce effective safeguards, with less responsible, more fanatical, and more unstable leadership, may intentionally or unintentionally cross the fatal line. Desperate governments may brandish and even use a nuclear weapon; revolutionary factions may seize and employ one; even guerrillas, terrorists, or criminals may piece together a primitive weapon and use it for blackmail; fatal accidents become more likely. In any of these cases the origin of the explosion may not be clear; one superpower may blame the other; confrontation and escalation can all too easily follow. A trivial incident that would in the nineteenth century have simmered harmlessly for months around some unpronounceable oasis in a thinly inhabited desert may in the late twentieth blow up in days or hours and scatter fallout around the world.

Before we conclude, one more element in the curious and intricate military competition among great powers requires brief examination. During these years the governments of the principal nations established ever-more-elaborate systems of "intelligence" gathering and analysis to determine the character of the foreign "threat," military, political, and economic, that they supposed they were confronting. This elaboration was given particular impetus during and after World War II by two factors: first, the development of technology making it progressively more and more possible to read other people's communications, listen to their conversations, and observe their military deployments in minutest detail from "spies in the sky"; second, the ubiquitous entry into the international intelligence arena of the Soviet Union, which already possessed the most massive, intrusive, and unscrupulous domestic intelligence apparatus known to modern times and quickly extended this network to global proportions. Other great powers, particularly the United States, soon paid the Soviets the compliment of slavish imitation in this field, down to the lowest of "dirty tricks."

My own experience with this apparatus over thirty-five years leads me to conclude that, except in wartime or as applied to weapons and weapons deployments in peacetime, its value is greatly overestimated for two reasons. First, the information supplied daily by the vast array of information media, supplemented by comprehensive diplomatic contacts and reporting, is as likely to enable an objective and experienced observer to judge an adversary's capabilities and to fathom his intentions as is the overload of "noise," chitchat, and conflicting rumors spewed out by competing intelligence services. The problem is not to collect more than one needs but to separate the true from the false, the significant from the trivial; to evaluate and assess correctly and draw sound conclusions quickly.

Here one encounters the second and principal difficulty—the settled predispositions of the recipient of intelligence, that is, the decision or policy maker, and the bureaucratic inclination of the purveyors not to offend or confront those predispositions too sharply. An expert in this field, Harry Howe Ransom, has coined two aphorisms on the subject: "Intelligence agencies tend to report what they think their leaders want to see and hear. The decision-making leadership sees or hears what it wants, no matter what intelligence is reported." These recall the remark of Alfred Binet, the celebrated inventor of intelligence testing: "Tell me what you are looking for and I will tell you what you will find." To illustrate the point, it is sufficient to recall how impervious were President Lyndon Johnson and his principal advisers, obsessed with the supposed strategic and domestic political consequences of "losing" another country to Communism, to all intelligence or counsel suggesting either that Vietnam was not vital to the United States or that it was not conquerable.

Similarly, a very large number of American military and political leaders have for many years refused to relinquish the delusion that their opposite numbers on the Soviet side are preparing to launch either a nuclear "first strike" against American land-based missiles or an all-out conventional offensive to drive across Western Europe to the English Channel. Whether or not the Soviets have or will have the capability to make these moves, which is dubious, there is hardly a shred of evidence from any sort of "intelligence," covert or overt, that they have ever had the slightest intention of doing either. Indeed the Soviet Union since 1920, has for the most part been conservative in the use of its own military power outside the sphere it already controls.

Raymond Garthoff, American ambassador to Bulgaria and a longtime student of Soviet affairs, has recently written: "Marxist-Leninist ideology sanctions the use of military power [and any other means] available to the socialist [Soviet] leaders whenever, *but only if,* expedient in advancing the Soviet cause and not jeopardizing the security of achievements already gained, above all the security of the Soviet Union. Military power is considered necessary to *defend* the socialist cause, may be used if expedient to *advance* it, but it is *not* seen as the decisive element in advancing the historical process, which will progress when conditions are ripe through indigenous action by the working class."

There could be no shadow of a doubt in the mind of any Soviet leader that to initiate a general war—that is, almost certainly a nuclear exchange—would jeopardize the security of the Soviet Union in the highest degree, would lead to the destruction of most of the great industrial base they have built up over sixty years, and very likely to the overthrow of their own régime. It is almost impossible for any sober observer to imagine any Soviet leadership, particularly the present array of septuagenarians and sexagenarians, risking such hazards. Soviet doctrine requires them to nudge history along in their direction but not to give it so brutal a shove as to send it sprawling—very possibly with themselves underneath.

It is very probable that these American misreadings of Soviet intentions, on which American military strategies, weaponry, and deployments are to a large extent based, have their mirror image in Soviet misperceptions of American, German, and Chinese intentions, which account for their strategies, weaponry, and deployments. The two reciprocating and continuously escalating misperceptions constitute another major potential cause of World War III. Each ascribes to itself only the best of motives and to its adversary only the worst. As the American theologian Reinhold Niebuhr has written: "The pride and self-righteousness of powerful nations are a greater hazard to their success in statecraft than the machinations of their foes."

This examination of major potential military effects of World War II—the nuclear arms race between the superpowers, the chronic military confrontation in the center of Europe, the political and military involvement of the superpowers and their allies in Third World conflicts—suggests that all three are multiplying rather than diminishing. None of the remedies so far applied, while they may have from time to time alleviated particularly glaring symptoms, has shown any capacity or promise of curing the diseases.

Traditional diplomacy, military establishments, military alliances, the search for "balance of power" or "equilibrium" in the style of

Metternich, Bismarck, and their predecessors, may have lessened the chances of war in some cases, but they have as often magnified conflicts of interest, enlarged their scope, and sharpened their intensity. Power cannot be accurately or even roughly balanced, because the balance depends on the uncoordinated and unpredictable input of two or more adversaries. Each keeps making additions to its power intended to balance what another has added or is perceived to have added. These additions, however, create in the eyes of adversaries imbalances, which must be corrected by additions on their side. Power in such an environment is almost certain to be both misconceived and abused. The ultima ratio, and reductio ad absurdum, of the balance of power has become the balance of terror. The pursuit of balance is therefore almost necessarily a self-defeating exercise. Clearly no nation, large or small, is ready to abandon these traditional instruments of "national security" in the absence of better ones, but equally clearly these instruments have in our times been as powerless to create a system and a sense of solid and durable security as they were before 1914 or have been throughout human history.

On the other hand, the imposing array of new international institutions established after World War II—the United Nations itself, including now almost every nation on the globe, the pacific settlement and enforcement powers of its Security Council, its tireless efforts to promote and negotiate measures of disarmament and arms control, all its vast family of specialized agencies for dealing with every variety of international economic and social problem, the regional organizations in Europe, the Americas, Africa, the Middle East, and Southeast Asia, all the elaborate panoply of modern multilateral diplomacy—all these have proved as ineffective as national instruments or alliance systems in assuring the international security and tranquility everyone claims to crave.

In a world as profoundly and intricately interdependent as ours has become, it is obvious that most of these multilateral instrumentalities are indispensable, but it is equally obvious that they are insufficient. There are no doubt serious flaws in their organization but, since their capabilities and limitations derive almost entirely from their members —the nation-states—the paramount flaws must lie in the will, wit, and wisdom of the latter. The causes of the inadequacy of international organization are essentially the same as the causes of the inadequacy of national military establishments, military alliances, and traditional balance-of-power diplomacy.

We shall return to this subject in the concluding chapter, where an attempt will be made to identify and scrutinize the imbalances arising from war and revolutions and to suggest some alleviations. Before concluding this chapter on military consequences of World War II, however, I should like once more to appeal to a few witnesses, distinguished in various disciplines, who have made comments that seem relevant.

The first is, perhaps unexpectedly, George Washington. His Farewell Address was often cited between the first two world wars in support of American "isolation" from those conflicts. Other portions of the address may better reflect what Washington had in mind and what Americans today, and others as well, would do well to recall.

"Observe good faith and justice toward all nations," the first President said. "Cultivate peace and harmony with all. . . . In the execution of such a plan nothing is more essential than that permanent inveterate antipathies and passionate attachments for others should be excluded and that in place of them just and amicable feelings toward all should be cultivated. The nation which indulges toward another an habitual hatred or an habitual fondness is in some degree a slave. It is a slave to its animosity or to its affection, either of which is sufficient to lead it astray from its duty and interest. Antipathy in one nation against another disposes more readily to offer insult and injury, to lay hold of slight cause of umbrage, and to be haughty and intractable when accidental or trifling occasions of dispute occur. . . ."

Early in World War II the great Italian historian, Guglielmo Ferrero, wrote a book called *The Reconstruction of Europe,* in which he described how the architects of the settlement of 1815, despite all their limitations, reestablished after twenty-five years of war and revolution a European compromise that lasted almost a century. In this book, even before nuclear weapons were invented, he wrote: "The usefulness of force to man is measured by his ability to control it, for it to be intensified is suicidal, and the use of force terrifies the one who commits it more than the victim."

Early in this century the Greek poet Cavafy wrote a poem called "Waiting for the Barbarians" in which he describes the emperor, the senate, and the people of an ancient city helplessly awaiting the arrival of the barbarians that day. All normal activity has ceased as officials and citizens in their finest garments and jewels prepare to welcome the barbarians.

But:

Why should this uneasiness begin all of a sudden, And confusion? How serious peoples' faces have become.
Why are all the streets and squares emptying so quickly,
And everybody turning home again so full of thought?
Because night has fallen and the Barbarians have not come.
And some people have arrived from the frontier;
They say there are no Barbarians anymore.
And now what will become of us without Barbarians?—
Those people were some sort of a solution.

⫸ 7 ⫷

Communism
1945-1979

In the short period from the victory at Stalingrad in 1943 to the end of World War II in 1945, the Soviet Union extended its domain from its 1939 borders, established after World War I when it was impotent, to the Elbe in Europe and the islands just off Hokkaido in the Japanese archipelago. It thus became, as the other European colonial empires disintegrated, by far the largest empire extant and the only surviving imperialism in which one ethnic group exercises dominion over a large number of others.

While Moscow of course imposed its social system on the territories it annexed or dominated, it did so not as a revolutionary but as an imperial power. The governments of its satellites, at least for many years, were obliged to serve Soviet interests primarily and only occasionally and incidentally national, popular, or even Marxist interests. The social system inside the Soviet Union, moreover, far from evolving progressively, tended more and more to congeal in rigid bureaucratic forms.

Stalin continued his purges of his Party comrades after the war and was probably about to embark on his most drastic one when death, natural or induced, intervened. He treated those around him like lackeys or conspirators. "You come to Stalin's table as a friend," Khrushchev quotes Bulganin as saying, "but you never know if you'll go home by yourself or if you'll be given a ride—to prison." "All of us around Stalin," Khrushchev adds, "were temporary people."*

*Krushchev Remembers.

This kind of atmosphere at the pinnacle of the bureaucracy was hardly conducive to independence of mind and an innovative spirit. It never had been. This was the price Communism paid for Leninist discipline. "The world has seen few heroes as ready to sacrifice and suffer as the Communists were on the eve of and during the revolution," Djilas wrote in *The New Class.* "It has probably never seen such characterless wretches and stupid defenders of arid formulas as they became after attaining power." The paralyzing effect of this oppression and terror on cultural life is well illustrated by a quotation from Dmitri Shostakovich's recent memoirs. "It didn't matter how the audience reacted to your work or if the critics liked it," the great composer said. "All that had no meaning in the final analysis. There was only one question of life or death: how did the leader like your opus. I stress, life or death, because we are talking about life or death here, literally, not figuratively. That's what you must understand."*

Khrushchev, certainly the boldest and most unconventional of the Soviet leaders since Lenin, shook up the system in a sensational and salutary fashion with his "destalinization" in 1956 and after. The pall of fear that had for twenty years hung over every Soviet citizen, no matter how exalted, loyal, or able, was partly lifted. Thousands of the innocent were "rehabilitated" and, like Solzhenitsyn, brought back from the Gulag Archipelago. It was impossible at that late date, however, to revive the vigorous spirit of innovation that had accompanied and immediately followed the revolution. State socialism requires an immense bureaucracy, and the tendency of any bureaucracy, public or private, is to adhere to routine and to cling to privilege. When the administrative and industrial bureaucracies, moreover, have superimposed upon them Party and police bureaucracies nurtured in the discipline of Lenin and the neuroses of Stalin, the whole ponderous apparatus stiffens and drags. Despite having "supreme power" for seven years, Khrushchev could not really shake it up or get it moving.

"The misfortune of Russia was and still is today," Djilas wrote in 1978, "that inevitable technological progress was brought to her by despotic forces, through which despotism expanded and took root." Technology reenforced despotism, and despotism hobbled technol-

---

*Testimony: the Memoirs of Dmitri Shostakovich (Harper & Row, 1979).

ogy. Nowadays the Soviets turn to the West for the innovations modern economics demand and their system cannot supply. Yet the vested interests of the various bureaucracies, combined in "the new class," are so powerful that they cannot be shaken by technological imperatives any more than by Krushchev.

What is left of "communism"? When Andre Malraux visited Mao in the 1960s, the Chinese leader described the Soviets as "revisionists moving toward capitalism." When Malraux disputed this judgment, Mao responded ironically: "In other words you think they are not revisionists because they are no longer even Communists." Actually the Soviet régime is not "moving toward capitalism," nor is it any more "revisionist" than Mao was. Its economic problems arise precisely from its lack of any genuine principle or any consistent progressive impetus.

The exiled dissident Vladimir Bukovsky wrote recently of Khrushchev: "I think he was the last Communist ruler who believed in the possibility of building Communism, nobody, besides him, believed it was any longer possible."*

Andrei Amalrik wrote ten years ago in *Will the Soviet Union Survive Until 1984?:* "The regime is not on the attack but on the defense. Its motto is 'Don't touch us and we won't touch you.' Its aim: Let everything be as it was. This is probably the most humane objective the regime has set for itself in the last half-century, but it is also the least appealing." Amalrik goes on to say, in implicit contradiction of his title: "However passive the elite is, it really does not need to make any changes, and in theory it could remain in power for a very long time, getting away with only the slightest concessions and minor measures of repression."

The fact is that more than sixty years after a revolution that has never been renewed or refreshed, the Soviet system has been drained of revolutionary content. The system is successful because it produces, because it feeds, clothes, and houses 250 million people, even though inadequately, because it has created an enormous, even though inefficient, industry and an equally enormous, and more efficient, military establishment, and because it supports in relative luxury its new class. It holds the loyalty of the Russian population, not because it is com-

To Build a Castle (Viking, 1979).

munist but because it is Russian.

Bukovsky has described with marvelous irony, in chapter II of his *To Build a Castle,* how the average Soviet citizen, who has completely lost faith in the system, nevertheless rationalizes his conformity to it and his failure to challenge the brainwashing of his children, arguing that sooner or later they too are certain to be disillusioned. Solzhenitsyn has expressed it best. In an interview shortly after he went into exile, he said: "80% of Russians have a pretty fair idea of the nature and merits of the Soviet regime. They think as I do. They've chosen to obey, that's all, but they live like emigrés of the heart."

The Soviet Union today, despite its ideological emptiness and its technological backwardness, is the world's second superpower because it has chosen ever since its revolution to spend an abnormal proportion of its national product, in recent years about 15 percent, on its military forces. Its nuclear arms are therefore today roughly equivalent to those of the other superpower, the economically stronger United States, and its conventional forces are considerably larger, if not demonstrably more effective. This military bias in national priorities does not necessarily reflect aggressive intentions, as both its western and eastern neighbors so frequently fear. It rather reflects, on the one hand, a national psychosis and, on the other, real vulnerabilities.

The unobstructed Russian plains have throughout history been notoriously tempting to foreign invaders. The Mongols swept across in the thirteenth century and remained in occupation or domination for more than two centuries thereafter. Teutonic Knights, Poles, and Swedes invaded repeatedly from the fourteenth until the eighteenth century. Napoleon penetrated as far as Moscow in 1812; the British and French occupied the Crimea in 1855; the Germans seized the Ukraine in 1918; British, French, and Americans moved in on three fronts to assist the Whites in 1919; Hitler's Wehrmacht drove as far as the Caucusus in 1942. In the latter war the Soviet Union lost about 20 million soldiers and civilians. In light of this history, it is not surprising that Russians have deep-seated anxieties about the ambitions of their neighbors and their own vulnerability, even when to their neighbors they seem most secure and most threatening.

Even discounting complexes, their actual military situation is not enviable. Unlike the United States, they have potential enemies on both east and west. The Chinese are stridently hostile. The West, in light of Russia's traumatic experience with the Germans in this century, are not perceived to be as benign as Americans and West Europeans assume themselves to be. Unlike the United States, the Soviet Union has no reliable allies. In case of major war the other members of the Warsaw Pact would at best contribute little, at worst defect to the other side. The United States is immensely superior technologically. It has always led the way in introducing new and more deadly strategic weapons. The Soviet Union has felt obliged, breathlessly and at great sacrifice, to catch up. Sometimes its momentum has carried it ahead in a particular program, but on each such occasion the Americans have promptly invented and deployed a new strategic system.

These considerations have been presented not in order to justify the exorbitant Soviet concentration on military force but to explain it. Large armies and massive artillery, including rockets, are traditional attributes of the Russian state, which they perceive as defensive. Manpower and arms are the only aspects of state power in which they can compete successfully with more advanced Western nations. In the struggle for influence in the Third World, they have only two useful tools, weapons and ideology, and the latter is proving less and less persuasive.

Domestically the Party, the police, and the Politburo seem in absolute control, certainly for the immediate future. However, the extreme nervousness with which they react to the handful of articulate dissidents reflects their underlying sense of insecurity. They are at least subconsciously aware that the majority of the population no longer believes in Soviet ideology, that they are, in Solzhenitsyn's words, "emigrés of the heart." The national minorities, the non-Russians, now constitute together a majority of the population and, since they have more children, that majority is growing; they may soon outnumber the Russians both in the labor force and the army. Soviet agriculture has been a disaster ever since collectivization. Even with large imports of grain and fodder, meat is constantly in short supply. Production of consumer goods has increased perceptibly but still falls vastly short of both the demand and expectations of the Soviet population. Only the "new class" leads the good life.

Though Soviet society may seem monolithic, it is beneath the surface at least as disjointed as any other. Amalrik refers to "the extreme isolation in which the regime has placed both society and itself." "This isolation," he points out, "has not only separated the regime from society, and all sectors of society from each other, but also put the country in extreme isolation from the rest of the world. This isolation has created for all—from the bureaucratic elite to the lowest social levels—an almost surrealistic picture of the world and of their place in it." How long can a whole society be kept in quarantine by their rulers and commanded to believe that the rest of the world is sick and only they are well?

A generational change at the top and all through the system is about to occur. No machinery or traditions exist for carrying out such changes smoothly. Those who come in are unlikely to differ substantially from those who have passed on, but the situation will be shaken up and cracks will probably appear. Psychoses, grievances, and tensions will be exacerbated. Stability, internal and external, may be harder to maintain. Neither an anticommunist nor even a Communist revolution is likely to occur, but the new leaders may perceive themselves as more rather than less vulnerable. On the other hand, it is to be hoped that new Soviet leaders will recognize, as the old presumably have, that their régime could not withstand either the physical or the psychological prostration that a general nuclear war would inevitably cause. The Soviet régime would under those circumstances collapse and disintegrate even more rapidly than did czarism.

Of course the same would be true of many other governments in case of nuclear war. The traditional symbiosis of war and revolution would reassert itself, perhaps to an extent unparalleled in history, at least since the breakdown of the Roman Empire.

Only a few words need be said about the countries of Eastern Europe, which used to be called and in fact still are Soviet satellites. If Soviet power should suddenly evaporate, their present governments would not last a month, perhaps not a week. Since it is not going to evaporate, they will endure, but they are undergoing a gradual and probably irreversible sea-change. They are becoming more national than Soviet, more popular than Party, more modern than Communist, more Western than Eastern. They are, on the one hand, reverting to their histories and, on the other, advancing more rapidly than the

Russians into the contemporary world.

A dissident Polish Communist and intellectual, Leszek Kolakowski, has written: "In the European Communist countries Communist ideology is for all practical purposes dead, in the sense that no one, neither rulers nor ruled, still takes it seriously. For the ruling Party however it remains absolutely indispensable, since in the absence of democratic forms of representation it is the only basis for legitimacy of the one-party tyranny." A dissident Czech Communist, Erazim Kohak, has also written: "The Czechoslovak Spring did not defy history; it anticipated it. Today we are waiting for history to catch up with us."

In an interview in March 1979 the Spanish Communist leader, Manuel Azcarate, said:

> The Czechoslovak experiment was an absolutely decisive move in the history of socialism in that it tried to give socialism an effective modern and democratic dimension and put its creative focus back into Western Europe. . . . The suppression of Czechoslovakia was a particularly odious demonstration of the fact that the backward and anachronistic nature of Soviet socialism has all the power in the world to prevent, if necessary by force of arms, the progressive strain in socialism from making headway. To the extent that the occupation of Czechoslovakia has killed or heavily retarded this development, we can only say that it has dealt a blow to the whole socialist movement, including, of course, its Soviet variant.*

The East European governments are straddling two systems, state socialist and postindustrial; two constituencies, Russian and national; two epochs, the past and the present. As the gap between each of these two elements widens, only Soviet power prevents an open rupture. These Communist bureaucracies are skating on very thin ice, most of all the Polish and Rumanian which are physically closest and nationally farthest from the Soviet Union. Their preferred model is probably the Yugoslav, where the Party survives but the system has been transformed. The Soviets, however, will not permit them to move that far. So they inch forward and backward, marking time until, as Kohak says, history catches up.

The Communist parties of Western Europe are in an even more

Encounter magazine, March 1979.

anomalous position. They are ambivalent about where their allegiance lies. Except for their ideological tie to Moscow and their own Leninist party organization, how do they differ from their Socialist rivals? Yet these ties separate them from electorates which are intensely national-ist and increasingly bourgeois. The only solution to their ambivalence is to remain out of power, where they do not finally have to choose. In opposition they can usually rely on the ineptitude and obduracy of the conservatives to keep them alive. The recent tactics of the French and Italian Communist parties, coyly advancing and retreat-ing before the prospects of power, reflect these ambivalences. Euro-communism is a stage in the evolution of West European Communist parties either to bourgeois respectability or to dissolution.

Chinese Communism, like everything else Chinese, is unique. The Chinese have one of the longest and most illustrious histories of any culture. Three and a half millennia ago they were creating some of the most beautiful bronze vessels ever made. Their periods of dynastic order at intervals during more than two thousand years—Han, Tang, Sung, Mongol, Ming, Manchu—their Confucian tradition of wisdom, gentility, and moderation, produced a high civilization, rhythmically decaying and reviving but persisting in its essentials until the present day. Their people have been immemorially schooled in diligence, sobriety, respect for authority, aptitude for fine arts and crafts, serene confidence in the superiority of all that pertains to the "Middle King-dom," the epicenter of the world.

Superficial similarities and common contemporary goals should not deceive us about the profound differences between Chinese and Occi-dental ways of thinking and organizing themselves politically. "Mod-ernization" and "democracy," two code words being proclaimed in China today, are misleading to Westerners, because they evoke images very different from what, even if Chinese leaders continue to pursue their present goals, will ultimately take shape there.

Despite the gentility of its manners and the urbanity of its social arrangements, there is an undercurrent of violence in Chinese society, which periodically breaks forth in unpremeditated acts of homicide or suicide, in brutal peasant revolts, in the overthrow of long-estab-lished dynasties. It is analagous to the strain of violence lacing Japa-nese conformity, though less tense and hysterical. It is perhaps the price any civilization pays for too rigid suppression of the assertive or aggressive impulses locked in human nature.

The differences between the Russians and the Chinese are far more profound than the "deviations" of Communist ideology. The two nations are even more widely separated by history than by geography. The continent between them has been twice bridged: in a moment of time by the ponies of the Great Khan which in the thirteenth century raced from the Gobi to the Adriatic; over several centuries by the Cossacks and the Czars inching from the Urals to the Pacific, carving chunks from the flanks of China as they moved. Poor fences make poor neighbors. Chinese and Russians have despised, despoiled, and feared each other for 700 years.

Lenin and Mao are perhaps prototypes of the two peoples, both deceptively camouflaged with a veneer of Marxism, neither deflected from his native genius by its alien Occidentalism, each molding his own people along the grain of their separate ethnicities. Nevertheless, each had his individual temper and his individual experience which influenced the nature of the revolution he inspired and manipulated.

In *Mao's Revolution and the Chinese Political Culture,* Richard Solomon notes:

> The one theme in Mao's personality which stands in sharpest contrast to China's traditional cultural pattern is his strong element of self-assertiveness, in a society which for millenia has stressed social inter-dependence and personal dependence. Mao's youthful opposition to the role of a filial son, his rebellion against the pain and manipulation suffered while dependent on paternal authority, however, acquired meaning beyond personal assertiveness. Mao's individual struggle merged with that of an age in which millions of Chinese witnessed the increasing ineffectiveness of the Confucian social tradition and suffered humiliation at the hands of exploitative foreign powers.

Of course self-assertiveness is necessarily characteristic of all revolutionary leaders, in Chinese history, for example, in the founders of the Ch'in, Han, and Ming dynasties, indeed in Sun Yat-sen and Chiang Kai-shek, not to mention Mao's own comrades, Chou En-lai, Teng Hsiao-ping, Lin Piao, Mao's wife, and the Gang of Four. The peculiarity of his personal approach to revolution was his emphasis on its continuing role, his refusal to allow it to freeze into a permanent mold, power structure, or "new class," his insistence on the "permanent revolution" (which recalls Thomas Jefferson's advocacy of a new revolution every twenty years).

According to Edward Rice, Mao was profoundly influenced by concepts, partly Eastern, partly Western, he picked up at the Hunan Provincial Normal School in Changsha, where he spent five years, 1913–18, from his twentieth to his twenty-fifth year. "These concepts," Rice writes "—that man is basically good, that human nature can readily be changed, and that the world can be transformed through a release of hidden human energies—were to influence Mao Tse Tung, many decades later, as he sought to guide China back to power and greatness and onward toward a communist society."* Mao always believed in, and eventually became, the wonder-working character who was the subject of one of his most celebrated fables—"the foolish old man who moved mountains."

Mao was keenly aware, however, that, after the revolution had cooled, these "hidden human energies" tended to flag and to be constricted in bureaucratic structures manipulated by those who dominated and profited from them. This was what he saw happening in the Soviet Union. Hence his untiring demand for renewed revolutionary impetus and effort, for the Great Leap Forward in 1958 and the Great Proletarian Cultural Revolution in 1966. Both of these produced economic and political turbulence and threatened to bring disaster. Both were carried on over the protests of many of his closest collaborators; indeed, he used them as a means of purging some of them, though in a less sanguinary fashion than Stalin had chosen. Indeed a central purpose of these recurrent revolutions was to reassert the paramount authority of Mao vis-à-vis the pragmatic managers like Liu Shao-chi and Teng Hsiao-peng, who, in their single-minded pursuit of efficiency and modernization, tended to elbow him out of real power and project him into the role of a celestial icon.

When I visited Communist China for the first time in 1973, the excesses of the Cultural Revolution had been ended by army intervention at Mao's reluctant command, and the ambitions of the military leaders had been curbed with the expulsion and death of Lin Piao. Through all these storms Chou En-lai had managed to hold the ship

---

Mao's Way (University of California Press).

of state together and was cautiously bringing it back on an even keel. However, the chief proponents of the Cultural Revolution, including Mao's wife, still closely surrounded the sage as he drifted into his dotage. Nevertheless, even at that murky time, I was struck, as were most in the freshening stream of foreign visitors, by the remarkable accomplishments of the Chinese revolution.

The first and most significant was that the entire population, estimated then at 800 million, was, probably for the first time in Chinese history, decently fed, decently clothed, and relatively free from disease. Gone were the ragged, starving, sickly masses in the city streets and country roads, the beggars, the dirt, the flies, the lice. The American economist Wasily Leontief wrote about that time: "The unique accomplishment of socialist China is the establishment and, for the time being at least, the effective maintenance of a social and economic order in which, in spite of very low average per capita income, abject poverty has been virtually eliminated." The ratio between highest and lowest earnings was, he estimated, only three or four to one, though other observers claim the gap is somewhat wider.

This miracle was achieved by a number of social, political, and economic devices. One was an extraordinary social discipline, part-Communist and part-Chinese, instilled by a pervasive propaganda producing a high degree of consensus, and lubricated by an element of participatory democracy at the grass-roots level in field and factory. In the critical area of agriculture, for example, there was collectivization, but the cardinal error of the Russian model was avoided and individual incentive preserved by permitting the production team (the former village) to retain whatever it produced over and above the government's tax in kind and by dividing this surplus among team members on the basis of work points individually earned. Moreover, most teams practiced self-reliance by producing some of their own tools and some simple consumer goods.

Health care was delivered to almost everyone by "barefoot doctors" employing simple remedies; for the seriously ill hospitals employing both traditional and modern medicine were available practically free of charge. The same network disseminated birth-control information and devices so successfully, reenforced by social pressure for late childbearing and small families, that a steady decline in birthrate was occurring and a stable population by the end of the century seemed possible. Traditional Chinese respect for the old continued to ensure an honored and useful place for most of them in their own households or villages.

There continued to be within the Party considerable dedication and enthusiasm for "serving the people" reminiscent of the spirit I encountered in the Soviet Union in 1929. The "new class" had been conspicuously chastened and was still in bad repute at that time. As Mao said: "Everyone on horseback must be brought down once in a while to share the burden of the long march as a correction to one's soul and behavior." Haughty, overprivileged, or insufficiently zealous bureaucrats were relegated for months, or sometimes years, to "May 7 schools" for reeducation in the fundamentals of Maoism.

The gap between study and work, between white collar and blue collar, so characteristic of the West and the Soviet Union, was at least partially bridged by the widespread distribution of workshops, of mandatory work with the hands, in most schools, by assignment of most students to farms and factories at intervals during the school year and, for the relatively few going on to higher levels, for two or three years between school and college. City youths were dispatched in hundreds of thousands to villages and frontier regions, to dirty their hands, humble their pride, build canals, open oil fields, level mountains.

Mass literacy and elementary and secondary education were being steadily and rapidly extended. University and graduate education, however, had been in practice eviscerated by adjusting standards and examinations to the modest level of those students who had distinguished themselves not by scholarship but by zeal in farm, factory, or armed forces. Little effort was being made to lift their intellectual level to meet the requirements of modernization. In higher education the Cultural Revolution was still in control. In the Party the struggle it had unleashed was dampened but still unresolved.

When I returned in 1977 all that had changed dramatically. The "Gang of Four" had been purged the year before. They were denounced everywhere, not merely ritually but in vials of righteous wrath from officials, teachers, factory and farm managers who had suffered under the Cultural Revolution and whose resentment at the revolutionary egalitarianism and primitivism of Mao, though his name was still untouchable, could now be spewed forth on the Gang.

Chou and Teng were the heroes. Science and technology, production and modernization were the watchwords. The practical goal was, first of all, to make up for the ten years lost, to resume the long march to great-power status that Chou had proclaimed as the objective for the year 2000. That remains the paramount objective today.

In a sense the course of Chinese history since about 1960, when Khrushchev withheld from Peking the secrets of the atom bomb and overnight broke off assistance to China's economic and technological development, has been determined by hostility toward and fear of the Soviet Union. The emphasis on self-reliance in proceeding with development, including nuclear weapons; the Cultural Revolution, which was, in part, Mao's answer to what he considered Moscow's betrayal of the Marxist revolution; the reaction *against* the Cultural Revolution when it seemed to be dangerously weakening the national economy and national defense; the treaty with Japan and "normalization" of relations with the United States, the two traditional enemies of the Communist régime; the dilution of self-reliance by a willingness to import technology on a large scale and to take loans from the West in order to do so; the invasion of Vietnam, to demonstrate to the Soviet Union that the Peoples' Republic was not a paper tiger that could be flouted in its own backyard—all these are evidence of an antagonism so deep-seated and deeply felt that it can deflect or overcome both the most cherished dogmas and the most pragmatic alternative concerns.

Churchill called the Soviet Union "a riddle wrapped in an enigma," but the phrase could be more aptly applied to China, a civilization even more mystifying to the West and a society much more in a state of flux, whose surprises and reversals are probably far from exhausted.

It seems plausible to suppose that China, after seventy years of turbulence and thirty years of Mao's idiosyncratic brand of communism, may now be settling down into the conventional role of an incipient great power, to which her history, population, resources, and skills entitle her. Such a role would imply vigorous modernization of the economy, though probably at a prudent pace and by "appropriate" means, more Chinese than Western; continued pragmatism in the domestic political process, with more emphasis on efficiency than on egalitarianism, on science than on ideology, more rewards and privileges for successful managers and officials; more openness to alien but contemporary cultures and folkways, more deference to human rights and popular expectations; closer association with Japan, the United States, and the West, but without undue dependence or commitment; undiminished hostility to the Soviet Union, corresponding reenforcement and modernization of the armed forces, sharper competition with the Soviets in the Third World, particularly in East and South Asia.

On the other hand, none of this is certain over the longer term. Both the outside world and the Chinese leadership itself have been faced with one stunning surprise after another during the last thirty-five years. Antagonism to the Soviet Union does not preclude a measure of accommodation, if and when both governments should perceive it to be in their interest. Even a limited accommodation could have considerable repercussions in each of the areas mentioned. Mao is dead but Maoism may be alive. If the "new class" presumes too much on the popular reaction to the excesses of the Cultural Revolution, it could provoke a renewed wave of populism and egalitarianism, which in its turn could generate either a larger measure of democratic liberalization or a tighter and more fanatical dictatorship. Mao, like Mohammed, may still in the late twentieth century have an unanticipated message for the Third World, even for the West.

Before ending this capsule survey of Communism in the latter part of the twentieth century and undertaking similar sketches of the democracies and the Third World, we should mention two points at which the two overlap—Vietnam and Cuba.

What is perhaps most remarkable, as we suggested earlier, is that there are only two. Of all the hundred or more countries in the Third World today, most newly liberated and groping for a new identity, only two have adopted wholeheartedly and carried out systematically the doctrines of Marx and Lenin, only two in the years of decolonization, liberation, and independence have voluntarily followed the example of the Soviet Union or China. Each of these two, moreover, has done so under special circumstances that have not yet and may not later be duplicated elsewhere.

In Vietnam the movement for national independence from France was captured from the very outset by a group of dedicated but indigenous Marxists—Ho Chi Minh, Pham Van Dong, Giap, LeDuan. Their eventual success, after forty years of revolutionary war against the Japanese, the French, the Americans, and even the Chinese, owes much more to their nationalism than to their Communism. Indeed had they been simply nationalist and not Communist, they would probably have won independence and national unity with much less suffering and travail, perhaps as early as the mid-1950s instead of the mid-1970s. Nonetheless, one must pay tribute to the dedication and discipline, at least partly inspired by this Marxist ideology, which enabled them to defeat two great powers—even while recognizing that they themselves by their fanaticism unnecessarily prolonged the armed struggle and the suffering of their own people.

The question that confronts the Vietnamese leaders now is whether they can ever stop fighting, whether during forty years their acclimatization to war has become so inveterate that they will have to be replaced before their people can at last find peace.

In Cuba Castro's revolution was both national and social, nationally directed against the United States of which Cuba had ever since its liberation from Spain been an economic satellite, socially against American and Cuban capitalists who in close alliance maintained a typical colonial system under which the overwhelming national majority worked at low wages and in deep poverty for the colonial power and its indigenous collaborators. Since the United States was not likely to support, even to tolerate, a revolution against a régime and a relationship from which it profited so substantially—as its execution a few years before of a coup against a similar revolution in Guatemala demonstrated—Castro, whatever his original personal convictions may have been, judged that only an open commitment to the doctrine of the rival superpower, and reliance upon it for essential military and material assistance, could ensure the survival of his revolution and his régime. Whether or not his calculation about the behavior of the United States was correct—and the conventional response by a liberal American President that brought about the Bay of Pigs fiasco seemed to bear it out—his gamble succeeded. However, the idiosyncratic character of his success in Cuba was shown by his failure, despite repeated efforts under the aegis of Che Guevara, to export his revolution elsewhere in Latin America. Still, it may well be that the evolution, or rather the weakness and muddle, of societies in the small countries in and around the Caribbean will in the future provide Castro with more fertile fields than Africa for the export of his brand of Communism. That would not necessarily demonstrate its virtues but merely the ripeness of these retarded societies for radical change.

As to Cuba itself, the Mexican socialist writer Octavio Paz has recently written: "A revolution can be gauged by its ability to transform an economy. Under Batista, Cuba was a monoculture of sugar. Under Castro, Cuba is still a monoculture of sugar. Cuba has changed its dependence, but not its economy. It was sort of an American brothel and now it is a Soviet barracks, a bureaucratic colony."*

*Interview in the *New York Times,* May 3, 1979.

≫ 8 ≪

The Democracies
1945-1979

The history of the democracies in the thirty-five years since World War II is a spectacle both more inspiring and more reassuring than that of the Communist states. Nevertheless, it is far from lacking in darker shadows that could be ominous for the future.

The West was singularly blessed in that during the five hundred years of Renaissance, Reformation, Enlightenment, and scientific revolution it had evolved remarkable diversity and flexibility of political structure, economic enterprise, and philosophic creativity. It had, therefore, achieved an intellectual and social level that enabled it to recover quickly even from the devastation and trauma of two world wars and to resume the elaboration of what came to be called "post-industrial" society. In so doing, however, it ran considerable risks.

For there are inherent risks—as the Greek city-states of the fifth century B.C., the Italian city-states of the Quattrocento, and the European nation-states of the early twentieth century discovered—in loose, competitive, undisciplined, innovative social structures. Their strength is that they adapt far better to changing circumstances than do authoritarian societies; their weakness is that their internal quarrels over adaptations may become so divisive, sometimes so mutually destructive, that even a very flexible social structure breaks down.

Western society has during the past 500 years been in an almost perpetual state of crisis, a state that has on the whole been immensely creative. There are now foreboding signs, however, that the accumulation of stresses and strains from the scientific and industrial revolutions and two world wars may be generating a crisis of unprecedented scope, to which even Western society may not be able to adjust sufficiently and in time. The intermittent, erratic, unpredictable coming together, drifting apart, and coming together again of the elements of this impending crisis make a study of our time both fascinating and perturbing.

The 1950s and most of the 1960s were great years for the Western European democracies. The Marshall Plan brought economic recovery and NATO military security. Behind these shields their blighted fields and factories revived and flourished like the green bay tree. Traditional membranes dividing class from class became for the first time pervious. Much of the working class, however they might vote, bought cars and rode happily into the bourgeoisie. The good things of life fell on almost all like the gentle rain from heaven.

A devastated, humbled, and guilt-stricken Germany clambered out of the shadows of Auschwitz and Nuremberg, contrived almost overnight the first genuine and respected democracy in German history, absorbed millions of refugees from the East, and built the most successful economy in Western Europe. Britain, it is true, had spent too many of its lives and too much of its fortunes in the two wars. On the shaky foundations that remained, without the nourishment of empire, the Labor party had to build a welfare state. It did so with remarkable success, but it paid a high price—the entrenchment of interests so self-seeking and single-minded that the nation soon began to suffer from a bad case of arteriosclerosis. However, it remained a lovely place to live. France, once it had shaken off its obsessions with the past, with Indochina and Algeria—which two courageous leaders, Mendes-France and de Gaulle, enabled it to do—also recovered with remarkable celerity the equilibrium and self-confidence it had so disastrously lost in the 1930s. Even Italy, which had not since the fall of Rome been well governed, prospered for a time under Alcide De Gasperi and, with its usual ingenuity and legerdemain, produced a cornucopia of economic miracles. Of course the Scandinavians, including the Finns, as well as the Dutch and Belgians, worked hard, lived well, and hewed to the golden mean as they always had. Best of all, under the inspiration and shepherding of Jean Monnet, the Treaties of Rome were concluded in 1958 and, out of the swamps and thickets of history, the concept of Europe began to take tangible form.

In Japan the political and economic recovery was even more scintillating, vertiginous, and substantial than in Germany. Soon no visible stigmata distinguished those who had lost from those who had won the war.

The scene in America was equally heartening and salubrious. The war had unleashed to the fullest the marvelous productivity of this people and healed the last wounds of the Great Depression. The United States was almost the only nation that came out of the war richer than when it went in. Nor did peace bring the economic relapse that had been feared. With no more than a brief pause for breath, the American economy resumed and redoubled peacetime production, commencing a rising curve of national, social, and individual affluence that continued with only minor interruptions until the 1970s.

Moreover, the quality of American leadership during the next twenty years, while occasionally flawed, was of a caliber sufficient to cope with most of the challenges it faced. The despised Harry Truman, from the moment of his taking office, displayed a resolution, a decisiveness, a flair both for leadership and for choosing superb lieutenants, which has earned him a significant place in the American pantheon. Faithful to the New Deal and the progressive tradition, he resurrected some of their major elements and, against all expert prediction, beat Thomas Dewey, Henry Wallace, and Strom Thurmond in 1948. He espoused and carried out, if he did not author, the Marshall Plan and the North Atlantic Treaty Organization. He responded without a moment's hesitation to the Berlin blockade and the Korean invasion.

The sickness that disfigured and weakened America from 1950 to 1954 was McCarthyism, the witchhunt not only against Communism but against "dangerous thoughts," which the demagogic and ruffianly Senator from Washington dominated but did not originate. Nixon, McCarran, Bridges, and a gaggle of other unscrupulous politicians had since the first blasts of the Cold War been quick to see the personal advantage they could derive from directing the whirlwind against their political opponents and riding it to popular fame and high office. McCarthy, however, in his contemptuous disregard for truth and justice, in the shameless exuberance of his calumny and vilification, outstripped them all. As I have said earlier, while his own career was blessedly brief, his effect on the political behavior of

American leaders for the next two decades was profound. The consternation of Eisenhower and Dulles, of Kennedy, of Johnson, even of Nixon, that they might be held politically responsible for "losing" another country to Communism was in large measure a posthumous exercise of power by Joe McCarthy. There lies buried not too deep under the skin of the American democracy a strain of bigotry and know-nothingism that demagogues can tap with frightening ease; leaders concerned for liberty should be eternally vigilant against it.

However, American democracy survived McCarthy, and for a dozen years after 1955 achieved one of its finest hours. Eisenhower presided over a prosperous, triumphant, complacent nation, which he symbolized and fostered. He left foreign policy largely to Dulles, intervening only if he thought things were getting out of hand—for example, when he blocked American military intervention in Indochina at the time of Dien Bien Phu. When I met him occasionally, I had the impression of a very decent man but not a great one. Perhaps as President he will be best remembered for his defense of the rights of blacks at Little Rock, and for his valedictory—his warning of the growing power of the "military-industrial complex." More and more Americans shared in the booming affluence, but they became increasingly "hooked" on it, impatient and resentful when the boom paused or fell short of their expectations. Moreover, toward the end of the 1950s, they began to get bored.

Kennedy was a breath of fresh air, a marvelously vibrant, stimulating personality, an intellectual with both style and the common touch. It is no wonder that, particularly in light of his premature and tragic death, he created a legend that enveloped his whole family and still persists. I saw him often in his thousand days and never failed to be impressed and exhilarated. He was the epitome of grace under pressure, of which the Cuban missile crisis was a classic display. Nevertheless, he was a conventional rather than a bold or innovative thinker, and his actions reflected his limitations. The Bay of Pigs debacle, the steady escalation of involvement in Vietnam, the prudence of domestic programs, were all in fact continuations and projections of Eisenhower-Dulles policies. They suited the mood of the people, who wanted a change of style but not really a change of content.

Yet that is what Lyndon Johnson gave them. He was truly a figure out of American legend, Paul Bunyanesque in his virtues and his

vices, overwhelming, ruthless, cunning, yet compassionate and vision-
ary, capable of incredible pettiness and meanness but also of prodigious feats of political performance. He could describe his Vice President in scatological terms or discard a carefully prepared plan of
action because someone had told the press what he intended to do.
Yet his "Great Society" and civil rights programs substantially diminished poverty and injustice in this country and were in the great
progressive tradition of Jefferson, Jackson, the two Roosevelts, and
Wilson. He was not an original thinker. His domestic policies were
those of the New Deal, amplified by virtue of the affluence the nation
had in the meantime generated. Yet even that affluence, as subsequent
events proved, was insufficient to support both massive internal trans-
fers of income and a modern war.

In foreign affairs Johnson simply extrapolated what he had learned
from the Cold War, adopted uncritically what the "best and the
brightest" told him was necessary, swore he would not be a President
who "lost" another country, and magnified in his gargantuan fashion
all the errors of his predecessors. As the cartoonist David Levine so
aptly revealed, Vietnam was the mortal wound on his belly. In many
ways his finest hour came in March 1968 when he faced reality and
bowed out.

The half dozen years from 1968 to 1974 can be said in retrospect to
have reflected a critical turning point both in the history and the
consciousness of the Western democracies.

In the opening months of 1968, Lyndon Johnson and his United
States, brutally awakened by the Tet offensive from the illusions of
power, confronted the realization that victory in Vietnam, if possible
at all, was not worth the costs. In May the Gaullist régime in France
was so shaken by riots of students and workers, erupting unheralded
out of the blue, that de Gaulle himself for a few days went underground and a year later withdrew abruptly from the political scene.
In August Europe was shocked when the Prague Spring, "Communism with a human face," was extinguished overnight by Soviet and
satellite armies. In the same month the quadrennial convention of the
American Democratic party was disrupted by hysterical displays of
violence and counterviolence, and shortly thereafter the despised and
rejected Richard Nixon became President of the United States.

There followed in the ensuing years the cynical and useless destruction of Cambodia and a further dilapidation of the American psyche; the sudden dethronement of the imperial dollar by suspension of its convertibility and then its devaluation; the emergence of political terrorism in Europe, particularly Germany, Italy, and Ireland; the Arab oil embargo and quadrupling of oil prices, and the degrading Watergate scandal, as a consequence of which an American President was for the first time ejected from office.

On the other hand, there were more auspicious developments: a "détente" of sorts between the United States and the Soviet Union, still richer in rhetoric than in substance; a beginning of modest "normalization" of relations between the United States and China; revivals of democracy in Greece, Spain and Portugal; a final ringing down of the curtain, even though an iron one, on America's Vietnam War.

Underlying most of these current events were the slow tides and tectonic shifts of human history which, sixty years after the upheavals of World War I, began to make themselves felt in the economics and politics of Western society. Shortly after the Second World War, the Spanish philosopher Ortega y Gasset had written: "There are many reasons for surmising that European man is lifting his tents from off that modern soil where he has camped these three hundred years and is beginning a new exodus toward another historic ambit, another manner of existence."* He added in the same essay: "We do not know what is happening to us, and that is precisely the thing that is happening to us—the fact of not knowing what is happening to us."

There was published in 1972 under the auspices of the Club of Rome, an "invisible college" of distinguished European, American, and Japanese men of affairs and scientists, a little book that shocked and outraged Western pundits and politicians but may have conveyed to their society the first inkling of that new "historic ambit" toward which it was moving. The book was called *The Limits to Growth*. Many of its graphs, extrapolations, and forecasts were ridiculed and contradicted, but its central message—that there *are* inevitably limits to growth—remained as incontrovertible as it was unpalatable. Three quotations from that book will convey both its flavor and its impact.

"The basic behavior mode of the world system is exponential

*Man and Crisis (W.W. Norton).

growth of population and capital, followed by collapse. . . . This behavior mode occurs if we assume no change in the present system or if we assume any number of technological changes in the system"; "Numerous problems today have no technical solutions. Examples are the nuclear arms race, racial tensions and unemployment. Even if society's technological progress fulfills all expectations, it may very well be a problem with no technical solution, or the interaction of several such problems, that finally brings an end to population and capital growth." The third quotation strikes a more cheerful note. "We believe," said the authors, "that the evolution of a society that favors innovation and technological development, a society based on equality and justice, is far more likely to evolve in a state of global equilibrium than it is in the state of growth we are experiencing today."* This remark, made in 1972, foreshadowed another little book of equally seminal import and effect, *Small Is Beautiful* by E. F. Schumacher, which appeared only a year later but, when it gradually percolated out to a wide audience, was more hospitably received than its more eschatological predecessor.

Before proceeding to comment on the events of the 1970s, which seem so bewilderingly to illustrate that "we do not know what is happening to us," it will be useful to recall what has been happening during the century so far to some of the economic and political assumptions, creeds, and structures to which the Western democracies, particularly the United States, still profess an unabated allegiance but which have lost so much of their original substance.

The legendary "free enterprise" system of Adam Smith and his followers has in the European democracies been competing for most of the century with various forms of "socialism." This competition has led in practice to a "mixed economy," in which some large industries are state owned and operated and others privately owned and operated, and in which small business, while politically free and in some sectors still flourishing, is in practice excluded from many other sectors by economic costs and constraints. The individual entrepreneur is free in principle but not in fact, unless he is a multimillionaire, to establish a new automobile-manufacturing or petroleum-distributing enterprise or a new metropolitan newspaper or television network.

---

*Dennis Meadows et al., *Limits to Growth* (Universe Books).

While socialism has not appeared as a significant political movement in the United States and the "mixed economy" there is characterized for the most part by forms of government regulation and subsidy rather than by government ownership, practical constraints on the exercise of "free" private enterprise are at least as decisive as in Europe. What used to be called trusts and to monopolize vertically all or much of a particular industry have now burgeoned into multinational corporations or conglomerates which own or control horizontally the most astonishing and incongruous assortment of totally unrelated enterprises at home and abroad. So-called economy of scale has often with wildest abandon proliferated into a meaningless extravagance of size for size's sake. Matching the corporation in scale, power, and unwieldiness have been two other indigenous components of the modern economic "system": huge private banks controlling hundreds of billions of assets around the world, and dictatorially managed trade unions embracing whole industries or several industries.

These developments led Adolph Berle twenty years ago to write in *Power without Property:* "The greatest part of American economic enterprise, formerly individualist, has been regrouped and consolidated into a few hundred non-Statist, collective cooperative institutions."* It is ironic that a society that so indignantly and self-righteously rejects "collectivism" should in fact have slipped imperceptibly into an economic system much better described as collective or oligopolistic capitalism than as the "free enterprise" it still fondly imagines itself to be. Indeed it could be argued that the essential difference between a large private and a large public enterprise today is that in the former the managers are relatively free from both supervision and harassment by the owners of the enterprise (the shareholders), while in the latter they are subject to both supervision and harassment by the owners (the politicians representing the public). The "free enterprise" system, therefore, insofar as it relates to large enterprises, has come in modern times to mean the freedom of the managers from the owners.

The managers of business enterprises, moreover, though they are in very large part college graduates, are not necessarily persons of

*(Harcourt, Brace & Co.).

In the Summer Palace in Pe-king, 1917.

Greeting former President Hoover in Bangkok on his global food survey, 1946.

At the Potsdam Conference, July 1945. Truman opposite with author standing behind. Stalin at left, Churchill at right.—SIGNAL CORPS PHOTO

Greeting Secretary of State Dulles on his arrival in Laos, 1955.

Chatting with Crown Prince Savany of Laos, 1955.

Greeting President Sukarno of Indonesia at Damascus airport, 1958. President Kuwa of Syria is just behind Sukarno.

Being received at the Royal Palace in Rabat before presenting credentials as Ambassador to Morocco, 1958.

Conducting King Mohammed V of Morocco and King Hussein of Jordan through the U.S. Pavilion at Casablanca Trade Fair, 1959.

After a flight in a jet fighter plane at a U.S. air base in Morocco.

King Mohammed reads a toast to President Eisenhower during latter's visit to Morocco, December 1959. The present King, Hassan II, is at the author's left and Prime Minister Ibrahim at his right.

A U.S.–Soviet call on U.N. Secretary General U Thant just after the Cuban missile crisis, November 1962. Among those present, from left to right, Soviet Ambassador Valerian Zorin, Vasili Kuznetsov, then Deputy Soviet Foreign Minister, John J. McCloy, Anastasi Mikoyan, then First Deputy Soviet Premier, U Thant, Adlai Stevenson, the author.

—UNITED NATIONS

The author and his wife chatting with Dean Acheson and Mrs. Dean Rusk at ceremony marking author's first retirement, 1966.—DEPARTMENT OF STATE

Speaking to the U.N. General Assembly in 1970. On the podium are U Thant, Assembly President Edvard Hambro, and U.N. Undersecretary Stavropoulos.—UNITED NATIONS

Casting the first U.S. veto in the U.N. Security Council, 1970. Yakov Malik is the Soviet delegate and Lord Caradon, the British.—UNITED NATIONS

Greeting Premier Chou En-Lai on visit to China as President of the National Committee on U.S.–China Relations.

Acknowledging applause following speech by Vice Premier Deng Xiao Peng at receptio during Deng's Washington visit, February 1979.—KENNETH R. SMALL

Testifying before the Senate Foreign Relations Committee in support of SALT II treaty with Mrs. Coretta King and former Senator McIntyre of New Hampshire.

great intellectual capacity or innovative talent, such as often were the founding fathers of modern industry. The present managers find it to their personal advantage to accommodate themselves to the system and to rise gradually through the hierarchy without "making waves." They are usually indistinguishable from the government "bureaucrats" they affect to despise, except in the location of the turf they defend and the size of the emoluments they receive. Quite a stir was created when Herbert Simon received the Nobel Prize in Economics in 1978 for demonstrating (in studies made thirty years before) that decision making among business entrepreneurs is not based, as economic theory would have it, on a rational search for alternatives to find the optimum course but on a much more haphazard and seat-of-the-pants groping for a satisfactory choice that permits the business to get along fairly well. As a matter of fact, anyone who had observed decision making in business or government over a period of years could have come to this conclusion without benefit of economic theory.

In consequence of these peculiarities of structure and management, there is very little consistent long-range planning. Indeed there is a popular prejudice against planning which business interests assiduously foster because they fear government planning would constrain their license to do as they like. The economy therefore tends to be driven primarily by two blind, anarchic compulsions. The first is the drive to make and sell whatever large numbers of people can be persuaded to buy, whether or not the comparative social utility of the product or its impact on scarce resources warrant its production. William Tombey has called this tendency a "whirling dervish economy dependent on compulsive consumption."

Robert Heilbroner describes the second prevailing economic drive as "technological determinism," the effect that geometrically expanding but incoherent and value-free technology, from nuclear weapons to pesticides to computers, has on modern societies. "Technological determinism," Heilbroner writes, "is peculiarly a product of a certain historic epoch . . . in which the forces of technical change have been unleashed, but when the agencies for the control or guidance of technology are still rudimentary."*

Between Capitalism and Socialism (Vintage Books).

Nevertheless the oligopolistic capitalism of the last thirty years, despite all these deficiencies and absences of mind, despite its irrationality, despite the arbitrary and often antisocial behavior of trade unions, banks, and conglomerates, has produced unparalleled affluence for many and a significant rise in the standard of living for most in the Western populations. Indeed the political difficulties of the 1970s, to which we shall come in a moment, arise primarily from the refusal of the majority of voters, who have graduated from the rugged individualism of an earlier day to what might be described as "upholstered individualism," to face the fact that this period of steadily rising real incomes may have been exceptional and may be coming to an end.

It is only fair to recall, moreover, that the free market has always been biased against poor people, which raises serious question about its supposed democratic character. Effective demand in such a market bears little or no relation to real need or optimum social distribution. The modern mixed economy has built into the system some considerable "upholstering" for the poor, in the form of social security and social insurance, but the poor remain nevertheless the most dispensable element of the economy and the first to suffer from recession, inflation, or the contemporary combination of both.

There is another curiosity of capitalism that in the past has been merely a somewhat unattractive reflection of human nature but in the modern context is proving to have serious economic and political repercussions. Adam Smith himself noted two centuries ago: "With the greater part of rich people, the chief enjoyment of riches consists in the parade of riches, which in their eyes is never so complete as when they appear to possess those decisive marks of opulence which nobody can possess but themselves." A hundred years later Thorstein Veblen elaborated the principle of "conspicuous consumption" in his *Theory of the Leisure Class.* In 1976, the centennial of *The Wealth of Nations,* the British economist Fred Hirsch (most unfortunately since deceased) published a remarkably perceptive study entitled *Social Limits to Growth** in which he demonstrated how difficult it is becoming under modern conditions for anyone "to possess those decisive marks of opulence which nobody can possess but themselves." His argument can be summarized, though at the expense of justice to its

*Harvard University Press.

richness and acuity, by a few quotations.

"Beyond some point that has long been surpassed in crowded industrial societies, conditions of use tend to deteriorate as use becomes more widespread." Hirsch cites as examples the accumulation of traffic and constraints on mobility as more and more people own cars, the frustration of the pursuit of wilderness and privacy as more and more build cottages and launch motorboats on once lonely waterways, the depreciation of the market value of higher education as a larger and larger proportion of the population gains access to it. More for everyone, he argues, must after a certain point become less for most. "What the wealthy have today," he writes, "can no longer be delivered to the rest of us tomorrow; yet as we individually grow richer, that is what we expect. . . . Instead of alleviating the unmet demands on the economic system, material growth at this point exacerbates them. The locus of instability is the divergence between what is possible for the individual and what is possible for all individuals." In other words, we are beginning to bump our heads against a social as well as a physical ceiling in the attainable growth of the economic system.

Hirsch has also drawn another more philosophical conclusion from his investigations. "The principle of self-interest," he declares, "is incomplete as a social organizing device. It operates effectively only in tandem with some supporting social principle. This fundamental characteristic of economic liberalism, which was largely taken for granted by Adam Smith and by John Stuart Mill in their different ways, has been lost sight of by its modern protagonists." Adam Smith's wonder-working "invisible hand," one might say, is able to perform successfully only when it is guided by Montesquieu's "spirit of the laws," which it now seldom is.

Another characteristic of modern economies, whether capitalist or socialist, should also be noted: the peculiarly attenuated and unsatisfactory nature, under contemporary conditions, of much of what has traditionally been conceived of as "property"—to which the economists of the eighteenth and nineteenth centuries attached such normative importance, and which their modern counterparts continue indiscriminately to exalt, without distinguishing between its totally different varieties.

Forty years ago the French social philosopher Simone Weil, who had a great respect for the kinds of property which, by their identification with the individual, are capable of comforting and sustaining the human spirit, wrote in *The Need for Roots* of her experience as a factory worker in England: "A great modern factory is a waste from the point of view of the need of property; for it is unable to provide either the workers, or the manager who is paid his salary by the board of directors, or the members of the board who never visit it, or the shareholders who are unaware of its existence, with the least satisfaction in connection with this need." This conclusion has been born out in the ensuing years by growing manifestations of workers' dissatisfaction with the mechanical, uncreative nature of the work in which most of them are engaged and with their exclusion from any responsibility or control of the enterprise to which they are devoting their working lives. Various devices to mitigate this alienation—more worker involvement in management at both the plant and shop level—are being successfully tried in several European countries, but so far they only scratch the surface of the problem. In the meantime worker frustration finds outlet in the growing volume and capriciousness of strikes and in political action, in some countries such as France and Italy in Communist parties.

The psychological and political aspects of this phenomenon have recently been emphasized by Heilbroner in his troubling book *An Inquiry into the Human Prospect.* "The lesson of the past," Heilbroner wrote, "may then only confirm what both radicals and conservatives have often said but have not always really believed—that man does not live by bread alone. Affluence does not buy morale, a sense of community, even a quiescent conformity. Instead, it may only permit large numbers of people to express their existential unhappiness because they are no longer crushed by the burdens of the economic struggle."

All these imperfections and distortions of the modern Western economic system, whether oligopolistic capitalism or democratic socialism or a mixture of the two, have accumulated to such a point in the 1970s that they are not only clogging dangerously the arteries of the system but are producing bewilderment and schizophrenia among economists and politicians who, like the common men, "do not know what is happening to us" or to themselves. Michael Blumenthal, addressing a convention of bankers shortly after he had been dismissed as Secretary of Treasury in 1979, frankly confessed: "Nobody fully understands the present situation. That includes all government officials making policy. They are as puzzled as you are when you open the paper in the morning."

Some years ago the economist Walt Rostow inquired: "What will happen when diminishing relative marginal utility sets in, on a mass basis, for real income itself?" That seems to be what is in fact occurring as population growth both impairs and strains finite resources, as the autonomy and the disorder of the Third World alter the terms of trade in those resources, and as scarcities, complexities, and structural overloads, economic and political, begin to outstrip the capacity both of unplanned and planned economies to change and adapt. We are more and more victims of our own success. As the biologist René Dubos wrote: "In all living systems, whether they are embryos, landscapes or cultures, organization limits the possibilities of reorganization."* Or as the ecologist John Holdren has pointed out: "Civilization tries to manage ecosystems in such a way as to maximize productivity, 'nature' manages ecosystems in such a way as to maximize stability, and the two goals are incompatible."

A conspicuous example of the impact of these misunderstood complexities is the new style of inflation currently afflicting most "free enterprise" economies. In the traditional view, inflation is caused by an excess of effective demand over available supply and to be corrected by constraining demand, most easily through reducing government spending and raising interest rates, and by encouraging investment to increase supply. This treatment remains the conventional wisdom and is being widely applied. If carried beyond an ill-determined point, however, it produces recession, and nowadays usually does so without curing inflation. This reminds one of the medical practice, which remained in unquestioned repute for centuries, of bleeding patients to cure them of practically anything. Whether recession is better than inflation is questionable, but certainly the conjunction of the two is the worst of both worlds.

The fact is that contemporary inflation is quite a new and different beast. The chief cause is technically described as "cost-push," but what underlies "cost-push" is not only the expectation but the insis-

*A God Within (Scribners).

tence of all organized elements of the population that their income must continue steadily to rise, as expanding technology, productivity, and other factors permitted it so delectably to do for a quarter-century after World War II. It has not yet penetrated the public consciousness, despite the conspicuous example of the oil crunch, that the economy is beginning to encounter certain physical, social, and political ceilings on growth, that rising incomes cannot buy more than there is to buy, that the issuance of too many tickets simply depreciates them. There are of course many other complementary causes of inflation, of which the toll exacted by politically powerful vested interests is the most important, but the appearance of these natural ceilings between us and the wild blue yonder is the heart of the matter.

One logical treatment for inflation of this sort would be wage and price controls on essential commodities, including rationing when necessary. Electorates, however, accustomed to a couple of centuries of free enterprise and several decades of rising affluence, are for the most part unwilling to constrain their freedom to pay more and more for less and less, or to admit that the exciting roller-coaster, whirling-dervish economy must begin to slow down. Until those facts of life are admitted, we shall bounce back and forth between curing inflation with recession and recession with inflation and usually suffering from both. This is not inherently so dreadful, since we in the West will continue to live very well indeed in comparison either with our forebears or with our contemporaries in the Third World. But the political consequences of the rather sudden "decompression" or "cold turkey" we shall have to endure already are serious and may become graver still.

In a book early in 1979 the political scientist Walter Laqueur encapsulated some of these consequences so exactly that this summary can be taken as a text for my appraisal. "Europe does face something like a crisis but it is not mainly economic"; he wrote, "it is political and, in the final analysis, cultural and moral. The roots are, first, the political system's weakness, the inability to resist conflicting demands of various sections of society, and, second, the clash between the urge for more freedom and the need for more order. . . . Social conflict has become less tractable precisely because it is no longer a clear-cut confrontation between classes, but between many interest groups; the general trend is toward fragmentation and conflict within classes.

Most of the recent strikes in Britain and France have been against the state and thus against society. . . . Europe's trouble is that nothing much has happened."*

This has been the case not only in Europe but in America and throughout most of the world. The 1970s, despite the seemingly sensational character of many of their events, have been essentially a decade of stalemate. As Derek Bok, president of Harvard University, recently remarked: "When so many groups organize to protect their special interests, the politics of activism can become a politics of immobility." This is due, as I have remarked, to overload of a system unable to adjust rapidly enough to rapidly changing conditions and, as Laqueur points out, to the fragmentation or impotence of many of its operating institutions, nations, political parties, local governments, in the face of entrenched group interests intent on seizing or holding shrinking points of vantage. We might be said to be suffering from the disproportional representation of single-minded minorities. So many of us seem to spend so much of our time fighting rear-guard actions against the future. We do not permit our governments to govern or our leaders to lead. Times are just bad enough to exasperate but not bad enough to inspire. This is a dangerous state of affairs and of mind, because the persistence of political stalemate and disorder tends to provoke resort to extreme remedies.

Almost two centuries ago James Madison remarked in a letter to Jefferson: "It is a melancholy reflection that liberty should be equally exposed to danger whether the Government have too much or too little power." At about the same time Benjamin Franklin, returning from the Constitutional Convention, was asked by his landlady: "Well, Mr. Franklin, what have you given us, a republic or a monarchy?" "A republic," he replied, "if you can keep it." Four years later, in 1791, Edmund Burke wrote in a letter to a member of the French National Assembly: "Society cannot exist unless a controlling power upon will and appetite be placed somewhere, and the less of it there is within, the more there must be without. It is ordained in the eternal constitution of things that men of intemperate minds cannot be free. Their passions forge their fetters." What a pity that so many modern "conservatives" so little heed the father of English conservatism.

A Continent Astray.

"The clash between the urge for more freedom and the need for more order," as Laqueur put it, the contrasting danger of too much or too little government power, to which Madison referred, have plagued mankind at least since the French Revolution. "There has developed in this century," wrote Walter Lippmann in *The Public Philosophy,* "a functional derangement of the relationship between the mass of the people and the government. The people have acquired power which they are incapable of exercising, and the governments they elect have lost powers which they must recover if they are to govern."

"When the modern corporation," John Kenneth Galbraith has written, "acquires power over markets, power in the community, power over the state, power over belief, it is a political instrument, different in form and degree but not in kind from the state itself." However, it is not only the corporation that behaves like a state within a state. Britain has in recent years been a captive of its trade unions. The military in the United States, the Soviet Union, and elsewhere conduct multibillion-dollar enterprises with little effective control by anyone outside their fraternity. Interest groups opposed to abortion or gun control destroy eminent political leaders who resist them. These "collectivities" are particularly alarming in a democracy because they are internally so undemocratic. Corporations, trade unions, military establishments, are structured and ruled like monarchies or dictatorships. If consistently undemocratic habits are built up in the institutions in which we pass our daily lives and in which our deepest loyalties lie, how can we be expected to preserve a democratic state based on these institutions? As Fred Hirsch remarked at the conclusion of his study quoted above: "We may be near the limit of explicit social organization possible without a supporting social morality."

In ending this exploration of the substructures of contemporary politics, let me mention three succinct diagnoses from three generations of modern political thinkers. Shortly before he died in 1924 Woodrow Wilson wrote: "In spite of all that has happened, I have not lost one iota of my great faith in the people. They act too quickly or too slowly, but you can depend upon them ultimately; you can depend upon their search for the truth and for what is right." In her *Crises of the Republic* a few years ago Hannah Arendt wrote: "Cracks in the power structure of all but the small countries are opening and widening. And while no one can say with assurance where and when the breaking point has been reached, we can observe, almost measure, how strength and resiliency are insidiously destroyed, leaking, as it were, drop by drop from our institutions." The contrast between these two perceptions reflects the toll that the years between the first and the last quarter of the twentieth century had taken of the "strength and resiliency" of peoples, of politicians, and of political "scientists."

In a response to a question about Solzhenitsyn by a *New York Times* interviewer in May 1979, Octavio Paz said:

> Obviously, everything he says about the West is correct. I also believe that in the West there is a serious moral failure. And obviously the West has been corrupted by money and pleasure. But Solzhenitsyn has a nostalgia for theocracy. He believes the West lives in decadence because it has abandoned God.
>
> That is not true. God dies and is reborn every day. The West's problem is different. First, it has economic and political problems which it must solve rationally. Secondly, it has problems of social justice which Solzhenitsyn does not see. The West is living a crisis of freedom.

In a similar vein the Canadian Prime Minister, Pierre Trudeau, wrote: "Inflation has not found its Keynes. I personally think the Keynes of inflation will not be an economist" but will instead "be a political, philosophical or moral leader inspiring people to do without the excess consumption so prominent in developed countries." It is suggestive, however, of the political hazards of so heroic a posture that Trudeau recently returned to power by overwhelming an opponent, Joe Clark, who had sought to inspire, or compel, his people to do without the excess consumption of gasoline.

Politically speaking, the 1970s in the Western democracies have, for better or worse, been overshadowed by three American personalities —Richard Nixon, Henry Kissinger, and Jimmy Carter.

Richard Nixon is one of the most curious figures in American history. A highly insecure and troubled personality, quite unscrupulous in dealing with real or imagined threats to a national security he naïvely identified with his own, at the same time calculating, reckless, and paranoiac, elevated to the Vice Presidency as the representative of McCarthyism and the Radical Right, bruised and battered in the reaction against it, he nevertheless, by indefatigable pertinacity and adroit opportunism, finally achieved against all odds his life's ambition of the Presidency, carried the country into a peace of sorts with its two great adversaries, won reelection by an almost unanimous electoral vote, threw it all away in trivial adventures and deceits inspired by his paranoia, and became the first American President to be forced to resign his office to escape impeachment.

Kissinger is quite another story. History will be puzzled to do justice both to him and to itself. He is in some sense a Renaissance figure, both Shakespearean and Machiavellian, a little out of his element in the late twentieth century, though perhaps the twenty-first will, for its sins, prove more compatible. He is an extraordinary and fascinating personality, a mind of great keenness and perceptivity that moves forward and backward at the speed of light, a wit that never fails except when he is crossed, a colossal vanity and ambition that he has learned to disguise by advertising them, a political animal with an instinct for the jugular and other organs, a man of total unreliability when his personal interests are at stake, but still a patrician by intellect endowed with a sense of history, of great issues and grand designs, of due proportion between the consequential and the trivial, of respect for the destiny of man, though not frequently for individual men. He has, however, created some deceptively intoxicating precedents. Henceforth all national security advisers will feel obliged to perform as media stars and will expect to become Secretary of State.

It is easier to understand why Nixon found it so difficult to extricate his country and himself from Vietnam than why Kissinger did. Of course both instinctively resisted to the last possible moment giving up anything they had. Both no doubt shared Lyndon Johnson's horror, inspired by McCarthy, of "losing" a country. Kissinger professed to fear a backlash from the Right if the United States was "humiliated," a backlash presumably to be directed in part against himself. I once tried to persuade him that if we turned over responsibility to General Thieu after sustaining and fortifying him for five years with half a million American troops and billions of dollars in American arms, and he still lost the war, the "humiliation" would be his, not ours. Kissinger was not persuaded. In the four years after Nixon took office, the number of American dead was doubled and neutral Cambodia was devastated and ruined. Otherwise we accomplished nothing. Thieu fell at the first serious blow and disappeared without a trace. America was traumatized but not humiliated. But for Watergate the Republicans would still be in office.

A few years later Leslie Gelb and Richard Betts concluded their study, *The Irony of Vietnam: The System Worked,* with this judgment: "The need for pragmatism more than doctrines, formulas and ideologies is the basic lesson of the Vietnam War. Americans are rightly known as a pragmatic people in their internal affairs and in their thinking. That so pragmatic a people have followed such ideological foreign policies is paradoxical."

This stricture can be applied to American foreign policy as far back as the Spanish-American War and World War I, and of course through all the Cold War. It is odd that it should, in the case of Vietnam, have ensnared two such committed and cold-eyed pragmatists as Richard Nixon and Henry Kissinger. Joseph Luns, Secretary General of NATO, once told me that Nixon had said to him that Johnson was a strong President but he had one weakness—he worried about what the intellectuals and the press said about him. I couldn't care less, bragged Nixon, what they say. Perhaps that was the trouble. Even pragmatists can ill afford to live in ivory towers.

Jimmy Carter reminds one of Wendell Willkie in his attractive image of the honest, idealistic, practical businessman, a quintessential, though in 1976 a somewhat old-fashioned, American figure.

Life in Washington, however, proved much more complicated than he and his provincial entourage of Georgians had imagined. Economic and political realities—the inflationary pressure of persistently extravagant habits on less and less elastic resources, the mutually neutralizing impact of all the pressure groups determined to prevent anything happening that would curb their indulgences—proved on the whole too much for Carter, as it had for many Western leaders. He was charged with lack of leadership because no one wanted to be led or would be driven. He drifted from Left to Right of Center, which may have been where he temperamentally always had been, but in any case was where the politically articulate among his countrymen for the most part momentarily were. (In actual fact the alleged "swing to the Right" may prove to be more simply a swing against those in office because they have been unable, for the reasons just stated, to deliver what electorates living in the past demand. When conservatives prove no better able than liberals to deliver, as they will, a "swing to the Left" will follow.)

Carter's "idealism" in foreign affairs—human rights, reduced defense budgets, nuclear nonproliferation, diminished arms sales—while winning praise in many quarters, foundered in practice on the intractability of adversaries he could not coerce, friends he could not persuade, and clients and neutrals he had to indulge. As so often in the past the cyclical behavior of the two superpowers was out of phase: the consequences of Soviet military decisions taken after the Cuban military crisis coincided, alarmingly to Americans, with the consequences of U.S. absorption for seven years in Vietnam. The identity crisis of the Third World was at the same time rising to new levels of passion and frustration, particularly in the Middle East, testing Carter as a man and as a statesman. He responded in Iran with an admirable mix of prudence and firmness but still found himself pushed back more and more into pre-Vietnam postures that he and the nation had sworn to forgo. It is much too soon to pronounce any verdict of history upon him, except to say that he is certain to end up, if he survives, a far different political animal than he seemed to be when first elected President.

The 1970s began with the Western democracies at last obliged to admit and confront the complexity of the internal and external problems that had been accumulating for twenty years but economic growth and the Cold War had concealed. They were not for the most part threatened with revolution but with accumulating frustrations, divisions, and malaise which, if unresolved over time, could eventually create revolutionary situations. The decade ended without anything having been resolved: the complexities of "postindustrial" society had proven to be more intractable than anyone had suspected; relations between East and West, between North and South, were more thorny and more dangerous than when the decade began: the interdependence between the three worlds had been more and more convincingly demonstrated, but effective prescriptions for the management of that interdependence had not been found.

◈ 9 ◈

The Third World
1945-1979

When World War II ended, there were only ten fully independent nations in the whole of Asia and Africa. At the end of the 1970s there were more than eighty. If one adds to this number those in Latin America, the Caribbean, and Oceania, which are also "developing countries," one arrives at a grand total of nearly 120.

These constitute the Third World, originally so called because these nations were supposed to belong neither to the world of the capitalist West nor the world of the Communist East. However, the supposed political nonalignment of some of them is questionable. Some tilt East and some tilt West, though usually not consistently.

In practice, economic factors determine which world a nation identifies with. While there are vast differences among the per capita gross national products of African, Asian, and Latin American countries—between Saudi Arabia and Brazil on the one hand and Chad and Haiti on the other—all of them feel a sense of solidarity as less developed countries and hence as members of an underprivileged class.

If one includes China, the Third World contains about three-quarters of the world's 4 billion human beings; if one excludes China, which is still a developing country but is politically sui generis, the Third World contains half the population of the globe. Most of the Latin American nations obtained political independence during the nineteenth century but continued thereafter to feel colonized economically. They still identify psychologically and politically with the nations of Asia and Africa. It is a sign both of the wisdom and the exhaustion of the European "imperialists," some of whose empires had endured for centuries, that after World War II they granted independence to most of their colonies without an armed struggle and continued to assist them thereafter. Vietnam, Algeria, and the Portuguese African colonies were notable exceptions.

This gigantic global revolution was, like the American Revolution and unlike the French or the Russian, essentially a political, not a social, revolution; its goal was simply national independence from a foreign master. It was completed almost everywhere, except in Southern Africa, in about thirty years.

The achievement of independence had little immediate effect on the class structure and distribution of income in most developing countries. They continued to be divided into poverty-stricken peasant majorities and privileged, educated elites. In nations where economic growth was substantial, the commercial and professional middle classes also expanded, but, because of rigid social barriers and rapid population growth, the "lower classes" remained abysmally poor and more numerous than ever. Despite startling progress in "development" in many countries, there are more poor people in the world than there were thirty years ago.

The economic and social revolutions that national liberation potentially unleashed have thus only just begun. They are likely to continue for many years on two levels: the international level through the striving of the loosely associated Third World for a "new international economic order" in which they would share more equitably in the benefits of the traditional system in trade, development, and growth; the internal level at which the vast, underprivileged, inarticulate majorities inside Third World countries will also strive for more equitable sharing of the national product of development and growth.

Neither political liberation nor economic development, no matter how desirable and necessary they are, should be expected to achieve the goals of their proponents without enormous disruption and turmoil. A society does not move suddenly from the seventeenth or eighteenth centuries into the twentieth or the twenty-first, as most Third World countries are doing or trying to do, without shaking its traditional structures to their very foundations. In the process, energies and passions capable of either amazing creation or appalling destruction—or both—are released.

Many years ago the philosopher Alfred North Whitehead wrote: "It is the first step in wisdom to recognize that the major advances in civilization are processes which all but wreck the society in which they occur." In 1969 in a report to the World Bank, the Canadian statesman and founding father of the United Nations, Lester Pearson, wrote: "Development is not a guarantee of political stability or an antidote to violence. Change is, itself, intrinsically disruptive."*Some years earlier Robert Heilbroner had written: "The central, inescapable and indispensable precondition of 'economic' development is political and social change on a wrenching and tearing scale. Economic development . . . is a process of institutional birth and institutional death. It is a time when power shifts, often violently and abruptly, a time when old regimes go under and new ones rise in their places. And these are not just the unpleasant side effects of development. They are part and parcel of the process, the very driving force of change itself."†

In light of these appraisals it is not surprising that the Third World has since 1945 been the scene of repeated eruptions, of wars between nations, of social, tribal, or religious struggles inside nations, of political revolutions, of coups d'état, assassination, genocide, and persecution. It is sufficient to mention a few examples: the separation of India and Pakistan on communal lines in 1947, during which about 15 million people fled their homes in terror and some 200,000 were slaughtered; intermittent, often fierce and murderous warfare in the Middle East, four full-scale wars between Arabs and Israelis, many lesser struggles among Arabs; conflict breaking out almost immediately after independence in the Congo (now Zaire), threatening dissolution of the country until suppressed by the United Nations, recurring sporadically thereafter in Shaba and elsewhere; communal strife and civil war in Cyprus, leading after a Turkish invasion to a virtual partition of the country; the overthrow of Sukarno and massacre of several hundred thousand Communists in Indonesia in 1965; almost continuous civil war in Burma and in Chad; a sanguinary dictatorship in Uganda finally overthrown by Tanzanian invasion; prolonged terrorism and counterterrorism in Argentina and Uruguay, violent overthrow of an elected leftist government in Chile, and civil war in

*Partners in Development.
†Between Capitalism and Socialism (Vintage Books).

Nicaragua; revolution in Ethiopia, overthrow of Haile Selassie, frontier war with Somalia and civil war with Eritrea; overthrow of the Shah and breakdown of stable government in Iran; civil war in Angola, Rhodesia, and Namibia, with intense racial conflicts in the latter two.

The extreme instability of governments in Africa is well illustrated by a paragraph from Edward Hoagland's recent book on the Sudan, where a cruel, bloody civil war between North and South went on for some fifteen years without receiving much world attention. "My first arrival in Khartoum," Hoagland writes, "had been delayed for several hours while the airport was cleared for Chad's head of state, General Felix Malloum, to fly in to discuss with Nimeiri [President of Sudan] the invasions staged from Libya . . . by dissenting nationals of their respective countries. And when I left, the news of that particular day was that Malloum had just survived an assassination plot by his own officers, who'd shot their way up the front steps of his palace in Ndjamena. Dusting himself off, he flew to Brazzaville to attend the funeral of Major Marien Ngouabi—the chief of state of the Congo— who had been shot while eating lunch in *his* palace by four of *his* officers . . . Nimeiri's closest friend among the neighboring presidents, Lieutenant Colonel Ibrahim el Hamdi of North Yemen . . . was successfully gunned down after three years in power by other officers, about six months after this."*

Lest this sanguinary roll call be taken to imply that the Third World is peculiarly susceptible to disorder and violence, it is well to remember that the history of Europe, not only in the Middle Ages, not only in the wars of princes during the Renaissance or the wars of religion during the Reformation, but especially in the two world wars of our own century, was equally disorderly and far bloodier.

Moreover, the European colonial powers, while they brought important material, educational, and sanitary benefits to the countries they colonized, are responsible in at least two respects for the instability that followed liberation. First, in the colonial scramble they divided territories among themselves haphazardly, often ignoring tribal (i.e., ethnic and linguistic) entities and loyalties or economic realities and requirements. The frontiers of many new nations, based on the

---

*African Calliope (Random House).

old colonial lines, often make no sense in either respect. Yet it is impossible to change them without risk of war. Second, the colonial powers for their own purposes sometimes fostered communal or tribal rivalries, dissolved long-established systems of governance and social cohesion, delayed too long, often until the last minute, the preparation of their colonial charges for self-government, created elites that were indeed better educated but in alien ways inappropriate to their native environment and separated spiritually from the fellow citizens they would be called upon to govern. So, while Third World leaders are both mistaken and demagogic in blaming all their ills on the departed imperialists, the latter are far from blameless.

It is, however, a futile exercise to try to apportion responsibility for the present ills of the Third World, except to show that responsibility is widely shared and that the ills have profound historical roots. The Third World is often reproached for its systems of government; but how could one expect societies just emerging from hundreds of years of feudalism, tribalism, or foreign domination to be prepared to govern themselves through modes of representative democracy developed gradually over hundreds of years in a few European and American countries? What could be more condescending and unrealistic than to attempt to "grade" such societies on the basis of their conformity or nonconformity to Western standards?

It is, however, necessary to scrutinize objectively the character of Third World governance in the three and a half decades since World War II. One should not be surprised that progress was discouragingly slow, indeed that regress often followed initial progress; but there is no denying that dictatorship, either of a single man or of an oligarchy, was in 1980 the prevalent form of government there.

It is a tribute to the prestige of the British parliamentary system that many nations withdrawing from the British Empire have sought to imitate it. A few have succeeded reasonably well; many have failed. India, despite the complexity of its ethnic and religious composition and the burden of its caste system, has thus far succeeded amazingly well in adapting to its needs an alien parliamentary system. Whether this success will continue in face of the horrendous and divisive problems India confronts is a question one cannot answer with confidence.

Of her neighboring fellow graduates of the Empire, Pakistan long ago fell under military dictatorship; Sri Lanka has done exceptionally well both with representative government and with equitable economic development; Burma has lapsed into a peculiarly obscurantist and stagnant autocracy engrossed in civil war. Singapore, almost wholly Chinese, has prospered under a brilliant but authoritarian leader; Malaysia, half-Malay and half-Chinese, beset by a prolonged Communist insurgency, has done considerably less well. In Africa some of the offshoots of the Empire—Kenya, Tanzania, and Zambia, for example—have consistently maintained fairly open socieites under charismatic and benevolent leadership. Others, such as Nigeria and Ghana, have drifted in and out of dictatorship, and one, Uganda, fell prey to a paranoiac monster.

All the former French, Belgian, and Portuguese colonies in Africa have, after independence, succumbed to authoritarian or oligarchic rule; some under astute leadership, such as Senegal, Ivory Coast, Cameroon, have prospered; others, Zaire, Mali, Central African Republic (or "Empire") have failed miserably; as to Mozambique, Angola, and Zimbabwe, the latest comers, the jury is still out.

Indonesia, the Philippines, South Korea, and Taiwan are all governed by dictatorships. The last two have achieved remarkable economic success, while the first two have achieved far less than their bounteous resources should have permitted. Climate, social discipline, a larger degree of ethnic uniformity may account for the relative success of Korea and Taiwan. Latin America, with the exceptions of Mexico, Venezuela, Colombia, and Costa Rica, has relapsed into traditional military dictatorship, masked by the republican forms adopted in the nineteenth century in imitation of the United States but never assimilated. Indeed it is both astonishing and sad that the Latin American countries, inheritors of a great culture, most of them richly endowed economically, have remained so backward politically and socially 150 years after independence. The barbarity of recent military régimes in Chile, Argentina, and Uruguay is more shameful and less excusable than that of the Spaniards against whom they revolted so long ago. Even in the milder autocracies of Mexico and Brazil, the social abyss between rich and poor is enormous and almost impassable. In Mexico the wealthiest 10 percent of the population gets 45 percent of the total income, while the poorest 40 percent gets 10 percent. Brazil, Colombia, and Venezuela, not to mention the rest, are probably worse.

The economic "systems" of Third World countries, if one can characterize by that term anything so haphazard, experimental, and inconstant, range from what might be called either state socialism or state capitalism, usually with strong surviving elements of private enterprise at the commercial level, to variations on the Japanese model of private enterprise guided and reenforced by state intervention. As we remarked earlier, only Cuba and Vietnam have chosen to adopt full-scale authoritarian socialism on the Soviet or Chinese model. Likewise few have chosen or are likely to choose an economic system permitting private enterprise as uninhibited a role as it enjoys in the United States. In most cases their indigenous private sector is not sufficiently strong and sophisticated to carry the responsibility for development and modernization, nor would their hostility to foreign "neocolonialism" and their distrust of multinational corporations permit foreign private enterprise to assume this responsibility.

Both political and economic paradigms in the Third World reflect, therefore, a concentration of authority in a small group, often around a single individual. In newly independent or newly modernizing societies where substantial political and economic elites have had little opportunity to grow and take root, government has to be jerrybuilt from the material at hand, which is likely to be military, since the military is the only organized and respected element in the society able to assert itself quickly and effectively. In some countries, under favorable circumstances, wider participation in both economic and political life can be generated in a few years. In others it may take generations. In relatively few are the transitions from authoritarian to more democratic rule likely to be orderly and uninterrupted.

During the 1960s the Third World, emboldened by its large accretion in numbers of states and votes at the United Nations, began to organize itself and to formulate explicit goals. Long before OPEC became significant, the so-called nonaligned nations had been convening under the leadership of Nehru, Nasser, and Tito. In the mid-sixties a parallel but larger "Group of 77" emerged, which included practically all the developing nations and has continued to the present day, though the "seventy-seven" now number well over a hundred. Also in the 1960s a new United Nations mechanism with universal membership, the U.N. Conference on Trade and Development, was set up at the insistence of "the 77," which wanted an economic forum that, unlike the World Bank and Fund or the GATT (General Agreements on Tariffs and Trade), they could dominate. They also proclaimed, through the General Assembly, a First and later a Second Development Decade, with a target of 6 percent growth for the less developed countries as a whole. This goal was in fact achieved, though most unevenly among countries and among populations inside countries. The Third World, therefore, despite its lack of military power and, until the consolidation of OPEC, of demonstrable economic power, did during these years acquire a modest amount of leverage vis-à-vis the industrialized nations and did make some notable progress in development. In the climate of initial success and boundless expectation they formulated and pressed their claim for "the new international economic order."

The rich countries' contribution to this process continued to be far less than the needs and claims of the poor, indeed even less then than their own repeated commitments. The United States, for example, has several times in the General Assembly joined in unanimous resolutions proclaiming the developed countries' intent to contribute annually 1 percent of their GNP to the development of Third World countries. I was myself, during my assignment as its U.N. Ambassador, instrumental in persuading the Nixon administration to reiterate this pledge in 1970. Yet we never remotely approached fulfilling it. On the contrary, by the end of the decade we were contributing only a quarter of that amount and had fallen from first place among donors of aid to fourteenth, in terms of percent of GNP. Moreover, most of what was provided, through both public and private agencies, had for many years been in the form of loans rather than grants, so that by the end of the 1970s many of the less developed countries had built up enormous debts, service of which sometimes amounted to as much as 50 percent of their annual export earnings. Such an unwieldy debt load created a most unhealthy situation, not only because it seriously inhibited development but because it contributed even more seriously to the fragility of the international economic apparatus. The debt burden of most developing countries was of course further significantly elevated after OPEC quadrupled the price of oil. It is by no means clear whether private Western banks, even bolstered by the International Monetary Fund, can carry indefinitely this constantly expanding load without repudiation or collapse.

Three conclusions that emerged from my participation in United Nations debates and operations seem relevant to the future evolution of the Third World. First, my involvement in the conduct of U.N. peacekeeping and pacific settlement in the Congo, the Middle East, Cyprus, India-Pakistan, Dominican Republic, and Indochina confirmed my conviction that conflicts and instabilities among and inside Third World countries are not only certain to keep many of them in intermittent turmoil for decades to come but will often draw in great powers and risk wider war. Second, the Third World's expectation of massive economic development, its passionate belief that its backwardness results from the political colonialism of the past and the economic "colonialism" of the present, its demand for a "new international economic order" which it will itself define—all these are inevitably leading to an acrimonious series of confrontations between developed and developing countries.

Third and most striking of all, the economic interdependence that has been imperceptibly growing up among all three "worlds" has already reached a stage of such intimacy and complexity that the binding knot can never be untied. North America, Europe, Japan, and Australia, at least, now share such a vital interest in the Third World's progressive development that the eventual result almost has to be some sort of a new international "order" reflecting, in a disorderly and unsystematic fashion no doubt, the interests of both. The most eloquent and effective exponents of this thesis during my years at the U.N. were those great international civil servants Ralph Bunche, the American who most deservedly won the Nobel Peace Prize; Paul Hoffman, a founding father both of the Marshall Plan and the U.N. Development Program; Maurice Strong, Canadian architect of the U.N. Environmental Program, and Barbara Ward, the eloquent and compassionate British advocate of an indivisible world inspired by justice.

This relatively optimistic conclusion about converging interests between North and South must be qualified by repeatedly stressing that the agonizing revolutions of the Third World have only just begun, that the "wrenching and tearing" process to which Heilbroner referred will go on for many decades, that the problems the Third World confronts are horrendous and perhaps insurmountable, and that, since the whole world is indeed interdependent and will become more so, those problems challenge the First and Second worlds almost as much as the Third. In order to have any idea where we stand and where we are likely to go, it is necessary to scan briefly the most formidable of these problems.

As frightening though not as immediate as the danger of nuclear war is the problem of explosive population growth. Three-quarters of the number of all the people who have ever lived are alive today, and numbers in much of the Third World are still exponentially increasing. This abnormal phenomenon, peculiar to the twentieth century, is frightening because it compounds—and if not eventually checked makes insoluble—so many other problems. In the present context its significance is, first, that in much of the Third World it contradicts and may frustrate the passionate striving for rising standards of living; second, it may consequently magnify both violent revolution within the Third World and violent clashes of interest between that world and the others.

In 1976, according to calculations of the World Bank, twenty-nine countries with a total population of over 1 billion, including India, Pakistan, Bangladesh, Zaire, Ethiopia, Tanzania, and Vietnam, had an annual per capita GNP of *less than $200.* Another thirty-six countries with a total population of about 1.3 billion, including China, Indonesia, Egypt, Nigeria, the Philippines, Thailand, Kenya, and Zambia, had a per capita GNP between $200 and $500. While small minorities in most of these countries no doubt live in affluence, and many like the Chinese live in relative decency, it would be safe to say that close to a billion people in those countries live in absolute poverty. Per capita GNP, moreover, is a deceptive measure because a country with a large GNP may, like Brazil and Mexico for example, distribute it so badly that a large proportion, even a majority, of its population may live in abject poverty. "Poverty" is a subjective not an objective term, but it would be safe to say that by the standards of developed countries, at least half of the world's population is poor, and one-quarter very poor—including, we should not forget to note, several millions in the richest country of all, the United States.

Certain other factors are relevant to the relation between population and poverty. During the year 1976 the rate of population increase in more than fifty countries, including Brazil, Pakistan, Mexico, Nigeria, Iran, Colombia, Algeria, and Venezuela was still, despite all national and international efforts to check it, more than 2.5 percent (1 percent being the rate necessary to maintain a stable population). Continuance at or near the 2.5 percent rate would double the population of those fifty countries by the end of the century.

Second, because of the large numbers of women of childbearing age already alive or certain to be born, it is estimated that a country would not reach a stable population level until about seventy years *after* it had arrived at a net reproduction rate of 1 percent. For example, if India, with a population of about 650 million now, should achieve a net reproduction rate of 1 percent in the year 2000, its population would eventually stabilize at about 1.4 billion; if it did not achieve the 1 percent rate until the year 2020, its population would eventually level off at about 2 billion. The same is of course true of all other countries with a high rate of population growth.

A third factor is the age level of the populations in Third World countries. In 1975, for example, between 40 and 45 percent of the population of the developing countries of Latin America, Asia, and Africa (nearly 50 percent in Mexico and Algeria) was under fifteen years of age, as compared with 26 or 27 percent in Europe and the United States. This disproportion has two consequences: the working population, for the most part poor, must support and educate an almost equal number who are contributing relatively little to the economy; within the next decade in countries already burdened with mass unemployment and underemployment jobs must somehow be found for these additional hundreds of millions. According to the International Labor Organization, the world labor force will by the year 2000 grow by about 900 million people, nearly equal to a quarter of the world's present population. Unless work and incomes can be found for these additional millions, political unrest will become even more explosive than it already is.

A fourth factor is the enormous confluence of Third World populations from the countryside into great cities, seeking employment which for many will never be found, confined to shantytowns where living conditions and hope of escape must both be minimal. Shanghai has more than 10 million people, Mexico City more than 8 million, Peking, Bombay, Cairo, Seoul, and Sao Paulo each more than 5 million, Jakarta, Tientsin, Rio and Teheran more than 4 million.

None of these cities is anywhere nearly equipped to support these numbers.

In an encyclical "Redemptor Hominis" issued in March 1979, Pope John Paul II, following in the footsteps of his predecessors John XXIII and Paul VI, called for a worldwide redistribution of economic resources to alleviate poverty and starvation in the developing world. "Areas of misery and hunger on our globe," the Pope declared, "could have been made fertile in a short time if the gigantic investments for armaments at the service of war and destruction had been changed into investments for food at the service of life." The Pope cited the contrast between food surpluses in some countries and "starvation and malnutrition" in others as one of the "symptoms of the moral disorder" in the world today. He also noted that mankind is "dilapidating at an accelerated pace material and energy resources and compromising the geophysical environment," thereby causing "the areas of misery to spread."

Unfortunately the Pope did not mention, nor have his predecessors, the link between the misery and hunger he so rightly decries and the population explosion for which the Catholic Church, by its opposition to birth control in those countries and communities where its word is still law, must share the responsibility. How long can the fathers of the Church blind themselves to this glaring contradiction between their compassion and their dogma, indeed between their current preaching and that "categorical" imperative of multiplying mouths and bellies which will ultimately prove inescapable?

In recent years it is becoming more widely understood that "the right to life" should mean the right to a decent life; "human rights" must comprehend, as the United Nations "Universal Declaration of Human Rights" explicitly does, not only political rights, freedom from tyranny and persecution, but economic rights, the right to food, shelter, health care, and education. This is a matter of simple justice. Failure to be explicit on this score has been one of the weaknesses of President Carter's human rights policy.

Satisfying basic human needs is, in the longer run, a matter of practical necessity. In this era of growing interdependence of nations, rapid communication between societies, rising expectations among the poor, and indiscriminate proliferation of weapons, no islands of affluence can insulate themselves for long from rising tides of resentment and revolt. We have recently seen how revolution in Iran is immediately reflected in economic stress among richer nations and political trauma in some. Failure to meet basic needs and offer employment to growing numbers of poor Mexicans causes them to flow in a rising flood into the United States.

After national independence the masses of the Third World were given to understand that the bounty of modern technology would soon become available to them. For the vast majority of them the "revolution of rising expectations" has proved illusory. As Francis Bacon said long ago: "Hope is a good breakfast, but it is a poor supper." The Third World is now beginning to experience "revolutions of frustrated expectations." These will become much more numerous and contagious if their causes are not removed.

The exasperation of poor nations with rich nations is also growing by leaps and bounds. One of the most perceptive thinkers in the Third World, the Indonesian Soedjatmoko, recently reported on a meeting of representatives of the "South" in Tanzania. "The most striking feature which characterized all the discussions," he recalled, "was the bitterness and anger towards the North for its unwillingness to accommodate very essential development requirements of the Third World. The depth of emotions displayed there was aggravated by the sense of powerlessness in dealing with their own problems. Still the feelings displayed . . . seemed to me the top of the iceberg, reflecting the kind of emotions that are bound to affect in the next ten years the behavior of nations and peoples in the Third World."

I shall have more to say about population, poverty, and their consequences in my concluding chapters. Suffice it to add here that these problems will in coming decades confront both poor and rich countries with moral and political dilemmas of the greatest magnitude. If they are not answered satisfactorily, if they *cannot* be answered satisfactorily for either physical or political reasons, the revolutions, the instabilities, the turmoil in the Third World will be magnified and will more and more critically spill over in a variety of ways into the First and Second worlds. The whole planet is now becoming a seamless web. If that web begins to unravel, there is no point at which its unraveling can be certainly arrested.

≫ 10 ≪

Recollections
1945–1979

Before going on to my final chapters, which will try to extract some rhyme and reason from the bewildering panorama of our times, I should like again to illustrate the preceding slices of history with some snapshots from my own memory. These may help sustain the credibility of a period that is in some respects so bizarre as, in retrospect, to seem implausible.

EUROPE

In January 1947, after ten months in India and Thailand and four at the first U.N. General Assembly in New York, I was sent to Czechoslovakia as First Secretary of Embassy. I drove in that month from Le Havre through Paris, Frankfurt, and Nuremberg to Prague across a dark and devastated Europe. The German cities were shattered shells, naked to the driving snow of the coldest winter in a hundred years. A pall of silence hung over the land. A man's labor or a woman's "love" could be bought for a handful of cigarettes.

Prague, however, had miraculously survived. The most beautiful urban antiquity in Europe, half-medieval, half-baroque, still adorned the hills along the Moldau. Only the old City Hall, dilapidated in a spasm of popular revolt just before liberation, the scorched earth of Lidice, razed to the ground in savage reprisal for the assassination of Heydrich, and the appalling roster of Jews transported to death, inscribed on the walls of a crypt beneath the old Jewish cemetery, bore witness to six years of Nazi occupation.

However, the soul of Czechoslovakia had been violated, its confidence and its courage sapped. Its betrayal at Munich by the Western democracies inflicted a blow to its morale and its trust from which it has never recovered. In free elections in May 1946, one year after liberation, the Communists won 38 percent of the vote, not because that proportion was Communist but because that proportion, having lost all faith in the West, believed that only the Soviet Union would protect them from an eventually resurgent Germany, seeking revenge for the expulsion of 3 million Germans from the Sudetenland.

Nevertheless, 62 percent of the electorate had voted for democratic parties. The government during the ten months I lived in Prague was a coalition presiding over a free society. New elections were scheduled for May 1948, and it was quite apparent that the Communists would lose heavily. That was of course the reason they carried out their coup in February of that year. My ambassador, Laurence Steinhardt, contemptuous of all Czechs and particularly the Communists, did not believe they would have the nerve to do it. After July 1947, when Stalin obliged the Czech government to rescind its acceptance of the Marshall Plan, I believed they would.

The Communists succeeded so easily not because they were strong but because their opponents were weak. It is true that Gottwald was Prime Minister, and his party held the ministries of Interior, which controlled the police, of Labor, which controlled the workers' militia, and of Information, which controlled the radio. These would not necessarily have prevailed had the democrats been united and strongly led and had they been firmly supported by the West.

The Benes I knew was old and sick, a broken man. He had stood foursquare against the Nazis in 1938 and been betrayed by his allies in the West. In 1948 he had no allies and no heart to resist. Alone in his great castle above the city, he fumbled, temporized, and surrendered. Jan Masaryk, one of the most charming, kindly men I have known, naïvely or wishfully persuaded himself he could be an impartial arbiter above the battle. The Communists used him and, when his usefulness was past, flung him out of a window to his death. The leaders of the democratic parties, wholly unprepared to go into the streets, fled across the borders in disguise.

The coup could perhaps have been forestalled if the United States had been willing to assure Czech military leaders that, should they resist and Soviet troops march in, American forces would come to their rescue. No such assurance was requested by the Czechs or seriously considered by the Americans. In 1947 the Cold War was just beginning; the U.S. Government was mobilizing opinion in defense of Greece and Turkey; it was in no mood, nor were the American people, to extend military commitments and risk war in the heart of Europe.

I recall a ceremony at which I represented our Embassy, when the citizens of the small town of Banska Bystrica in Slovakia conferred posthumously on Franklin Roosevelt the freedom of their city. Since they felt politically obliged to confer the same "freedom" on Stalin, the ceremony was also attended by Gottwald, the Communist Prime Minister, who was so drunk he could hardly stand or talk throughout the whole affair.

I recall the Fourth of July party in our ambassador's garden in Prague during which we were dismayed to hear—the report rippling like a hot breath of wind across the assembled dignitaries—that Gottwald, Masaryk, and Drtina, the Minister of Justice, had been abruptly summoned to Moscow. We later learned Stalin had upbraided them like delinquent schoolboys and forced them to withdraw ignominiously their acceptance of the Marshall Plan.

When our ambassador was on leave in September and I was in charge, I reported an aborted Communist coup in Slovakia and speculated that the next attempt would be in Prague and that it would be carried through. The last time I saw Masaryk was when I wished him Godspeed at the Prague airport on his departure for the U.N. General Assembly in New York. He knew this might be his last chance to save his country, but, as usual, he was not unhopeful. Later I learned from his close friend Marcia Davenport that Truman and Marshall, then Secretary of State, had refused to receive him in Washington. What could they have said to him?

In November 1947 I was unexpectedly transferred to Vienna, where a new counselor of legation was needed. Vienna, like the German cities I had seen, was a sad spectacle, somber, dreary, strewn with shattered buildings and acres of still acrid rubble, its most famous monuments—Saint Stephen's Cathedral, the Opera, the Burg Theater —reduced to charred skeletons. The people were hungry and cold.

The country was divided into four occupation zones; unpredictable and often rowdy Russian soldiery held all the east as far as the Enns River; Vienna, where the ruling Allied Council met and the celebrated "four men in a jeep," military police of the occupying powers, patrolled together the inner city, was deep in the Soviet Zone; Americans, French, and British needed Soviet passes, separately issued for each trip, to move in and out of the city and consequently suffered from cumulative claustrophobia. On one occasion an American aid official was kidnapped and killed; many of us were detained inexplicably for hours; the atmosphere was never comfortable.

I recall vividly one tense night in the American headquarters. At great risk and pains the CIA had been able to persuade two Soviet pilots to defect and fly one of their most modern aircraft into the American sector of Vienna. The Soviet military high commissioner demanded the immediate surrender of pilots and plane. Since the Western sectors of Berlin were currently being subjected to blockade and he feared a like fate for those in Vienna, our general hesitated. All through the night we debated by telecon with Washington. Only as dawn broke did those of us insisting on refusal prevail. The pilots were spirited off to the West, and the plane returned only after it had been dismantled and studied. No blockade ensued.

Despite these tensions, hazards, and hardships, even at the end of 1947, and increasingly as the years passed (I returned to Austria in 1953 as Deputy High Commissioner), Vienna throbbed with life and gaiety. Free elections had also been held in Austria shortly after the war, but here, where no Munich trauma warped the national psyche, the two democratic parties won 95 percent of the vote. Moreover, although they had spent the interwar years fighting each other, they realized that only by union could they now survive and so firmly maintained a coalition until long after occupation ended. Leaders like Figl, Schärf, Helmer, Raab, and hundreds of their colleagues manfully resisted the most blatant intimidation, and in political campaigns in the Russian Zone did not hesitate, though some were arrested and never seen again, to denounce openly Soviet oppressions. The irony was that in Austria, an ex-enemy, in contrast to Czechoslovakia, a wartime ally, the Western states had contractual responsibilities as occupying powers and so firmly supported the Austrian government. The Marshall Plan poured in millions of dollars to rebuild the blasted economy; the Western zones, in contrast to the dilapidated East, blossomed like gardens.

Not only government but the people were courageous, even exuberant. Deprived of all but the barest essentials, they revived almost immediately, in makeshift quarters, their magnificent opera and symphony orchestras (where one heard Bruno Walter, Furtwängler, Karajan, Elizabeth Schwartzkopf, Sena Jurinac, Lisa della Casa, Hilde Güden, Erich Kunz, Walter Schöffler, and scores of other great artists), their classical and their comic theaters, their fantastic carnival season with nightly balls for weeks on end. This was not mere frivolous diversion but a spontaneous challenge to adversity and demoralization. It succeeded amazingly.

When in 1955 Stalin's successors felt it advisable to make a concrete display of "détente" to the West, they chose Austria as the offering least profitable for them to hold. The long-delayed "State Treaty" was concluded in a rush, Austria evacuated and its liberties fully restored. Twenty-five years later it exhibits one of the firmest democracies and strongest economies in Europe. The schilling, of which in my day one could buy packages for a carton of cigarettes, is now more solid than the dollar. There are advantages in living cheek by jowl with the Iron Curtain, if one has the nerve to stand up and the astuteness to make one's fortune doing so.

I spent three years in Greece from 1950 to 1953 as minister at the Embassy. The civil war had just ended with defeat and expulsion of the Communists. The United States was administering enormous military and economic aid programs with almost equally enormous missions of American advisers and supervisers. The responsibility of the Embassy was to ensure that the charming but incorrigibly combative Greek politicians maintained a government stable and efficient enough to bring about economic recovery and to prevent a drift back to the Left. Since there was a multiplicity of parties under mutually incompatible leaders, and since the Palace, manipulated by that indefatigable intriguer Queen Frederika, was constantly fishing in troubled waters, this was not an easy task. At one point when I was chargé d'affaires King Paul asked for my recall, but Dean Acheson blandly replied that I probably knew what I was doing. The political problem was eventually resolved, at least for some years, when the hero of the civil war, Marshal Papagos, formed a political party, received the

American blessing, won an overwhelming majority in an election, and inaugurated a series of stable governments, which lasted for ten years until the Marshal's successor, Karamanlis, went into voluntary exile in a fit of pique. That brought on another period of political disorder, ending in the Colonels' coup in 1967 and the even more ill-starred coup in Cyprus in 1975. Greek democracy in the twentieth century is as lively, as creative, as contentious, and as unstable as it was in classical times.

During my sojourn there I visited almost every part of that beautiful land, from Corfu and Yanina to Olympia, Sparta, and Mystra, from Nauplion, Mycenae and Tyryns to Delphi and Hosios Loukos, from Hydra and Volos to Metsovo, Salonika and Kavalla, across Homer's wine-dark sea to Rhodes, Crete, and other islands of the Odyssey. I saw the frescoes of Santorini, the gold and bronzes of Phaistos, the tombs of Mycenae, the Charioteer of Delphi, the Poseidon, the Acropolis—and those evocations of earliest Christianity, the Byzantine churches of Salonika, Mistra, and Daphne. I read Greek philosophy, poetry, drama, and history. I immersed myself in the wellsprings that underlie and nourish Western culture. None of my assignments was as intellectually and aesthetically rewarding.

Incidentally, it was during my time in Greece that I had my one personal brush with McCarthyism. To my astonishment I received from the State Department Loyalty Review Board a lengthy "interrogatory" about my associations over the past twenty years, including those with Alger Hiss, Karl Frank, and Noel Field. Apparently the answers were satisfactory as I was "cleared," though the whole process was painfully repeated after the Republicans came to power two years later, and even then needed a year or so more finally to fade away. It later turned out that the chief ground for suspicion in my case was that, in his debriefing by the FBI many years before, Whittaker Chambers had produced a list of young men in State he said Hiss had proposed to "recruit," and my name was among them. I was fortunately able to persuade the authorities that if Hiss had ever tried to recruit me, he had done it so subtly that I was blissfully unaware.

Of course many others in State, no more "guilty" than I, did not escape so easily; their careers and their lives were ruined. I recall a fiercely anticommunist Austrian leader once telling me that McCarthy's performance was "the most un-American activity" he had ever witnessed. Unfortunately the monomania and the intemperance of the Radical Right, while never since so venomous and so successful, are still with us and still, in my judgment, a much more serious, because more indigenous, threat to American democracy than Communism is or ever will be.

My final assignment in a Western democracry was as Minister in our Embassy in Paris from 1956 to 1958. What a joy it was to turn the clock back nearly thirty years and discover how little Paris had changed, physically and culturally at least. I climbed on the same bus I used to take as a student from the Madeleine on the Right Bank to the Place de la Contrescarpe behind the Pantheon on the Left and was delighted to find that in three decades but one new building, the Ecole de Médicine, had been constructed along that entire route through the heart of the city. There has been more building since then, but not much.

Politically, however, the climate was less nostalgic and salubrious. Those were the years of the Algerian war, which split French society as sharply as had the Dreyfus case. An anachronistic and crazy interlude was introduced when Nasser nationalized the Suez Canal and the British and French Governments, elevating him in their bitterness and frustration to the stature of Hitler and Genghis Khan, invaded Egypt to throw him out. To their amazement, not only Khrushchev but Eisenhower and John Foster Dulles denounced them. Eden (though not Guy Mollet) lost his nerve, and their crusade collapsed like a pricked balloon; they had to scuttle out of Egypt with their tails between their legs. For some weeks Americans in Paris, if spoken to at all, were addressed only in the loudest decibels. Fortunately the next year was the Bicentennial of Lafayette, and in the exaltation of banquets and ceremonies all, or at least much, was forgiven.

Nevertheless, confronted by the incessantly revolving governments of the Fourth Republic—there were three during the eighteen months I was in Paris—it seemed obvious to me that de Gaulle, whether or not one liked him, whether he liked the United States, was almost certainly coming to power and would provide France the only means of escaping from the Algeria morass. I therefore cultivated those closest to him, Michel Debré, Geoffroy de Courcel, and others, which I hope was subsequently of some use. Indeed, though the Algerian war did splutter on in a welter of atrocities for several years more, de

Gaulle finally ended it. Today French and Algerians coexist quite happily in mutual respect and cooperation.

As events later proved, while de Gaulle slowed the consolidation of Europe by about a decade, he saved France from political degeneration in the Italian pattern and strengthened the new intimacy with Germany, which is the key to a coherent Europe. His contribution was therefore great. I talked with him for the last time at the White House at Eisenhower's funeral in 1969, a stately, lonely, laconic figure in the uniform of the France he loved and symbolized.

FAR EAST

Though I had been prepared to go to Czechoslovakia in September 1945, the eternally astonishing roulette of State Department assignments sent my wife and myself by Air Transport Command to Delhi with only one week's notice. In those days it was a flight of three days and three nights on bucket seats, uninterrupted except for refueling stops at Bermuda, the Azores, Casablanca, Wheelus in Libya, Cairo, Abadan, and Karachi. Our ultimate destination was Bangkok, where I was to be chargé d'affaires until a Far Eastern expert, George Atcheson, could be pried loose from MacArthur's staff. But since we had not yet resumed diplomatic relations with Thailand after the wartime break, I was temporarily assigned as political adviser to General Wheeler at Lord Louis Mountbatten's Southeast Asia Command in Delhi and at Kandy in Ceylon.

I remember my first courtesy call on Mountbatten in Delhi. I was led through the interminable corridors and chambers of the colossal Viceregal Palace, symbol of a 200-year-old empire that had only two years to live. I remember sending from Kandy unheeded telegrams expressing dismay that the British were facilitating the return of French forces to Vietnam and Dutch forces to Indonesia, fateful decisions that Roosevelt, had he lived, would almost certainly have prevented. I remember a farewell party given a relaxed and genial Mountbatten and his beautiful, sharp-witted Lady by the departing OSS detachment, all of us nostalgically singing together, in a Kandy bungalow, the Yale Whiffenpoof song.

I recall our tropical mansion in Bangkok, open to the four winds, the ghekkos gurgling on the ceilings, the owls hooting through the night in the branches that brushed our windows, the intermittent gunfire in the darkness from rebels, cops and robbers, the Japanese prisoners docilely cleaning up our yard under the disdainful guard of a bearded and turbaned Sikh. I remember the shy young king and his brother, brought back reluctantly from a carefree life in Switzerland to reign not rule, driving madly about the Palace grounds in a jeep, playing saxophones in sad harmony, shooting off revolvers the OSS had given them. I remember the mysterious death of the King in his bed, killed with his own revolver, and the exotic funeral in the Buddhist temple, inlaid with gold and green, the tall golden urn before us in which the slim corpse must have been propped upright. I remember the instant clamor of the rightist parties to exploit the royal death to discredit Pridi Panomyong, the leader of the wartime resistance and of one of the few relatively democratic governments Thailand has ever enjoyed.

Finally, I recall two emissaries to Bangkok of the Chinese Nationalist government: one a Scotch-imbibing ex-warlord who assured me that with Chinese manpower and American wealth and know-how, we could conquer the world; the other, China's first postwar ambassador to Thailand, whom I was later to encounter teaching in exile in Connecticut, still later a converted repatriate instructing young Communist diplomats in Peking, later still visiting a beautiful daughter married to one of the affluent overseas Chinese of San Francisco. Revolutions muddle the lives of both public and private persons.

In 1954, just after the first Geneva Accords dividing Vietnam and marking the withdrawal of the French from Indochina, I was named first American resident Ambassador in Laos. This country was at that time something of a small Shangri-La, peopled by a gay and gentle folk, peacefully cultivating rice in their valleys and opium poppies on their mountain slopes. War had intruded in 1953–54 in the form of two successive Vietnamese invasions, but a famous blind bonze or Buddhist priest had prophesied they would not reach Luang Prabang, the royal capital, and they had not. There were fewer than a thousand native Communists or Pathet Lao in the whole country when peace came in 1954. Since the French had in effect withdrawn, it became a U.S. responsibility to provide the aid needed to keep a Lao government in being. It was my object to induce all the nonCommunist politicans to work together to preserve and develop their country, which for a number of years they did. Unfortunately, Washington in those days saw everything in black and white, or rather in red and red, white, and blue. "Better dead than red" was too often their motto. After I had left, "neutralists" and middle-of-the-roaders like Prince Souvanna Phouma were ousted from power by U.S. machinations and replaced by true-blue hardliners. The result in 1960 was to alienate the center, rekindle the civil war, provide the Vietnamese with a golden opportunity to intervene once more, and link the war in Laos indissolubly to the war in Vietnam. These events led in the ensuing years first to the devastation and then to the Vietnamization of Laos. When I revisited the country briefly on an official mission in 1977, the city of Vientiane was half-deserted, most of the merchants had fled across the river to Thailand, and the officials of the puppet government did not dare venture outside the city without armed escort.

I have considerably less personal experience with China than with Russia. As a small boy of nine in early 1917 I accompanied my mother and another recent widow seeking distraction in travel on a venturesome expedition (China was involved at that time in civil war), which took us to Hongkong, Shanghai, Nanking, up the Yangtse by riverboat to Hankow, by train to Peking, and eventually out through Mukden to Korea. We were in China about a month. I recall most vividly the crowds in the great cities, ragged, malnourished, pockmarked, fly-speckled, with running sores and snotty noses, the panting, sweating ricksha men and sedan-chair bearers, the sabers and pistols hung on the walls of riverboats for defense against pirates, the fortified diplomatic compound in Peking which had survived the siege of the Boxers seventeen years before, the long, cold ride on a donkey over barren hills and plains to the Great Wall and the Ming tombs.

At the United Nations I labored through seven General Assemblies under the burden of the perennial question of "Chinese representation," whereby the United States successfully maintained the fiction that the Nationalists represented China for more than twenty years after it had been driven from the mainland to Taiwan. Our mission under Adlai Stevenson recommended in 1961 that we move to a "Two China" policy whereby both Communists and Nationalists would have been represented. President Kennedy was attracted to the idea but, for domestic political reasons, put it off until his second term.

After our involvement in Vietnam, partly designed to counter a supposed Chinese intention to take over the country— to which of course the Vietnamese Communists would have been even more violently opposed than we were—the idea of "two Chinas" was dropped until, after the Nixon-Kissinger rapprochement with Peking, it ceased to be a practical solution.

In 1973, after my retirement, I visited China as president of the National Committee on U.S.-China Relations, an organization established to promote American understanding of the People's Republic and to arrange cultural exchanges. During this visit our delegation, of which Michael Blumenthal, later Secretary of the Treasury, was also co-chairman, was received for two hours by Chou En-lai. Chou was undoubtedly one of the most consummate statesmen and attractive personalities I have met in political life. Though seventy-six years old and already suffering from the cancer that killed him two years later, he was still almost single-handedly holding the Peking government together after the disruptions of the Cultural Revolution and the aborted coup of Lin Piao. In our conversation he was friendly, sharp, witty, thoroughly conversant with world politics, speaking in Chinese but frequently correcting in English his interpreter, whom he playfully accused of having slept badly.

Chou denounced American policy in Vietnam and Cambodia and welcomed the recent revulsion against it by the American people and Congress. He blamed most American sins on "the bad seed sown by Dulles," who was his *bête noire,* perhaps because he was so outraged by Dulles's refusal to shake hands with him at Geneva in 1954. This discourtesy had left so painful a scar that, nearly two decades later, Chou referred to it no fewer than three times in our conversation.

The United States had overextended itself after World War II, he tells us. It sent troops and money everywhere. Now its prestige is the lowest in twenty-five years. The United States cannot return to isolationism; the times will not permit it. However, there is no vacuum in Asia or among the less-developed countries. People will fill their own vacuums.

The Soviets will never give up hegemony, he insists. They will not disarm, indeed are expanding their armament. They are "social imperialists," more dangerous than any other imperialists.

Chinese policy, he said, is threefold: dig tunnels, store grain, never seek hegemony. President Nixon is right in saying we are a potential great power, but, even if we develop, we will try to avoid great-power chauvinism. Mao has always told foreign friends that if we ever become expansionist, you will have the right to oppose us. China will never be the first to use nuclear weapons. We only want to break the monopoly of the big powers. We would prefer to abolish them altogether. They are a terrific waste of resources.

The difference between the American and Chinese peoples, Chou says, is that you are anxious—automation makes people nervous. We are slow and patient. There are many advantages in moving slowly. We take agriculture as a base, then light industry and finally heavy industry. A nation of 700 million people (the figure used at that time) must develop first its agriculture. It cannot rely on others; China's basic principle is self-reliance. It believes in "walking on two legs," using both traditional and modern methods.

Four and a half years later, in the fall of 1977, I headed another delegation to the People's Republic. Chou and Mao had died, the "Gang of Four" had triumphed briefly and then been thrown into outer darkness, Hua Kuo-feng was Chairman and Teng Hsiao-peng, Chou's right hand, twice purged and twice restored, was at seventy-two still the indefatigable organizer of Party, government, and the economy. He too received our delegation for two hours in the Great Hall of the People.

He is a short, stocky man with bristly hair, dancing eyes, and little hands that weave expressive patterns in the air. He spits frequently into a large spittoon at his side. He is a pragmatist who has said that it does not matter whether cats are black or white; if they catch mice they are good cats.

China is still a backward country, he acknowledges, and has lost a further ten or eleven years because of the Gang of Four. (He does not mention the Cultural Revolution, but that is what he means.) Now we must hasten to catch up and modernize if we wish, as Chou said at the Party Congress two years ago, to become a great power by the year 2000. We wish to be as self-reliant as possible, but we need to learn from the science and technology of others. Education was sabotaged by the Gang of Four. We have lost half a generation of university graduates. We must catch up. We intend to mechanize agriculture much more, but have to consider carefully what is appropriate technology for the size of our farm plots and the number of people per hectare. We do not want to drive people into the cities.

In an interview at the same time with the chairman of Agence France-Presse, Teng said: "The global war plan cooked up by the Soviet Union must be destroyed. I hope that this effort will be made by the whole world—the Third World, the Second World and even including the First World, the United States."

We visit the mausoleum of Mao, through which a stream of curious, docile visitors swiftly moves, and a neighboring building, in which an exhibit of memorabilia celebrates the life of Chou. Here one can barely move among the awe-stricken, grief-stricken crowd.

When Teng came to Washington in January 1979, I chaired a reception sponsored by four world-affairs socieites at which he spoke. His tune had not changed. He said: "The zealous pushing of a global strategy for world domination by the hegemonists cannot but increase the danger of a new world war. It has become an urgent task of all countries and people who cherish independence and peace to combat hegemonism. . . . Some say that we Chinese are warlike, and they even allege that China is a potential source of world war. But in fact, China has throughout modern history been a victim of aggression, and even today it is under the threat of aggression. . . . How can China, with its limited and defensive military capabilities, start a world war?" Nevertheless, shortly after Teng returned to Peking, China did start a war with Vietnam—to punish her for her invasion of Cambodia and to warn the Soviets that they cannot with impunity play around in China's backyard. Neither "lesson" seemed to have much effect.

MIDDLE EAST

For three months in early 1958 I was Ambassador to Syria. I was coolly received because shortly before my predecessor had been declared persona non grata when Syrian intelligence had penetrated and "blown" a particularly clumsy CIA plot to overthrow their government. My tenure was brief because at that juncture Syria chose to join with Egypt in the United Arab Republic. I was witness to the delirious welcome an excited multitude accorded Nasser as, from a balcony on a public square, he denounced a Saudi attempt to block the union by bribing Syrian officials committed to Nasser. In those years he was the hope and the darling of Arabs everywhere. Three years later, however, he himself, by his heavy-handed insistence on imposing Egyptian ways and Egyptian officials on proud Syrians, brought about dissolution of the union.

I was also exposed during my brief sojourn in Damascus to three other aspects of a particularly passionate Arab nationalism. The first was their profound and intractable resentment against what they saw as an unjust intrusion into historic Arab lands by a Jewish state, imposed by Western powers, especially the United States, concerned only to purge their own sense of guilt for their failure to avert the Holocaust. The second was a parallel resentment against the contemporary "Eisenhower Doctrine," an exercise conceived by the American government to check Soviet influence in the Middle East, but interpreted by Syrians and other Arabs as merely an "imperialist" device to preserve an obsolete status quo in the region. The fragile structure on which the "Doctrine" rested soon collapsed with the revolution in Iraq and assassination by the Baghdad populace of the pro-Western King and Prime Minister. Syrian resentment on this score was vividly brought home to me on one occasion when my official car, with myself inside, was caught in a hostile crowd which for the better part of an hour hemmed it in and beat on windows and roof, shouting, "Down with the Eisenhower Doctrine."

A final demonstration of the intensity of Arab nationalism was conveyed to me by a group of most respectable Syrian ladies, wives of ministers, officials, and wealthy businessmen. They called to plead for American intervention to obtain clemency for an Algerian girl condemned to death for blowing up a considerable number of French women and children with a bomb planted in a cinema. I protested that I was certainly sympathetic to the Algerian desire for freedom, but blowing up women and children seemed a dubious way of pursuing it. The good ladies were unimpressed, indeed quite puzzled, by this argument. In a war of liberation, they argued, all means are justified. Had not the United States in World War II, they impolitely asked, blown up thousands of women and children by aerial bombing of cities?

From mid-1958 until early 1961 I was ambassador to Morocco, which had, with a minimum of violence, achieved independence from

France only three years before. Its ruler, Mohammed V, a wise and courteous scion of an old dynasty, felt both an obligation and a political need to assert a vigorous Moroccan nationalism in two respects: by associating himself on the international scene with "radical" African states—Egypt, Ghana, Guinea—in the so-called Casablanca group; and by insisting on the evacuation of four large American strategic air and naval bases installed some years before under agreements with the French but without Moroccan participation or consent. Negotiations on the latter subject were prolonged and arduous, reflecting both Moroccan and American complexes. The Moroccans publicly insisted on immediate evacuation, while in fact not wishing too seriously to offend the Americans who were supplying substantial aid and who provided an attractive alternative to French economic predominance. Negotiation inside the American government was, however, even more difficult than with the Moroccans. Although alternative strategic air bases were nearing completion in Spain, General Curtis LeMay gagged at giving up those in Morocco and spoke grimly of "bombing them into the Stone Age" if the Moroccans should use force. He was gently reminded that, first, the Moroccans could shut down the bases without violence simply by cutting off their water supply, and, second, the American image of gallant defender of the "Free World" would hardly be improved by the devastation of a newly independent and friendly country. The matter was eventually settled when President Eisenhower visited Morocco by an agreement to evacuate after a decent interval.

Despite my subsequent efforts to elude involvement in what seemed to me the most intractable and impassioned of regional conflicts, I found myself during my assignments at the United Nations and afterward repeatedly swept into the vortex of the Arab-Israeli confrontation.

In May 1967 I was sent on a futile mission to Cairo to assist our new ambassador there in avoiding what soon became the Six-day War, with the unhappy consequences we are still experiencing. During my stint as Permanent Representative to the United Nations from 1969 to 1971, I participated in the fortnightly Four Power meetings in which we, along with the British, French, and Soviets, sought a means of implementing Security Council Resolution 242 and were repeatedly thwarted by the intransigence of one or both parties. This exercise culminated in a rather discreditable episode in which the United States strongly encouraged the Secretary General's representative, Gunnar Jarring, to submit a compromise proposal to Egypt and Israel and then, when Egypt accepted but Israel rejected it, ignominiously failed to give our point man any support whatsoever. Had we had more political courage, the 1973 war might have been averted and the reconciliation between Egypt and Israel taken place six years earlier.

After my retirement in 1971 I traveled frequently to the area and had long interviews with Sadat, Fahmy, Rabin, Peres, Begin, Assad, King Hussein, and various Lebanese leaders. My conclusions, derived from this long and intimate association with the problem, about what sort of compromise settlement might eventually bring the Arab-Israeli conflict to an end were largely embodied in a study, *Toward Peace in the Middle East,* prepared in 1975 for the Brookings Institution by a group of knowledgeable Americans of diverse views, of which I was the rapporteur. This study did in fact form the basis of the Carter administration's pursuit of a comprehensive settlement during its first ten months in office, but Sadat's dramatic visit to Jerusalem in November 1977, courageous and salutary as it in itself was, most unfortunately diverted negotiations into narrower and less profitable channels, from which at this writing they show no signs of emerging.

UNITED NATIONS

In January 1961 Adlai Stevenson asked me to be one of his deputies at the United Nations. Although I was subsequently offered embassies in Yugoslavia, Greece, and Austria, I remained there until his death in 1965, and for one additional year under Arthur Goldberg. Both my chiefs, different as they were from each other, were a joy to work for and most admirable and dedicated representatives of their country in a most difficult post.

The United Nations was, when I arrived, just beginning to undergo the sea-change that followed the great wave of decolonization in the early 1960s and transformed the U.N. from the cozy club composed mostly of Europeans and Latin Americans that emerged from San Francisco into the quasi-universal, panoramic, polyglot conglomeration now comprising more than 150 members. This overwhelming dark-skinned influx once prompted a white delegate, on encountering another in the Delegates' Lounge, to remark, "Dr. Livingston, I presume."

This new institution was obviously, from the American point of view, far less manageable and hence congenial than the old, but it was, as Dag Hammarskjold said, "a reflection of the world as it is"; hence, Daniel Patrick Moynihan to the contrary, it could be neither ignored nor browbeaten. Indeed, in the 1960s at least, the United States found means of accommodating itself to the diversity and fractiousness of those with whom it inescapably shared the planet and of making better use than it has since of the peacemaking and peacekeeping capabilities of the international institution it had had so large a part in creating.

I was involved in the long-drawn-out Congo operation whereby the United Nations, under the skillful aegis of Hammarskjold, U Thant, Ralph Bunche, Andrew Cordier, Brian Urquhart, and others, recruited around the world and melded together from incongruous contingents an efficient military force which, against all odds, held the vast Congo basin together in a single nation. I remember the crucial meeting in the Cabinet Room of the White House at which President Kennedy, belatedly but decisively overriding the qualms of British, French, Belgians, and some of his own advisers, agreed to supply to the U.N. forces the arms Bunche said they needed to wipe out the Katanga mercenaries and secessionists. Within two weeks his forecast was borne out, and the Congo, now Zaire, achieved a unity it still maintains.

I sat behind Stevenson during his dramatic confrontation with Zorin, that shark with gold teeth, over the Soviet missiles in Cuba and, after the immediate crisis was past, took part in the negotiations in which Stevenson, McCloy, and Kuznetsov hammered out an East-West standoff on Cuba. Though often since threatened by the impetuosity and pretensions of all three governments involved, it has survived for nearly twenty years.

I was actively involved in the protracted effort to induce the two ethnic communities in Cyprus to live peacefully together and to prevent their quarrel from causing a war between two of our NATO allies, an effort moderately successful until Mr. Kissinger, in a fit of absence of mind, permitted the Greek Junta to initiate a coup in

Nicosia that provoked a Turkish invasion. Of course Archbishop Makarios, much too sly a fox for his own and his country's good—I talked with him often, butter wouldn't melt in his sanctimonious mouth—could have had peace with honor a dozen times if he had been willing to concede the Turks a fraction of the latitude he demanded himself.

I sat through interminable sessions in the Security Council during the India-Pakistan War of 1965 while Krishna Menon ranted and Bhutto wept and Arthur Goldberg, imperturbable and indefatigable behind the scenes, hammered out the compromise that ended it.

In the course of seven years in those turbulent halls, I had occasion to meet and do business with such distinguished or colorful figures as Lester Pearson, Harold Macmillan, Harold Wilson, Paul-Henri Spaak, Willy Brandt, Aldo Moro, Tito, Ceauşescu, Bourguiba, Nyerere, Kaunda, Mobutu, Haile Selassie, Golda Meir, King Faisal, the Shah of Iran, Nehru, his sister, and his daughter, Sukarno, Carlos Romulo, and, later in Vietnam, Pham Phan Dong.

Best of all perhaps I remember at the funeral of Eleanor Roosevelt lunching in a small room in John's house at Hyde Park with three Presidents at their ease—Harry Truman, Dwight Eisenhower, and John Kennedy. I believe Lyndon Johnson was there as well, but not in the inner circle.

It was of Eleanor that Adlai Stevenson said: "Better to light a candle than to curse the dark." They were a pair. One can no more write a thumbnail sketch of either of them than one can describe a smile or the touch of a hand. No one is perfect, but they came closer, without trying, to "loving thy neighbor as thyself" than most people do, trying hard. Have you seen that photo of their profiles together, serene, simple, human? They were both great and very simple—a rare, refreshing combination. I shall try to write about them at length, as they deserve, another time. I think I am the better for having worked with Adlai for four years. At least I should be.

I had another experience, which may have been good for me in another way. I had resigned from government in 1966, a little weary of the eternal repetitions of General Assemblies, to write a book, *The Insecurity of Nations,* for the Council on Foreign Relations. I was therefore at liberty, for the first time in more than thirty years, to take part in the political campaign of 1968 and headed with enthusiasm

Hubert Humphrey's Task Force on the United Nations. I was therefore intensely astonished in mid-December, after Humphrey's defeat, to be summoned to the penthouse of the Pierre Hotel in New York and, having assured William Rogers and Henry Kissinger that I was indeed a Democrat, to be ushered into the presence of Richard Nixon and offered the position of Ambassador to the United Nations.

It had become apparent from my preliminary conversation with Rogers and Kissinger that this strange offer to an inconspicuous political adversary was made because Nixon had decided to make a gesture of bipartisanship at low cost by offering this job to a Democrat. Humphrey had turned him down, and Sargent Shriver had attached unacceptable conditions to his acceptance. The fact I was a Career Ambassador in the Foreign Service and had served five years at the United Nations would enable the President-elect to cite my appointment as evidence of his commitment both to bipartisanship and to professionalism. In fact, as his bland but transparent assurances during our first conversation did not conceal, he had a low opinion of the United Nations, at least as a channel for great-power relationships, though he claimed it would be his principal instrument for dealing with North-South relations.

Obviously this offer to serve in high place a President I had always disliked and distrusted, both for his personality and his policies, presented me with a considerable dilemma, particularly since I was about to become director of the Atlantic Institute in Paris. My acceptance was motivated not only by the prestigious character of the position but also by three other considerations: first, a naïve hope that Nixon would carry out his campaign promises "to bring us all together" and to end the Vietnam War, and a feeling that after the appalling national traumas of 1968 everyone asked owed it to the country to assist him in that endeavor; second, a belief that, if a third Democrat turned him down, Nixon would abandon his experiment in bipartisanship and professionalism and appoint some Republican party hack without experience in or commitment to the United Nations, an institution to which I was devoted; and finally, the terms of a letter I had received shortly before from Hubert Humphrey thanking me for my assistance in his campaign. In that letter Humphrey wrote: "I am a strong believer in continual interchange between the government and the academic and professional communities. I hope that President-elect Nixon shares this view. Some of you may be asked to submit ideas for his Administration. A few may be asked to serve. To the extent that the foreign policy of the Nixon Administration is consistent with your own views, I hope that you will respond affirmatively."

During the first year of the administration, affairs went reasonably well. With the realization of his life's ambition a "new" Nixon seemed indeed to have been born. I participated regularly in cabinet meetings, in meetings of the National Security Council having to do with matters in which the U.N. was involved, such as the Middle East and Southern Africa, and each fortnight in New York in the Four Power meetings on the Arab-Israeli conflict. My access to the President, Kissinger, and Rogers was easy, though I did most of my business with Rogers. My one gnawing concern was the slow pace of withdrawal from Vietnam. Though at the U.N. I had no official involvement in this matter, I gave Secretary Rogers in October 1969 a memorandum for himself and the President in which I urged greatly accelerated disengagement and transfer of responsibility to the Saigon government. I never had a reply. I suppose I should not have expected one.

After the beginning of 1970—with the Haynsworth and Carswell nominations to the Supreme Court, the "incursion" into Cambodia in May, and the hysterical gearing up for the fall election, the "old" Nixon, to whom all opposition was sinister and threatening, began to slough off his benign masquerade. I was indignant at Cambodia and in many other ways felt like a fish out of water. I sensed a growing coolness in the White House toward an unreconstructed outsider, tainted in Nixon's eyes by both the Democratic party and the State Department, and decided to retire gracefully at the end of the next General Assembly. Nixon beat me to it. In November on the floor of the Assembly word leaked out that I was being replaced by Pat Moynihan. While the U.N. was spared this particular cross for another five years, announcement of my replacement by George Bush followed shortly thereafter. Curious as it may seem, I never had a single word from Nixon, either before or after the event, as to what he intended to do or had done. At two recent encounters with him, at a White House dinner for U Thant in July and at the U.N. when he came to speak at the opening of the Assembly in September, he had praised my performance effusively. He is a shy man who cannot bear to say unpleasant things to anybody face to face.

As to his policies during the two years I served under him, I welcomed his initiatives toward détente and arms control with the Soviet Union and toward normalization of relations with China. I found him moderately, though not enthusiastically, supportive of my efforts to improve relations with the Third World, by contributing to the First and Second Development decades, by giving lip service at least to self-determination in Southern Africa, and by putting forward, even if he subsequently abandoned, the Rogers Plan for an impartial settlement in the Middle East.

On the other hand, I found it increasingly hard to stomach his persistence in clinging so long, at heavy cost in American lives and treasure, to a losing and useless game in Vietnam, against which I had protested in vain. It was certainly not that I believed the Vietnamese Communists were morally right—they were fighting to dominate both southerners who in free elections would have voted against them, and their Laotian and Cambodian neighbors who considered them foreign interlopers and oppressors—but there was no vital American interest that justified sending thousands of young men to fight and die there. In any case, in retrospect, I wish I had protested more and left earlier.

To bring my involvements in foreign affairs since my second retirement up to date, I might simply mention that from 1971 to 1979 I have participated in two groups, the Dartmouth Conference and the United Nations Association, which met once or twice a year in the United States or Russia with representatives of Soviet foreign-affairs institutes; that beginning in 1973 I headed the National Committee on U.S.-China Relations and in that capacity paid the visits to China in 1973 and 1977 to which I have referred; that I maintained my association with the Middle East by membership on the Board of Trustees of the American University in Cairo, by annual visits to the area, by taking part in the Brookings Institution study I have also mentioned, and by serving from 1975 to 1978 as director of an Aspen Institute program of cultural exchanges with Iran; and that in 1979 I was co-chairman of an organization called Americans for SALT whose purpose was to support Senate ratification of the SALT II agreement. Also, during those years, I taught at the Columbia School of International Affairs and the Georgetown School of Foreign Service and wrote a weekly syndicated newspaper column on foreign affairs and two books, *The Insecurity of Nations* and *The Conduct and Misconduct of Foreign Affairs.*

❧ 11 ❧

The Scientific Revolution

The most characteristic, the most astonishing, and the most subversive phenomenon of the twentieth century is the scientific revolution and the technology it has generated. No man or woman, no bird or beast, no landscape or ocean depth has been untouched by it. It is impossible to understand our century so far or to have any conception how it might end or what might follow without throwing at least a cursory glance at the miracles and misadventures of science, at its technological achievements and its ethical absences of mind, at the scientist as lawgiver, benefactor, and sorcerer's apprentice.

"If I had to say a single thing about my lifetime," wrote Jacob Bronowski, the lately deceased expositor of the ascent of man, "I would say it quite simply: that I have lived in the twentieth century in the most prodigious time of discovery that the human race could imagine."

A recent textbook on biology makes a similar point: "If the evolution of the mind should turn out to be a successful biological trait, rather than a device accidentally built to self-destruct, we have aeons of human and social evolution ahead of us. Each generation has reason to think it stands at a crossroad. Our generation certainly has good cause to feel that way."*

From the strictly human point of view, the most striking triumph of twentieth-century science has been the conquest of many diseases and the lengthening of life expectancy, at least in developed countries, to the proverbial three score years and ten. This statistical expectancy has, no doubt happily, been achieved more through the survival of

*James D. Ebert, Ariel G. Loewy, Richard S. Miller, and Howard A. Schneiderman, *Biology* (Holt, Rinehart & Winston, 1973).

infants than through the longevity of the aged, though the latter is also notable.

Antibiotics, sanitation, and improved prenatal and child care have drastically reduced infant and child mortality. Smallpox, tuberculosis, and plague have been almost wiped out. My maternal grandparents were deafened for life in childhood, one by diphtheria, the other by scarlet fever. These and other childhood diseases have now almost disappeared. Miracles of surgery cure or arrest maladies, repair wounds and injuries that previously would have been fatal. Human life has not only been extended but ameliorated and enlivened by better diets and exercise, more widely available health care, and a far more sophisticated understanding of our physical and mental constitution and its requirements. All these extraordinary achievements, for the most part occurring within my lifetime, are so well known and taken for granted that to mention them seems almost superfluous.

Alas, even the blessings of medical science are not unalloyed. Its most momentous, and potentially calamitous, side effect is the population explosion. Homo sapiens required some 100,000 years before building up, by about 1800, a population of 1 billion; only a century was needed for accumulating the second billion, fifty years for the third, twenty-five for the fourth. Population experts estimate that there will be about 6 billion human beings in the year 2000. Continued growth by geometric progression, doubling in shorter and shorter periods, would eventually result, if the earth would submit to such abuse, in the surface of the globe being densely carpeted with a living species no longer describable as Homo sapiens. Already such an infestation is being approximated in some megalopolitan areas, such as Shanghai, Tokyo, Mexico City, New York, Bombay, and Cairo.

Fortunately, the rate of population growth is beginning to slacken, rapidly in developed and a few developing countries, slowly in many countries where the largest populations are concentrated. Nevertheless, numbers of women already born or soon to be born who will be in their childbearing years after the turn of the century ensure that world population will, in the absence of gigantic global catastrophes, continue to grow substantially thereafter—to 8 or 9 billion according to the most conservative estimates, to 12 to 15 billion according to less sanguine demographic experts—before it finally levels off and becomes more or less stable.

There is already, with a mere 4 billion, serious question about the carrying capacity of the biosphere, the sufficiency of natural resources and governability of such large agglomerations, more than half composed in the case of most developing countries of ill-educated, undernourished young people under twenty. Such vast and growing masses of people require vast and expanding quantities of cropland, of livestock, of fish, of forests, of oil, coal, and electricity, of minerals, of shelter and utilities, of industries, of transport, of means of employment, of hospitals and schools. The natural limits imposed by a finite environment on some of these are already being approached. Exceeding these limits in many cases proves self-defeating, producing dustbowls, saline soils, diminishing water tables, poisoned air, streams, and seas, shrinking forests and fisheries, indigestible accumulations of toxic gases and wastes, possibly disastrous modifications of climate. There is no assurance at all that in all these respects a planet already strained by the appetites of 4 billion human beings can satisfy or even tolerate those of 6 or 8 billions. Science is miraculous, but the bounds of nature are not infinitely elastic.

There is no escaping the conclusion, therefore, that science in the twentieth century has let *two* genies out of the bottle—the chain reaction of the atom and the chain reaction of unbalanced natality. A wise and benevolent despot bestowing upon his people the bounty of modern death control would have scrupulously balanced it with a measure of birth control adjusted to maintain population, not necessarily in static but in healthy equilibrium. Unfortunately, most human despots are neither wise nor benevolent, and those that are are far less powerful than the blind surges of instinct and social tradition. Everyone wants health and long life, so that death control enjoys instant popularity and distribution. Birth control, on the contrary, confronts prevailing religions, social and masculine prejudices and seems to run counter to the self-interest of the poor in poor countries, for whom numerous children are often the only available form of old-age insurance. Since both science and governments are reluctant to face down these prejudices or otherwise to care for these interests, several generations pass before birth control catches up with death control. It has done so in a few countries, it is doing so in others, but many are still, willy-nilly, producing far more children than they can possibly care for, or very possibly than the world as a whole can assimilate.

No nation is an island unto itself. The excesses of Mexico spill over into the United States and those of its former colonies into Britain. This outpouring will happen on a far larger scale around the world until the prevailing doctrine becomes not "the right to life, but "the right to a decent life," and until the choice can be much more widely made not by men and churches but by the women most concerned.

To return to medicine, the science is still young. A distinguished biochemist, L. J. Henderson, has speculated that not until about 1912 did the chance that a doctor visiting a patient would do him more good than harm become better than fifty-fifty. There can be little doubt that many medical prescriptions and surgical operations are even today harmful or unnecessary. An estrogen widely prescribed to ease the female menopause has been found greatly to enhance the possibility of uterine cancer. The extensive use of X rays, antibiotics, tranquilizers, and food additives may turn out to have side effects more damaging than the benefits they bring. Biologists, despite the apprehensions of many lay persons and some of their own community, are now enthusiastically working to reproduce and apply DNA, the code of life engraved on the double helix. Whether the result will be boon or bane for mankind no one can really know.

Since men and women still have to die, though a little later, other diseases have stepped in to play the role of those medical science has banished. The new ones are more recalcitrant to science than many of their predecessors, because they tend to arise not from one but from a variety of causes, not from a germ or a virus but from a way of life. Dr. Umberto Saffiotti, an associate director at the National Cancer Institute, has said: "Cancer in the last quarter of the 20th century can be considered as a 'social disease' whose causation and control are rooted in the technology and economy of our society." Thus the U.S. government, while prescribing that each cigarette package display a warning that smoking is dangerous to health, subsidizes the production of tobacco. The overconsumption of drugs, heroin, amphetamines, barbiturates, marijuana, even our old friend alcohol, may also be considered as social diseases, as indeed should automobile "accidents," which are mostly due to the recklessness or intemperance of drivers and are one of the leading causes of death in modern society.

Nevertheless, despite social diseases, polluted environments, and overzealous physicians, health in modern developed countries is no doubt better than it has ever been in human history; and this we owe to science. A cynic has said that the advances of medicine are enabling more and more of us to achieve senility, but that is only part of the story. Senility is being put off; it is also being sequestered. Society has not yet had the courage—will it ever?—to decide when and how to terminate it.

Similar, though less measurable, advances in science have contributed to the alleviation of mental disease, a condition that hitherto in history has aroused more horror than compassion. Now illness of the mind is at least understood to be natural and as deserving of scientific treatment as that of any other organ.

"Science" in this case is still even more experimental and controversial than in many others; modes of treatment change from year to year; there is a perennial battle between proponents of psychiatric and of chemical therapy; many people confined in mental institutions are probably no more abnormal than many outside. Indeed no one is quite sure what constitutes normality. As the Quaker said in the old story: "Everyone is a little mad but thee and me, and sometimes I wonder about thee." Nevertheless, miraculous cures are increasingly performed and "devils" exorcised that in all the ages past would have blighted lifetimes. No doubt this branch of medical science is in its infancy, and far more dramatic progress in mental healing may be expected.

Perhaps even more significant than cures of the mentally sick or rehabilitation of the mentally deficient has been the more sophisticated exploration of the complexities of normal human motivation, which novelists and poets have often ventured but which Sigmund Freud first treated as a science. He has therefore been rightly considered, along with Einstein and Marx, as one of the innovative movers and shakers who has most decisively shaped the twentieth century.

As the theologian Paul Tillich has written: "Despite what critics have to say of our time, one of the great things to have come out of it is the difficulty of anyone's being able to hide permanently from himself and others the motives for his actions." Probably Tillich is too sanguine. Men and women still have remarkable capacity for deceiving themselves and others about their motives, when it is personally or politically troubling to face and acknowledge why they are acting as they are. Unfortunately, consciousness of the unconscious and of the irrationality of our motives has not yet served to make them much more rational.

Still, as Tillich remarks, self-deception has become more *difficult,* and hence the Socratic injunction "know thyself" somewhat easier to obey. To the extent that we can all better understand why we think and behave as we do, how often many of our motives are indeed irrational and our actions contrary to our own best interests, human societies will become more healthy, politics somewhat more sensible and serious, less a conflict among separate interests and more a search for common interest.

Yet psychoanalysis, like other branches of medicine, has its deleterious side effects. Karl Kraus, a Viennese contemporary of Freud, called it "that spiritual disease of which it considers itself to be the cure." That criticism may be excessive, but there seems little doubt that obsessive preoccupation with one's own psychological traumas and complexes, of which we all have our share, has a crippling effect on many individuals. Excessive anxiety about anxiety, upon which both human survival and progress after all depend, can create epidemics of hypochondria as debilitating to society as they are profitable to psychiatrists.

It is true that decline of faith in priests, of trust between parents and children, and of the presence of the old-fashioned family doctor have driven many for consolation and for relief from the perplexities of modern life to psychoanalysts, psychiatrists, and psychologists, as well as to astrologists and religious cults. To the extent any of them afford consolation, human and social ills may be mitigated.

It is probable, however, that just as the early Victorian industrial environment warped the perceptions and doctrines of Marx, other aspects of the same environment unwholesomely biased the mind and doctrines of Freud. In his *Civilization and Its Discontents* he wrote of ". . . my intention to represent the sense of guilt as the most important problem in the evolution of culture, and to convey that the price of progress in civilization is paid in forfeiting happiness through the heightening of the sense of guilt." Thanks perhaps largely to Freud himself, we would now be more inclined to recognize that a socially pervading "sense of guilt," which was indeed a principal unconscious ingredient of Victorian culture, is itself unhealthy and demoralizing, is rather a problem indigenous to the peculiar culture of the Victorian age than a common characteristic of civilized society.

Similarly, while Freud's analysis of the unconscious aspects of human motivation and behavior were enormously perceptive and valuable, the role he attributed to sex in the unconscious and in mental illness may have arisen more from contemporary Victorian attitudes and the repressions they dictated than from a universally applicable understanding of the mind of civilized man. Of course an illegitimate association between sex and guilt has periodically—for example, under the inspiration of Saint Augustine—poisoned man's peace of mind and warped his social attitudes. Freud's innovative therapy has the capacity to ease this unnatural association or to magnify it.

Actually, one of the most refreshing and healthy aspects of social life since World War I has been the growing candor and naturalness with which sex is treated. The human body has at last escaped from swaddling clothes and is accepted unadorned as almost as respectable, though still fortunately more exciting, as the bodies of other living creatures. Not since the classic Greeks has nudity been so widely thought of as an aesthetic revelation rather than a moral outrage. Of course this particular shift in vision is still so new that the pornographers are, with broad popular connivance, carrying it to extremes that may eventually provoke an equally extreme reaction.

The applications of modern science and technology to the production and distribution of material goods has often been described as "the conquest of nature." These miracles are so much a part of our landscape and our way of life that they have ceased to astound us or even attract our attention, except when they are interrupted through some abnormal event like an oil embargo.

Yet the production and distribution of both essential and superfluous goods on a scale to stagger the imagination of every generation before the last four or five is another principal benefit of the modern scientific revolution. Economically, the availability of these goods has raised the immemorially stagnant living standards of a substantial proportion of the world's people; socially, it has in developed societies elevated into the middle class that majority of the population that previously constituted the "peasantry" and the "proletariat"; politically, it has, through these benefits, made possible a substantial extension of democratic government.

Like other aspects of science and technology, the industrial and agricultural revolutions, the mass production and distribution of goods and the means for doing so, have had side effects that have proven pernicious and, if indiscriminately continued, could become disastrous. One of the first and most eloquent spokesmen of the scientific revolution, Francis Bacon, noted, "Nature cannot be conquered except by obeying." The fact subsequently revealed is that it cannot be conquered *even by* obeying. It is not possible for a minute constituent of an enormously complex system to conquer or control that system. What the human constituent can do, through the development of consciousness, is better to adapt itself to nature and, later, adapt some aspects of nature to its needs. Even, however, if man is able to understand and manipulate aspects of nature, he will be far from certain he is obeying her laws because, once again, the side effects of what he is doing are only tardily revealed. Conclusions and extrapolations from the most meticulous scientific observations often go astray either because highly specialized scientists have not troubled to observe outside their specialties or because an extravagant application of initial success vitiates it by changing significantly what was originally observed.

The achievements of large-scale mechanized agriculture in multiplying many times the quantities of food produced by a few hands may, at the same time, dissipate fertile topsoil and promote desertification, drain water tables and pollute streams with the runoff of fertilizers, displace much of the rural population and drive them into cities unready to house and employ them, grossly overfeed majorities of the population in rich countries and minorities in poor countries with ill-balanced diets dangerous to their health, while failing to provide minorities in the former and majorities in the latter with sufficient food to nourish them adequately.

Similarly, large-scale industry has tended by its insatiable appetite to deplete natural resources, to pollute the atmosphere, rivers, lakes, and seas, to concentrate populations in unwholesome and incommodious urban ghettos, and then, by becoming more capital-intensive, to disemploy them. It often does so, moreover, in order to produce not necessities but luxuries or trivialities. The invention and rapid dissemination in the twentieth century of means of rapid transport, the automobile and the aircraft, while expanding fantastically human horizons and capabilities, has in many respects changed human life for the worse. The shift of populations to the suburbs, stimulated enormously by the automobile, has blighted much of the inner cities and condemned commuters to spend much of their lives in exasperating traffic jams. The airplane, as was noted earlier, has been misused for warfare, most atrociously for bombing civilians, almost as much as it has been benignly used to move people and goods. Even in its unique capacity to make odysseys to all the wonders of the world available to the middle classes, it has often tended so to congest and homogenize those wonders as greatly to depreciate their charm.

Finally, there is the fundamental question whether the character of the work most widely offered by industrial society is likely to promote enduring personal satisfaction or, in poorer countries, even to meet the real needs of the society itself. The most eloquent recent skeptic on this score has been E. F. Schumacher, author of *Small is Beautiful.* He has pointed out that "the type of work which modern technology is most successful in reducing or even eliminating is skillful, productive work of human hands, in touch with real materials of one kind or another." He has vigorously argued that the common criterion of national economic success—growth in gross national product—is very likely, particularly in poor countries, to be deceptive. Even while the gross product increases, its distribution is so skewed that the poor majority of the population gets poorer rather than richer, loses rather than gains opportunities both to earn a decent living and to make their lives meaningful. It is far more important, Schumacher says, that everybody should produce something than that a few should produce a great deal. "What is it that we really require from the scientists and technologists?" he asks in regard to the means of production. "I should answer: We need methods and equipment which are

—cheap enough so that they are accessible to virtually everyone;
—suitable for small-scale application;
—compatible with man's need for creativity."

A cautionary example of the hazards of exuberantly exploiting a newly discovered technology before its assets and liabilities—its "bottom line" in the broad social sense—have been thoroughly explored and assessed was "the peaceful use of atomic energy," a wonder-working capability enthusiastically promoted by the Americans in the

1950s, both as a "clean" replacement for coal and oil and as a palliative to their sense of guilt over military use of this technology. Only twenty years later did it become apparent, first, that the proficiencies required for peaceful and for military use were essentially inseparable and, second, that the liability of any human enterprise to occasional error might in this case create unacceptable risks. As Walter Creitz, president of Metropolitan Edison, which managed the celebrated Three Mile Island plant, remarked in a classic piece of understatement: "Anything that man makes will not operate perfectly."

Indeed a Nobel Prize physicist, Hannes Alfven, sardonically pointed out some years ago:

> Fission energy is safe only if a number of critical devices work as they should, if a number of people in key positions follow all their instructions, if there is no sabotage, no hijacking of the transports, if no reactor fuel processing plants or reprocessing plant or repository anywhere in the world is situated in a region of riots or guerrilla activity, or no revolution or war—even a "conventional" one—takes place in these regions. . . . No Acts of God can be permitted.

In the same vein, the textbook *Biology* states:

> Since there is a linear relationship between dosage and mutation rate, any increase in the amount of radiation experienced by the human population will naturally produce a proportional increase in genetic abnormalities. . . . It should also be emphasized that nobody knows as yet how much of an increase in genetic variability our species can take before the normal regulatory processes of evolution break down and an inevitable deterioration of our genetic constitution occurs. In the absence of any definitive knowledge we are well advised to treat assurances from military or industrial sources with the greatest skepticism.

Despite intense political efforts by some of those nations that already have nuclear weapons and nuclear energy to prevent the proliferation of the former and some modes of the latter to those who do not have them, the technology continues to be diffused. As long as nuclear weapons are considered essential to defense and nuclear energy to the economies of some nations, it is almost inevitable that others with the capacity to produce or acquire them will do so. Indeed some of the present possessors of these technologies find it commercially profitable or politically advantageous to abet in practice the process of proliferation they denounce in principle. Under these circumstances, it seems extremely improbable that the conditions Alfven asserted to be necessary for the safe use of fission energy will be consistently or widely met. The momentum both of politics, in a world of competing nations, and of technology, in a world dependent on shrinking energy resources, is likely to prove irresistible—unless and until Alfven's judgment is tragically vindicated.

Such apocalyptic visions are now causing a number of scientists to reassess their original judgments of the usefulness of atomic energy. The sometimes startling contrasts between attitudes thirty years ago and today may easily be illustrated.

"I recall a conversation with Enrico Fermi after the War," Werner Heisenberg, the great physicist reported, "a short time before the first Hydrogen Bomb was to be tested in the Pacific. We discussed this proposal, and I suggested that one should perhaps abstain from such a test considering the biological and political consequences. Fermi replied: 'But it is such a beautiful experiment.' This is probably the strongest motive behind the applications of science. The scientist needs confirmation from an impartial judge, from Nature herself, that he has understood her structures."

Nevertheless, as we have seen in chapter 6, Fermi ultimately came to oppose development of the hydrogen weapon. Some contemporary scientists have gone farther. In a letter to the *New York Times* shortly after the Three Mile Island accident, Bernard F. Erlanger, a professor of microbiology at Columbia University, wrote: "As a young scientist, I participated in the development of the atomic bomb. I can remember, when World War II finally ended, how we all felt that our efforts would be vindicated by the many beneficial uses of atomic energy in peacetime. Now I am afraid that, aside from the use of isotopes in science and medicine, the development of atomic energy must be regarded as an event totally without socially redeeming value."

The scientific community as a whole, not to mention the political and the military community, is far from having reached such a negative judgment on nuclear energy. There is, however, a clear drift in that direction which another more serious accident would certainly accelerate. In any case, the dialogue between Fermi and Heisenberg, with the coda by Erlanger three decades later, does raise the broader question whether and to what extent scientists have the right to impose unpredictable, and sometimes calamitous, consequences on society simply in order to satisfy their own passionate curiosity about the workability of one or another of their theories. What in these circumstances are the rights and responsibilities of society and its political leaders? What indeed are their capabilities, confronted by an esoteric scientific knowledge that they cannot judge because they cannot comprehend?

Yet some sober-minded scientists have shown a marvelous modesty. In 1978 Lewis Thomas, president of the Sloan-Kettering Cancer Center, wrote: "The solidest piece of scientific truth I know of, the one thing about which I feel totally confident, is that we are profoundly ignorant about nature. Indeed I regard this as the major discovery of the past 100 years of biology." In the same vein Geoffrey Burbridge, the distinguished British astronomer, has written: "Cosmology has much in common with religion; both rely on a very small measure of information and a very large measure of belief."

One other aspect, perhaps potentially the most significant, of the contemporary scientific revolution is the astronomical proliferation of education, information, and communication. Many more people are literate, go to elementary school, to secondary school, to the university; more teach, perform research, conduct scientific experiments, than ever before in any society or civilization. Ninety percent of all the scientists who have ever lived are said to be alive today.

More people read more newspapers, magazines, and books than ever before. Hundreds of millions, whether they can or cannot read, listen to transistor radios or watch television. A single speaker can be seen and heard simultaneously anywhere on the globe. Quadrillions of words are recorded on tape and stored in libraries. More and more compact and sophisticated computers can retain and retrieve seemingly limitless amounts of information and can calculate with a speed and precision that multiplies many times the capabilities of scientists, engineers, and laypersons. They may prove to be the most innovative and powerful tool since the paleolithic hand ax or the neolithic plow.

Again, however, the educational and communications revolutions have had unforeseen, confusing, and disruptive side effects. Many societies are turning out more university graduates than their economies need, thus causing extensive white-collar unemployment, personal alienation, and political unrest. If words of wisdom can be more readily recorded and widely transmitted, so can deceptions and inanities. Thus far television wastes time more than it enriches. The voice of Hitler was more widely heard than the voice of Einstein. The volume of current news that pours out over the airwaves to the average man, and the even greater volume of "intelligence" that flows in to the political decision maker, constitute an information overload that cannot be usefully assimilated and that confuses or deceives as often as it illuminates. "Crises" that in earlier times would never have been heard of until they had passed now agitate our breakfast tables and provoke demands on political leaders for instant, and usually escalatory, "action."

"The communications society" confuses quantity with quality. More is not necessarily better, nor is either John Q. Citizen or the President of the United States more likely to resolve a pressing problem wisely because all the information stored in the world's data banks is potentially at his fingertips. He may often be better served by what the Germans call *Fingerspitzengefühl*—folk wisdom or sound judgment. After all, the computer's knowledge and opinions are simply those of the fallible human who programmed it. It is an instrument that believes everything it is told and repeats or rearranges what it is told until told something different. It can be an enormously useful tool, but it should not be canonized. Like all other tools, its effects can be good or bad, depending on how we use it.

It only remains to say a word about the place of the social sciences in the twentieth-century scientific revolution.

There has always been serious question in my mind whether it may not be inappropriate, even profoundly misleading, to use the same word, "science," to describe such inherently dissimilar branches of knowledge as on the one hand, physics and chemistry and, on the other, economics and sociology. The former are more properly called "exact," although elements of subjectivity on the part of the observer can never be wholly excluded, and scientific "laws" are constantly being revised by further observation and experiment. Nevertheless, these two sciences, and to a lesser but growing degree biology, have acquired the capacity to confirm their revelations by repeated experiments on controllable matter and by the efficacy of their applications.

The social sciences, on the other hand, deal with the behavior of man, an unreliable subject at best, who is constantly breaking out of the Procrustean bed of statistical treatment and confounding the extrapolation of naïvely plotted curves. Anyone who has observed through a lifetime the record of economic and sociological prediction —that is, of the application of these "sciences" to life—must have the gravest doubts whether they are justly so described. The desire of the economists and sociologists to appropriate for their professions a term that has won such enormous prestige during the past century or two is natural, but this confusion of apples and oranges has been a source of recurrent disappointment and sometimes disaster.

In a speech to the American Association for the Advancement of Science in January 1980, its president, Kenneth Boulding, said, with a considerable dose of understatement: "The uncritical transfer of statistical techniques, which are entirely appropriate in some epistemological fields, into fields in which they are quite inappropriate has been the source of a great deal of wasted scientific effort, especially in the social sciences."

The subject has been treated at some length by the distinguished modern psychologist Jean Piaget in an essay called "The Place of the Sciences of Man in the System of Sciences." "A scientist is never completely objective," Piaget writes, "but is always at the same time committed to some philosophical or ideological attitude. This point is only of secondary importance in mathematical, physical or even biological research (we already reach a frontier region in the latter case), but it may have a great influence in some of the problems dealt with in the sciences of man."

Of his own discipline, psychology, he writes: "The introspecting subject is modified by the object of his inquiry in that his entire activity, introspection included, is influenced to varying degrees by his past history, which is unknown to him because his memory of the past is the work of a very biased historian who forgets certain sources and distorts others." In discussing sociology he remarks: "We know that the many political comments with which Pareto embellished his famous 'Tratto di sociologia generale,' and which he somewhat ingenuously regarded as evidence of his scientific objectivity, were due to an attitude acquired from reacting against a father of progressive convictions."

Piaget's essay, on the whole, is far from depreciating the philosophic and existential value of the sciences of man. It does nevertheless candidly pose a number of reservations about their claims to be
"scientific" in the more rigorous sense which applies to disciplines
that can be much more readily based on controlled experiments.

Finally, it will be pertinent, even if it may seem impertinent, to say
a few words about the connection between politics and the twentieth-
century scientific revolution. Not only laypersons but some of science's greatest protagonists have questioned whether its prized "objectivity" is compatible with ethical concerns which our times may
even more desperately need.

Einstein wrote in 1944 to Max Born: "The medical men have
achieved amazingly little with a code of ethics, and even less of an
ethical influence can be expected from pure scientists with their mechanized and specialized way of thinking." Nevertheless in a more
hortatory speech at the California Institute of Technology in 1931
Einstein had said: "It is not enough that you should understand about
applied science in order that your work may increase man's blessings.
Concern for man himself and his fate must always form the chief
interest of all technical endeavors, concern for the great unsolved
problems of the organization of labor and the distribution of goods—
in order that the creations of our mind shall be a blessing and not a
curse to mankind. Never forget this in the midst of your diagrams and
equations."

The rest of mankind would be justified, in the closing years of the
second century of scientific revolution, in addressing several significant questions to the scientists. Are they concerning themselves as
assiduously with their responsibilities to society as with their allegiance to their discipline? Does their devotion to pursuit of knowledge, which they passionately enjoy and of whose benefits they and
their associates are the sole judges, give them the right to disengage
themselves from the uses to which their knowledge is put? Is it proper
that in a democratic society clusters of the most brilliant minds should
be busily conceiving and applying new systems that may alter the lives
of millions for better or for worse, with little effective popular participation or sanction?

Indeed, is it not high time that that great and growing community of enormously talented men and women, in whose hands so much of our future rests, should begin to turn their attention to content rather than process, to ends rather than means, to constraining rather than elaborating weapons, to the messages to be communicated to bewildered humanity rather than merely the means of communication, to humane objectives of production, to the moral values without which science and technology are just as likely, through all their marvels, to contribute to the destruction as to the betterment of mankind?

"We claim to live in a scientific era," writes one of America's most eminent biologists, René Dubos, "but the truth is that, as presently managed, the scientific enterprise is too lopsided to allow science to be of much use in the conduct of human affairs. We have accumulated an immense body of knowledge about matter, and powerful techniques to control and exploit the external world. However, we are grossly ignorant of the effect likely to result from these manipulations; we behave often as if we were the last generation to inhabit the earth."*

Somewhat more surprising is a letter written July 1, 1970 to Congressman Emilio Daddario, then chairman of a Subcommittee on Science, Research, and Development, later first director of the congressional Office of Technology Assessment. The author of the letter was Charles Lindbergh. He wrote: "The critically important fact that man is beginning, vaguely, to realize in this 20th century A.D. is that the impact of the human mind on life's evolution has been negative, and that major changes in his thought and action are essential. We see our surface-of-the-earth environment breaking down at the same time our genetic defects are increasing—both rapidly.

"Our science and technology are at once responsible for the rapidity of breakdown and our realization that a breakdown is taking place. Speaking fundamentally, the human intellect is becoming aware of the vulnerabilities that accompany its power, that a crisis exists, and that to avoid self-destruction it must exercise control over its accumulating knowledge."†

Before concluding this interlude on twentieth-century science it would seem useful, since so much of this book is about war, to report

So Human An Animal (Scribners, 1968).
†Reprinted *Science* magazine, June 29, 1979.

briefly what modern anthropologists and ethologists have to say about biological and cultural causes of this increasingly lethal practice. Recorded history has been predominantly a chronicle of wars. Is this because animals are incorrigibly prone to killing each other? Modern ethologists, students of animal behavior, for the most part say no.

Darwin's "law" of the survival of the fittest has often been distorted by less careful scholars. Obviously those that survive are "fit" to survive, but fighting ability does not necessarily determine fitness even between species. The mole survived the tyrannosaurus and the cockroach will almost certainly survive the tiger. Each has its niche and its ways of adapting to that niche.

Ethologists assure us that among animals other than man, there is little lethal combat within the same species. That is one reason they *have* survived. Intraspecific "fighting" is common but in most species is limited to a trial of strength or a show of force, a locking of horns, a display of tooth and claw, wounds in nonvital places. The weaker or less resolute combatant usually yields to the display of force or the exhibition of superior strength. The victor rarely kills his rival.

Animals are "aggressive" in asserting their claims to territory, to prey, to mates but not in the sense of a genetic impulse to slay their own kind. An animal that behaved consistently in that fashion would have to be judged psychopathic, a deviate hostile to species survival.

Presumably the earliest hominids evolving into man did not behave differently from other animals. They probably drifted into their habit of "intraspecific aggression," of regularly fighting each other to the death, as a malign side effect of an otherwise benign development— the association of men and women in small bands for the purpose of hunting large game and better protecting their own young. Such bands competing with each other for food and territory, especially as territory became more crowded, may have, out of a mischievous combination of need and vainglory, gradually shed their inhibitions against murder of their own kind, first against rival bands and then, as custom inured them to this exciting practice, even occasionally within their own communities.

Thus, the same impulses that led to the coalescence of human beings into tribes and eventually societies, with all the implications for progress, culture, and civilization that had, may have also led to the institutionalization of warfare, the first considerable example of organized intraspecific aggression in several hundred million years of animal experience. There is no evidence of an imperative to genocide built into the human genes that makes wars inevitable and efforts to constrain them useless. An infant may be born "aggressive"; it is not born fratricidal.

On the other hand, one can hardly question that several hundred successive human generations, particularly of males, have been culturally imprinted with the belief that manhood is chiefly demonstrated by combat with other men, even, paradoxically from the point of view of survival of the fittest, by death in combat. A curious combination of noble self-sacrifice for the welfare of the community —*dulce et decorum est pro patria mori*—and of virile competition for heads, scalps, or notches on a rifle has, since the first tribes collided, tainted the claim that human society conduces to the general welfare.

So, while irresistible instincts to warfare with our own kind are not built into our genes, we have been culturally conditioned for so long to consider war both convenient and thrilling, both materially and psychologically rewarding, that those who argue the contrary, most of all Jesus Christ, have always been voices crying in the wilderness.

There is another related and compatible explanation of this melancholy characteristic of mankind.

Bertrand Russell has remarked: "Wars are due, in the main, to the insane and destructive impulses which lurk in the unconscious of those who have been unwisely handled in infancy, childhood and adolescence." Similarly the British biologist C. H. Waddington has remarked: "I think that aggressiveness depends enormously on the particular way society handles its young children, on children's relations to their parents, on the relation of women to men, and on other matters of that sort."

According to this theory, the causes of human aggressiveness should be sought not in nature but in nurture. Those fecund aspects of human evolution that prolonged childhood and dependence far beyond the span found in any other animal also created, through that protracted relationship, psychological tensions on both sides and, more critically, imposed obligations on parents that are, at best, onerous and irritating and, at worst, impossible for many to bear without explosions of wrath and loss of control.

The French biologist Jean Rostand has said: "I think that we can demand very much of a man if we do not begin by maltreating him and disheartening him when he is a child." Yet it is difficult to think of an animal whose progeny are more often maltreated or disheartened in infancy than man's. I speak not so much of outright child abuse, though there is enough of that, as of neglect, indifference, thoughtless and corrupting example, careless severity or laxity, absence of love. The instinct of human parents to care for and nurture their young seems more often than with other animals overshadowed by the distractions of society or the temptations of self, of "doing one's own thing." The consequences are apt to be disastrous, not only for the personality of the small creature set adrift without rudder or anchor but for the socialization of the adult and the health of the society of which he and many like him are constituents.

An American ethologist, Sally Carrigher, writes: "Just as in birds or animals, for a child too there may be a definite and quite limited time in which fellow feeling can be established. In the human infant it is thought by some experts to extend from about the sixth week through the sixth month. If, during that period, he makes his bid for affection and there is no response, something—trust?—dies in the small heart."

Whether one accepts the judgment that the critical period of imprinting and confidence-building is so short, or whether one thinks it extends through the second or a later year, there can be little doubt that there is such a period in the formation of human personality. Many children emerge from it frustrated, rejected, alienated, consumed by complexes, mistrustful of their fellows, ripe both to seek scapegoats for their own defects of character and to pass these defects on to another generation.

Such an ordeal, for so many among us, cannot help but affect profoundly the temper of a society, its instinctive reactions to what are perceived or proclaimed to be internal or external threats, its disposition to violence or, in time of crisis, to war.

This thought may serve as an introduction to the next chapter, the last before our conclusions and forecasts. It will attempt to make some fleeting insights into the cultural and spiritual climate, which, as much as wars and revolutions, as much as science and technology, determined the events of our century so far and will determine those yet to come.

❧ 12 ❦

Life-styles,
Visions, and Moods

Every era is more than the catalogue of its events or the deeds and
misdeeds of its heroes. An ambience envelops each, a tone that distin-
guishes each from its predecessor or successor: a vision, even though
blurred, on which its dreams and hopes are fixed. Indeed these secular
moods sometimes seem to contradict events in the external world.

Barbara Tuchman has rightly described the fourteenth century as
"calamitous"; yet Chaucer's pilgrims cheerfully storytelling on their
way to Canterbury do not reflect a sense of calamity. What would be
calamity to us was to them commonplace. The fifteenth century was
distinguished both by the most exquisite flowering of the Renaissance
and by an obsession with death gruesomely depicted in much of its
art. Death, particularly after the plague began to recur every few
years, was also commonplace, though still fearsome.

The historian Johan Huizinga, speaking of that century, wrote:
"The men of the Middle Ages lived in a continual mental crisis. They
could not for a moment dispense with false judgments of the grossest
kind."* Parenthetically, one might remark that no generation, even
the most "rational" or "scientific," has been able to dispense with false
judgments.

The sixteenth and first half of the seventeenth centuries, in revulsion against the corruption of the Church, dissolved into a welter of
sects, intolerances, and religious wars of most un-Christian ruthless-

*The Waning of the Middle Ages.

ness and intensity. Yet this same period produced one of the richest harvests of Western literature and art, some of the most significant movement toward democratic government, the gestation of much of eighteenth-century rationalism and nineteenth-century science. On the other hand, the eighteenth century found itself in midcourse unable to endure its own rationalism and veered away into sentimentality, romanticism, evangelicism, eventually political terror and continental war.

The most significant triumph of the European spirit throughout all this time was that there was never a prolonged collapse of morale. Within an amazingly few decades after the calamities of the fourteenth century, the religious wars of the sixteenth, and the political turmoil of the late eighteenth, there was a recovery of purpose and achievement. This has not been typically the case in other great centers of civilization—China, India, and the Middle East—where the downfall of a dynasty repeatedly led to anarchy and collapse of morale, lasting sometimes for centuries. The central question we will be asking in the next and final chapter is whether the contemporary recovery from the thirty-year war of 1914–45 is solid and enduring, or whether the weakening of political structures and the sapping of public morale has been so pervasive that its worst effects are still to come.

"Without social history, economic history is barren and political history is unintelligible," wrote G. M. Trevelyan.* The purpose of the present chapter is to take a rapid reading of the mood of our century thus far, as reflected in its art, its beliefs, its life-styles. This reading may, more than an account of more solemn happenings, offer the best clue to an answer to the question just posed. "What people think and believe," wrote the historian John Lukacs, gleefully turning Marxism upside down, "is the real substance of their lives and of their histories —and the material institutions of society—indeed the material organization of the world—is merely the superstructure of that."†

Only within the past few years has the expression "life-style" become popular; yet the sharpest discontinuity in manners and morals in our century, perhaps in any recent century, occurred immediately after World War I, when in the brief span of seven or eight years skirts

English Social History (Longmans, 1942).
†*The Last European War.*

shot up from ankle to thigh, alcohol and extramarital sex became as respectable for women as for men, and divorce conventional for both. The "jazz age" prefigured almost every aspect of the revolution in morals that occurred throughout the next half-century.

What might be called the entropy of established ideas did, however, intensify as the century ran its course. Four-letter words became humdrum and printable—indeed, like explicit sex, practically obligatory for any popular novel. Other words, in a curious sort of reverse Victorianism, suffered euphemistic distortions: homosexuals became "gays," pornography "adult entertainment," and TV commercials "messages." Homosexuality tumbled so exuberantly out of the closet that "straights" began to feel a little old-fashioned, as did those heterosexuals who had been married only once. Permissiveness tended to shade into compulsiveness.

The nuclear family, while surviving in isolated pockets, in many cases dissolved and left its debris scattered around the courts, schools, highways, and bars of the nation. The Census Bureau, a little out of its element, reported that "households which contain two unrelated adults of opposite sexes" had more than doubled between 1970 and 1978 and estimated that nearly half of all children born today will spend a "meaningful" portion of their childhood with only one parent.

Seventy years ago Ambrose Bierce had written: "Women would be more charming if we could fall into their arms without falling into their hands." This "male chauvinist" dream has now been realized— at the insistence of women! Women are "liberated" to behave like men in every way physiology permits. Almost no profession, occupation, club, or bar is closed to them. They have been admitted, by economic pressure or "affirmative action," into all the onerous and boring employments hitherto reserved for males. If they all went home again, the economic system would collapse.

Mobility, hitherto characteristic of mankind chiefly in mass migrations and crusades, has been enormously facilitated for the individual, indeed for the "lonely crowd," by the automobile, the airplane, and the peripatetic corporate employer. People have poured into cities, rebounded into suburbs, and, more recently, drifted back to abandoned farms, wildernesses, or counterfeit Shangri-las. The transformations, displacements, and inconstancies of the landscape, man-made or man-mangled, have contributed to a gnawing feeling of uprootedness that has afflicted so many. This is perhaps the first settled and civilized society in which people normally outlive buildings. Not one of the five substantial houses in the small town in upstate New York in which my extended family lived and I spent most of my childhood is still standing. "Progress" devastates almost as thoroughly as war.

While young people have traditionally revolted against the nuclear family and the immobile home, the sudden disintegration of both has probably been more shocking to them, who have not yet found their feet, than to any other generation except the very old. These instabilities have aggravated the problems caused by the extended adolescence of our times. In the United States in 1870 less than 5 percent of the relevant age group was in high school; today more than 85 percent is; moreover, nearly one-third of the 18- to 21-year-olds are in college, and a substantial proportion continue on to one, or even two, graduate schools. Education is an admirable and, in so complex a society, a necessary privilege, but it is being administered in indigestible doses. Too often it prepares its acolytes for jobs that are not there, but not for the tribulations and frustrations that will be. As Ellen Goodman has said: "Adolescence isn't a training ground for adulthood now. It is a holding pattern for aging youth."

A professor of history at Princeton University, Laurence Stone, recently wrote:

> There is already apparent a growing reluctance among students to permit discrimination among sheep and goats, to reward excellence and punish sloth or stupidity; a widespread contempt for any form of learning which does not have the crudest kind of relevance to the contemporary scene; a decline of respect for that infinite capacity for taking pains which is so essential for success in any form of intellectual endeavor; and, worst of all, the rise of the cult of unreason, emotion and free self-expression, regarded as somehow superior to logic, clear thinking and self-discipline.

In unconscious confirmation of this shift in values, the poet Rod McKuen has said: "I don't believe in history and I get very bored by any kind of study. You can fill your mind with theory instead of feeling." One can hear the voice of Rousseau echoing down the corridors of time.

At the end of the 1970s the pursuit of feeling was leading "students" in Iran and elsewhere into the most extraordinary throwbacks and paroxysms. It beguiled many Westerners, young and not so young, into "doing their own thing," "blowing their minds" in the most literal sense, with amphetamines, barbituates, LSD, cocaine, and heroin. Many were lured into a variety of cults, some fraudulent, a few crazy, some otherworldly and austere. Eager young people, adrift and looking for causes, were to be found stranded on all kinds of desolate beaches around the globe.

In some ways these seemingly exotic phenomena were new in form but not in substance. The profuse variety of religious sects in the seventeenth, eighteenth, and nineteenth centuries reflected the same search for transcendental certainties and distinctive life-styles as the modern cults. Addiction to drugs and its consequences are no more spectacular than Gin Lane as portrayed by Hogarth in the mid-eighteenth century, or the abuse of the saloon that prompted Prohibition in the United States in the twentieth. Still, the modern varieties of these withdrawals and excesses seemed to represent a more widespread and decisive "dropping out" from society, more of a commitment to self-indulgence or self-destruction, than the more positive, strenuous, or genial commitments of earlier times.

In Europe, with its more intellectual tradition, the youth revolt has more often taken a political form to which Marxist professors have contributed considerably. In some cases, particularly in Italy, Germany, and parts of Latin America, the politics of frustration and naïve utopianism has been carried to an appalling extreme, in which young people arrogate to themselves the right to administer the death penalty to those with whom they disagree politically. On the other hand, others seem more American in the unfocused nature of their insubordination. One French student, a young woman, was quoted as saying at the time of the "events" of 1968: "Quand vous savez ce que vous voulez, vous êtes déjà embourgeoisée."

This malaise of youth, which has swept over not only the Western world but the young elites of many developing countries, is often attributed to a so-called identity crisis, an expression taken from the psychoanalyst Erik Erikson. Erikson himself, however, has been sufficiently annoyed by the misuse of this phrase to clarify what he meant. "I must register a certain impatience," he wrote in *Identity, Youth and Crisis,* "with the faddish equation, never suggested by me, of the term identity with the question 'Who am I?' This question nobody would ask himself except in a more or less transient morbid state, in a creative self-confrontation, or in an adolescent state sometimes combining both; wherefore on occasion I find myself asking a student who claims that he is in an 'identity crisis' whether he is complaining or boasting. The pertinent question, if it can be put into the first person at all, would be, 'What do I want to make of myself, and what do I have to work with?' "

A century and a half ago Emerson wrote: "Young people should be very careful about what they want, because that is probably what they will get." Have the young people of this generation, who go into the streets or onto the road, reflected seriously about what "identity" and what society they really want, and whether they would be happy with what they suppose they do? Would it, all things considered, be better or worse than what they have?

In fact, many young people are enjoying what William Styron, contrasting it with the sufferings of his heroine in *Sophie's Choice* at Auschwitz, has called "unearned unhappiness." Of course it is not only the young who so indulge themselves, as the extravagant dependence of educated Americans on psychoanalysis suggests. André Malraux reports that a chaplain of the Resistance, Abbé Magnet, once told him that the fundamental fact he had learned from fifteen years of taking confessions is "that there is no such thing as a grown-up person."

There is of course comfort, when one reflects on this panorama of social disintegration—erosion of the family, trivialization of sex, abuse and neglect of children, severance of physical and intellectual moorings—in recalling that soothsayers of every civilization have denounced its demoralization and predicted its downfall. "With the gradual relaxation of discipline, morals gave way, then sank lower and lower, and finally began the downward plunge which has brought us to the present time, when we can endure neither our vices nor their cure." That complaint was written by the Roman historian Livy in the time of the Emperor Augustus, generally considered to be one of the highest peaks of Roman civilization. The Roman Empire, moreover, survived in the West for four centuries after Livy wrote and in the East for fourteen. Of course its morals continued for the most part to be deplorable throughout both periods.

Now let us turn briefly to the art by which our century has expressed its emotions and to the beliefs that have nourished or troubled its spirit.

Art, architecture, music, literature often express more powerfully and more poignantly, at least to posterity, the quintessences of an age and a civilization than do its politics or its philosophy. When we think of the Middle Ages we think first of Chartres, Mont-Saint-Michel, Giotto, and Dante; of the Renaissance we think of Donatello, Michelangelo, Titian, Rabelais, Shakespeare, the palaces along the Grand Canal, the chatêaux of the Loire; of the Baroque, we think of El Greco, Rubens, Bernini, Monteverdi, Cervantes, of the great churches of the Counter-Reformation; of the eighteenth century, we think of Bach, Haydn, and Mozart, of Voltaire, Goethe, and Chardin, of Sans Souci, the Petit Trianon, and the decorous squares of London; of the nineteenth Beethoven, Ingres, Turner, the great Impressionists from Manet and Monet to Renoir and Cézanne, the great novelists from Dickens, Stendhal, and Balzac to Tolstoi and Dostoevski.

What will posterity think of the art, music, and literature of the twentieth century, of form and content distorted and sometimes tortured to a degree quite unprecedented in the history of human culture? Will posterity look on what survives as the troubled scribblings of autistic children, poor creatures subjected to more torment than they could stand? As the posturing of jesters in exile with King Lear? Will it, with astonishment and some contempt, compare our aesthetic response to the torments of our times with that of Chaucer's pilgrims and cathedral builders to the calamities of the fourteenth century? Will it understand at all what our artists were trying to say—as we understand the ancient Egyptians, the classical Greeks, and the Chinese of Han and Tang?

There was in my view much great art and music produced in the first half of the twentieth century, but almost all of it by artists and musicians who began their careers before World War I. Matisse and, with reservations, Picasso deserve a place in the timeless pantheon that began with the wall paintings of Lascaux and Altamira. Debussy, Stravinsky, Bartok can stand on a level with many of their great predecessors. The novel never displayed more consummate understanding of the human spirit than with Proust, Conrad, Thomas Mann, and James Joyce. Yet of all those who came later, who began their artistic careers after World War I, few seemed able to transcend their own private nightmares, to bring to the troubled generations to whom they spoke a firmer grasp of reality rather than simply a deeper anguish.

Much of art and music suffered, beginning even before World War I, a disintegration that, as though by some supersensitive sonar, caught the accumulating echoes of disasters to come. This decomposition may have occurred for at least four reasons: first, the culmination of half a century of artistic effort, which found its greatest expression in Cézanne, to penetrate to the heart of reality, to lay bare the visual balances and imbalances that exist in every landscape, every visage, every object, to convey emotion by these structural and chromatic accords and disaccords rather than by representation or anecdote; second, an urge among Cézanne's followers to carry these experiments to ever greater extremes, to strip the skin from the flesh, the flesh from the bone, the bone from the dust, all in the belief that the less visible and less human had to be more "real" and more "honest"; third, a conventional revolt against all the conventions not only of the past but of the present, so that it became obligatory to invent a new style each half a dozen years, both to show one could and to sell more pictures; finally, there was the outraged response of the sensitive artist to the horrors of battlefields, mass murder, extermination camps, political torture, and chronic civil violence to which the twentieth century so casually exposed its populations.

There was much that was profound and much that was humane in the best of these aesthetic reactions. As they worked themselves out over the years, however, they tended to separate the artist more and more from his public, as his subject matter, in pursuit of his private vision, became more and more abstract or misrepresentational. This aberration took particularly ugly and meaningless form in modern sculpture: pieces of scrap iron or holes in megaliths were allowed to disfigure public plazas in the name of art. Such tendencies ultimately provoked an equally extreme reaction into the representational but childish triviality of Pop Art. Another curious influence was the vogue for African and Polynesian masks; the fetishism, witchcraft, and nightmares of primitive peoples were imported to confirm the anxieties of the civilized.

"Cézanne, you see, was sort of a god of painting," Matisse once said. "Dangerous his influence? So what? Too bad for those without the strength to survive."

Unfortunately, very few, among whom Matisse was of course notable, *had* the strength to survive. Cézanne himself said, "I remain the primitive of the path I discovered." Conceivably that may turn out to be true, but as far as one can tell at present he remains at the pinnacle of a slope; those who endeavored to climb higher slithered down or suffered from vertigo.

A critic, Jean Clay, wrote of Matisse: "Each picture seems an answer to the question: up to what point can one reduce the representation of a tree or a still life, the space of a room or a landscape, without their becoming incomprehensible." Cézanne and Matisse, in their genius, were able to answer that question affirmatively; very few others have been.

In my opinion Picasso was a very great artist who wasted much of his own talent and caused many others to waste all of theirs. He once said: "I have less and less time, and more and more to say. I've reached the moment, you see, when the movement of my thought interests me more than my thought itself."

This was the demonic (or calculated?) impulse that led him to change his style repeatedly, usually for the worse. He did his greatest work when he was a young man in the first decade of the century and during a few months at the age of seventy-two when he produced a series of drawings and lithographs of deceptive simplicity and profound genius. Most of what he did in between—cubism, *Les demoiselles d'Avignon, Guernica*—was an indulged eccentricity. Posterity will not know what to make of it—or of us.

All this prestidigitation deceived and demoralized the artists who came after him. They became convinced, and dealers and critics confirmed them in this delusion, that each new season demanded a new style. The public accepted docilely whatever was offered, because they felt guilty and insensitive at having failed to recognize so many great artists in the late nineteenth and early twentieth centuries and did not dare risk being mistaken again.

Perhaps the most trenchant word on much of modern art and modern literature was said more than sixty years ago by the Viennese critic Karl Kraus (already quoted in his disrespectful description of psychiatry): "There is a distinction between an urn and a chamberpot," Kraus said, "and it is this distinction above all that provides civilization with elbowroom. Those who fail to make this distinction are divided into those who use the urn as a chamberpot and those who use the chamberpot as an urn."*

A few words about twentieth-century literature. Of the greatest writers mentioned earlier, Proust and Conrad died in the 1920s, Joyce during World War II, and Mann in the 1950s. Joyce, incidentally, played a role in literature similar to that of Cézanne in painting: he developed a radical clairvoyance and an idiosyncratic way of expressing it which were too "dangerous" for imitators and carried most of them beyond their depth.

The infirmities of modern writers are, however, more spiritual than formal. "In a not altogether rhetorical sense," Francis Hope has written, "all poetry written since 1918 is war poetry." That is true not only of poetry. World War I administered, and World War II repeated, a cultural shock, a blow below the belt, to the sensibilities and the Weltanschauung of Western intellectuals. They can hardly be blamed, but many of the most admired writers and artists of the past fifty years, even those who never heard a shot fired in anger, have been all their lives among the walking wounded. They rarely seek, moreover, to hide their wounds but rather, like the maimed children of professional beggars, expose them for pay in public thoroughfares.

Franz Kafka, whose antenna were so extraordinarily receptive that they registered horrors that had not yet materialized, made no bones about his own disorientation or the irrationality of the world he perceived about him. "Yet I felt no certainty about anything," he wrote in his diary, "demanding from every single moment a new confirmation of my existence—in truth, a disinherited son."

An American writer, Tennessee Williams, said in an interview with the *New York Times* in 1965: "I have always been more interested in creating a character that contains something crippled. I think nearly

*Quoted in *Wittgenstein's Vienna* (Simon & Schuster, 1973).

all of us have some kind of defect, anyway, and I suppose I have found it easier to identify with the characters who verge upon hysteria, who were frightened of life, who were desperate to reach out to another person." In this respect he was typical of many others in the years after World War II.

Much as one might sympathize with those emotionally "crippled" in this way, and indeed appreciate much of their work, still one could not help but question whether they qualified to be mentors of a generation already sufficiently bewildered and disheartened. A Polish writer, Czeslaw Milosz, who actually experienced the horror others only wrote about, said some years ago: "The war years taught me that a man should not take a pen in his hands merely to communicate to others his despair and defeat. This is too cheap a commodity."* This reflection recalls William Styron's reference to the "unearned unhappiness" of those whose unhappiness comes from within rather than without. I cannot help but feel myself, in observing modern literature, that it is as shameful to offer nothing but uncertainties as it is to offer false certainties.

"We live now amidst the ruins of a civilization," John Lukacs has said, "but most of those ruins are in our own mind."

Anyone who undertook to explore the mind of the twentieth century would be entering a labyrinth from which he might never escape. For our purposes, we need a reasonably clear understanding of those trains of thought, circulating through the collective consciousness, or the collective unconscious, which have affected or seem likely to affect our times in distinctive and decisive ways.

It has been said that the three personalities who have most profoundly affected the twentieth century are Marx, Einstein, and Freud. Our last chapter has dealt with some aspects of the influence of science on our times, though the impact of science has only just begun to be felt.

We have also had much to say about the practical consequences of Marxism, so different from what its founding fathers expected or even imagined. The historian Siegfried Kracauer has remarked: "Marx once declared that he himself was no Marxist. Is there any influential

The Captive Mind.

thinker who would not have to protect his thoughts from what his
followers make of them? Every idea is coarsened, flattened and distorted on its way through the world."

Nevertheless, Marxism, even though coarsened and flattened, or
perhaps because of the coarsening and flattening, has had an enormous impact on twentieth-century society. The harassed and bewildered human spirit still remains more responsive to thaumaturgy than
to science unadorned. As Leszek Kolakowski, a lapsed Marxist, has
noted, "The influence that Marxism has achieved, far from being the
result or proof of its scientific character, is almost entirely due to its
prophetic, fantastic or irrational elements."

Nevertheless, whatever its authenticity, this doctrine has determined the thought and lives not only of hundreds of millions who live
in countries governed by "Marxists" but, paradoxically, of intellectuals all over the world. They, much more than "the masses," desperately crave a "scientific" explanation of injustice, of poverty in the
midst of plenty, and of how to remedy both in an orderly grand
design. While the loyalty of some has wavered in recent years, it is
amazing how many managed to reconcile themselves to the great
purges of the 1930s, to the Nazi-Soviet pact of 1939, to armed suppression of the Hungarian "national liberation" struggle and of Czech
"socialism with a human face."

On the other hand, it is only fair to note that intellectual distortions
and political derelictions can also be ascribed to those at the other end
of the political spectrum. Ira Progoff, in his study of modern psychology, remarks of Alfred Adler: "The frequency of the neurotic condition in modern times is thus, in Adler's view, directly attributable to
the competitive individualism that dominates Western culture, for it
results in a type of personality whose social feelings are severely
underdeveloped and whose drives toward self-indulgence display the
main characteristics of the pampered child."*

As a matter of fact, the one value on which capitalism and communism are in total agreement is what is loosely called "materialism" or
"consumerism"—the implicit, though usually unavowed, elevation
above all spiritual or political ends of ever increasing material prosperity. As heaven, and the virtues required to reach it, lost credibility

---

***The Death and Rebirth of Psychology* (Julian Press, 1956).

in the popular mind, an earthly heaven, dispensing wealth and leisure, at least for the right-minded and the hard-working, replaced it as the promised land. These are natural human inclinations, but the industrial and scientific revolutions for the first time made it possible to gratify them on a large scale. Wealth has always been popular with those who had the means to obtain it, but with the proliferation of machines its superlative value became almost axiomatic for almost everyone.

By the late 1960s, it is true, a reaction had begun. A growing concern with the effects that uninhibited indulgence of materialism was having on the human environment, an incipient boredom with repetitive and uncreative work and with its trivial products, was causing a growing number of people, usually young and privileged, either to mobilize political opposition to commercial excesses or, as we remarked above, to drop out. Both these movements, however, embraced only small minorities; the vast majority remained ardently faithful, if not to hard work, at least to its material rewards.

The most subversive influence on the twentieth-century mind, however, was almost certainly the consecutive social calamities that assailed it almost from its birth: the two world wars, the Great Depression, the Holocaust, the Cold War, Vietnam. Thoreau had written a hundred years before: "A man needs only to be turned around once with his eyes shut in this world to be lost." The people of this century were turned around many times. When they opened their eyes from time to time, they could hardly believe what they saw.

When the novelist Georges Bernanos asked André Malraux in 1945 what he considered the most important event of our time, Malraux replied: "The return of Satan." Malraux was a melodramatist, but the events of the previous thirty years had certainly reminded mankind, as Freud had earlier, what fanatical polarities, what slumbering horrors, still persist in the human heart.

One of the intellectual and moral responses to this "return of Satan" before and during World War II (one foreshadowed long before by Kierkegaard) was existentialism, a philosophic rationalization of the extreme predicament that men and women confronted in Occupied Europe under the Nazi Gestapo, later in Eastern Europe under the Soviet KGB, and elsewhere under all the other apparatuses of political terror installed by modern régimes of Right and Left. As

Jean Paul Sartre wrote of his wartime experience: "At every instant we lived up to the full sense of this commonplace little phrase: 'Man is mortal!' and the choice that each of us made of his life and of his being was an authentic choice because it was made face to face with death, because it could always have been expressed in these terms: 'Rather death than. . . .' "*

Some years later, in a more philosophic mood, Sartre described the conclusions he as an intellectual had drawn from this daily confrontation with mortality. "Man is nothing else," he wrote, "but that which he makes of himself. That is the first principle of existentialism. . . . When we say that man chooses himself, we do mean that every one of us must choose himself; but by that we also mean that by choosing for himself he chooses for all men. For in effect, of all the actions a man may take in order to create himself as he wills to be, there is not one which is not creative, at the same time of an image of man such as he believes he ought to be."†

Ever since the breakdown of the ecumenical Church in the sixteenth century, faith has disintegrated into a motley of sects, causes, and superstitions and for many men and women has simply withered away. Churches, still marginally powerful in many places, have become repositories of conventions and taboos rather than of gospel and inspiration. The modern theologian Paul Tillich has said, "The church is the perpetual guilty conscience of society and society the perpetual guilty conscience of the church." The church has in fact become much more responsive to society than society is to the church. As Arnold Toynbee and others have pointed out, the chief object of human worship in this century is the nation-state; any conflict between church and state usually ends in a victory for the latter.

Still, any sort of belief seems to exist nowadays only at a low temperature. Even loyalty to the nation is sapped and qualified by, on the one hand, a welter of petty regional nationalisms—Basque, Croat, Kurd, Biafran, dozens more—and, on the other, by the equally numerous welter of parochial interest groups which, while vociferously proclaiming their patriotism, actually place the supposed welfare of their group above that of the whole community.

The disintegration of traditional beliefs, moreover, leads not only

---

The Republic of Silence (Harcourt Brace, 1947).
†*Existentialism and Humanism* (1946).

to alienation and anomie, to susceptibility to demagogues and mass hysteria, but to a revival of superstition and mysticism, a resort to astrology, transplanted Oriental cults, quacks, fads, and nostrums. We are surprised to find these anachronistic throwbacks in a scientific age, but the anthropologist Robin Fox has warned us, "Those who think that superstition will decline with advances in knowledge and technology will be disappointed. Not only can man not stand too much reality; he cannot stand too much rationality."*

Modern man confronts an agonizing dilemma. He has as strong a will to believe as his ancestors had, but he finds his efforts to anchor his belief to any solid rock constantly frustrated. The old-time religion has been discredited by science, and attempts to reconcile the two lead to such a dilution and abstraction of religion that it provides little nourishment. Science itself constitutes a sufficient faith for many of its ardent practitioners, but for the mass of mankind, who accept its "laws" and its technologies more or less on faith, it is nevertheless, in Fox's words, "too much reality" or "too much rationality" to be spiritually satisfying. The community or tribe, as organized contemporaneously in the nation-state, elicits passionate devotion in wartime and more perfunctory loyalty in peacetime, but it seems only among fanatics to provide steady spiritual sustenance.

So too often the child of the twentieth century, if he is of an introspective bent, ends up like Kafka, feeling "no certainty about anything, demanding from every single moment a confirmation of my existence—in truth, a disinherited son." In contrast, compare the people of the Middle Ages. According to Egon Friedell, "They believed in every vision, legend, rumor or poem; in true and false; in wise things and crazy things, saints and witches, God and the Devil. But, what is more, they believed in *themselves.*"†

Which is better? Which is happier? Is it possible to find a golden mean that marries the best elements of the two and excises the worst? Certainly the spiritual and ethical vacuum of the present day leaves too much room for sick fanatacisms and mass hysterias, for voracious greed and cynical privilege, for tribal passions, ambitions, and fears, which may in time fester, burst, and tear society apart. Thus far we have survived and even prospered, but, with the liberation since 1945

Encounter with Anthropology.
†*A Cultural History of the Modern Age.*

both of the atom and the multitudinous populations of Asia, Africa, and Latin America, the margins are closing in.

Our final chapter will chart those margins and explore how and where they might be strengthened and held.

⚹ 13 ⚺

The Next Twenty Years: What Is To Be Done?

Human history has from its beginning been a spectacle of turbulence, war, appalling problems rarely resolved but gradually receding into the background as new ones overshadowed them. In this perspective the tragedies of our century are neither novel nor desperate. Civilization has triumphed over much worse catastrophes.

The nineteenth century after 1815 was exceptionally peaceful but also, by being innovative in so many fundamental ways, unusually disruptive of established order. The twentieth century dawned just as these disruptive tendencies reached a critical point. It has not, however, been more violent or more disorderly than the fourteenth, the sixteenth, the seventeenth, or many others. Why then should we be more concerned about the human predicament today than were our forefathers at any time in the last two or three millennia?

There are now present in our global society five factors, all direct or indirect consequences of the scientific revolution, which no previous human society, no earlier century, has ever had to confront. These five factors, taken together, represent a qualitative change in our condition and our predicament.

The first is the presence and proliferation of nuclear weapons, which, if used on a wide scale, could profoundly cripple or wholly destroy our civilization.

The second factor is the population explosion which, unless comprehensively curbed before the end of the century, could place such intolerable burdens on the environment and on the structures of society that both might break down.

The third factor, arising partly from the second and partly from the extravagances of modern industrialism, is that certain raw materials on which modern societies depend both for sustainment and for political stability may be dangerously diminished before either substitutes are devised or greater austerity becomes politically tolerable.

The fourth factor is that a global juxtaposition of peoples, an uncomfortable interdependence of disparate and sometimes hostile societies, has been created by the revolution in communications brought about during the past half-century by the airplane, radio, television, satellites, computers, and the new habits and appetites these have generated.

The fifth factor is the drastic compression in time of the social strains and transformations that flow from the coincidence of the several revolutions of modern times.

If these five novel factors, profoundly disquieting as they are, are nevertheless confronted soberly and resolutely by all of us individually and collectively, there is no essential reason why all of them should not be successfully dealt with and overcome. Nuclear weapons, despite our addiction to them, certainly need not be used. Population growth can be slowed and stabilized, late but not too late. Critical raw materials can be conserved, recycled, even forgone if necessary, until substitutes are found or life-styles adjusted to their absence. International interdependence, exasperating as it may often be, can be accommodated to and effectively managed to the mutual advantage of most if not all peoples. Social transformations, disruptive and violent as they will often be in our times, can nevertheless be contained and eventually digested. There is nothing intrinsically insoluble about any of these problems.

The question is whether human societies as currently organized, nationally and internationally, as psychologically conditioned by their past and present social environments, *will* deal with these problems rationally and decisively, *will* make the necessary psychological, political, and structural adaptations in time. Each individual's answer to this question will determine whether he ends this survey in a mood of hope or of despair. I strongly incline to hope.

The remainder of this chapter will be devoted to examining briefly what might happen in our society during the brief balance of this century and what we could, but may not, do to cope effectively with these five new interlocking global challenges to our well-being and survival.

I. PORTENTS OF WAR

Since 1945, there have been several substantial international wars, a series of "wars of national liberation," and innumerable civil wars, but there has been no great or general war. Almost certainly we owe this immunity to nuclear weapons. The appalling holocaust that would inevitably overwhelm instigator and victim of nuclear aggression, the wholesale annihilation of hundreds of millions of lives and of the cultural and industrial legacy of many generations, must wonderfully concentrate the mind of any leader contemplating an act that might have such consequences. As Dean Rusk has rightly said, World War III would be the last act of organized governments in the Northern Hemisphere. No one in his right mind is likely seriously to contemplate such a risk to his country and to himself, except conceivably if the only alternative were abject surrender.

Yet this unprecedented prudence and the relative equilibrium it has brought are qualified, uncertain, and precarious. Madmen do sometimes reach great office, and sane men do go mad. Both active and armchair generals do from time to time seriously contemplate some "limited" use of nuclear weapons—on the battlefield or against the missile launchers of the other side—under the delusion that such use would not provoke, in the unimaginable stress of the occasion, an elevated nuclear response, a response to that response, and, within days or even hours, a full-scale strategic nuclear exchange.

When one attempts to divine the probable course of events during the 1980s along the East-West line in the center of Europe—the old and somewhat frayed Iron Curtain, still the critical point of confrontation between the two worlds—one is tempted to assume stability, because it is so much in the interest of each adversary both to maintain a sufficient military presence to discourage attack by the other and to refrain himself from provoking a war of such unpredictable character, scope, and outcome. The nature of weapons has changed so fundamentally in the thirty-five years since the full range of them was used that over and above their annihilating effect on cities and civilians, it is not even sure that soldiers could long tolerate that infernal environment. Competition and escalating military buildups on both sides of the line are therefore not only costly and unnecessary but provocative and counterproductive; reciprocally they aggravate rather than moderate the threat both sides self-fulfillingly perceive.

Nevertheless, while calculated aggression in Europe seems for these reasons extremely unlikely, there is always risk of accidental clash, instantaneously generating tension, overreaction, and escalation. Henry Kissinger has predicted that if World War III should ever occur, it would arise not from a World War II but from a World War I scenario, that is, a war neither plotted nor intended but suddenly breaking out from a series of moves on some geopolitical chessboard where each side has supposedly "vital" assets that it is endeavoring, rashly but without war, to enhance or protect. Meanwhile, within this murky framework, one can foresee the members of the two alliances maneuvering across the thickly sown minefields, each endeavoring on the one hand to derive political advantages from its arms and on the other to negotiate some limits to their excess. Neither enterprise will in my estimation be likely to achieve much in the near future. Nuclear blackmail is unprofitable when both sides are aware how implausible it is that nuclear weapons would be intentionally used. On the other hand, limits on weapons in such a hideously complicated situation, with one alliance monolithic and the other passionately pluralistic, with one superpower close at hand and the other distant, are appallingly difficult to achieve. As the French say, *rien ne dure comme le provisoire.*

The nuclear game of war and peace, life and death, is further complicated by the fact that the chessboard is no longer exclusively, even primarily, Europe; moreover, the new pieces are not the docile instruments of two players but are intensely independent nations having, like the Serbians and Austrians in 1914, ambitions and fears they are by no means prepared to suppress at the behest of a great ally. The Soviet Union and the United States, if they should both deeply involve their prestige, interests, and even elements of their armed forces in the Middle East, Southern Africa, Korea, Indochina, Yugoslavia, or Cuba, might suddenly find themselves to their common dismay swept into confrontation by the impetuosity of their clients and thus faced with the alternative either of standing fast and raising the stake or of capitulating. If both chose the former course, they might find themselves involved first in conventional, then in limited nuclear, finally in strategic nuclear war, almost before they knew what was happening.

How easily such escalation might occur is curiously suggested in the recent memoirs of one of its most experienced modern practitioners. "In my view what seems 'balanced' and 'safe' in a crisis," Henry Kissinger writes,* "is often the most risky. Gradual escalation tempts the opponent to match every move; what is intended as a show of moderation may be interpreted as irresolution. . . . A leader must choose carefully and thoughtfully the issue in which to face confrontation. He should do so only for major objectives. Once he is committed, however, his obligation is to end the confrontation rapidly. For this he must convey implacability. He must be prepared to escalate rapidly and brutally to a point where the opponent can no longer afford to experiment."

The onetime historian has apparently in this case forgotten that the scenario he prescribes for confrontation is almost exactly that followed by Count Berchtold, the Austrian Foreign Minister, in July 1914. Berchtold chose the issue carefully—as he perceived it, the preservation of the Hapsburg Empire from dissolution by detachment of its Slavic constituents. He escalated rapidly and brutally by moving from his ultimatum to Serbia to a declaration of war against Serbia in five days. He conveyed implacability by refusing to pause, even when his German ally urged him to do so. He ended the confrontation rapidly, with the cooperation of Russia, by escalating it into World War I nine days after it began. The fatal mistake Berchtold made, and Kissinger makes, is in overlooking the possibility that the opponent, in Berchtold's case Russia, may be prepared to "experiment" just as "brutally" and "implacably" as he is, and that in that case war will almost certainly result. A sensible man does not play "chicken" with nuclear weapons.

The dire contingencies we have been discussing would become considerably more probable if nuclear weapons, as the saying goes, "proliferated" beyond the present five members of the "club." Israel,

The White House Years.

India, and South Africa probably already have the capability; others could shortly acquire it. Many who could would be likely to have both less sense of responsibility about initiating use and less expertise in preventing theft or accident. Primitive nuclear weapons could fall into the hands of revolutionary or terrorist groups or even blackmailers. This dispersion would be bad enough in itself. Yet the presumption might persist, if an atomic explosion occurred, that one of the two superpowers was responsible. "Signals" between them, grossly imperfect at the best of times, could under such circumstances become fatally confused and misleading. Given sufficient proliferation, a situation could arise in which literally thousands of obscure individuals could, either advertently or inadvertently, trigger a nuclear war and perhaps a nuclear holocaust.

The danger of war, including world war, arises of course not only from nuclear weapons. The possession of nuclear weapons may be an effective deterrent to attack on a nation possessing them, but it has not prevented and will not prevent conventional wars between heavily armed middle-sized states, which could in turn escalate both horizontally and vertically, that is, could spread to other states than those originally involved and could eventually graduate to the use of nuclear weapons. More than $400 billion a year is now being spent for armaments; by far the largest proportion is for conventional arms, and a considerable part is spent by developing countries not aligned with either NATO or the Warsaw Pact. Efforts to limit the international arms traffic, by which most of these latter countries are supplied, has proved unavailing, because the buyers want the weapons and the sellers do not want to risk losing "clients."

It would not be unreasonable to conclude: (1) that conventional wars in and among Third World countries with unstable régimes, unstable populations, and unstable frontiers will continue to occur with at least their present and perhaps with increasing frequency; (2) that great powers, particularly the superpowers, unless some benign revolution in their current practices occurs, will be indirectly or directly involved in some of these conflicts; (3) that any of them could escalate horizontally and any in which a superpower is involved could escalate vertically, that is, to the use of nuclear weapons; (4) that, therefore, despite effective deterrence against calculated nuclear attack by one superpower against the other, there remains a disconcerting variety of ways in which they could unexpectedly find themselves in confrontation or at war with each other, and in such cases under great compulsion to use their nuclear arsenals.

The presence of this mortal hazard, ignore it as we will, reminds us that the need for far more effective conflict management and control, so dramatically demonstrated in July 1914, so insufficiently met since that time either by the League of Nations, the United Nations, or conventional diplomacy, remains as imperative as ever. Since in a world of nation-states, still emotionally resistant to their growing interdependence, there is not now and is not likely soon to be any world policeman with sufficient power to prohibit war at any level, the paramount immediate necessity of our times is for much more efficacious international machinery for preventing wars from breaking out and, if they do, for preventing them from spreading.

Before concluding this recapitulation of what I have to say about the risks of war, one other neglected factor needs to be mentioned. That is the climate of public opinion, the state of the public mind and temper, which, most of all in democracies but also in dictatorships, always circumscribes and often determines the action of leaders.

We have observed how a pernicious accumulation of social and psychological frustrations racked the nerves and exasperated the passions of European populations before World War I. These in turn generated the mood that made descent into war so easy and so rapid. We have also observed how violence unleashed on such a monumental scale in that war, far from purging the passions that inspired it, seemed to imprint them even more firmly on the human psyche, to contribute to the rise and success of fascism and to all the malignant disorders of the 1930s that led to World War II.

Alas, the climate of violence has not in any sense been alleviated since that time. An increasing number of governments protect their tenure by the most brutal oppression of their fellow citizens, execution, torture, cruelties reminiscent of the Inquisition applied in the name of "order," "justice," or even "freedom." Terrorists and "freedom fighters" respond in kind in equally barbarous ways, assassinating public figures or blowing up innocent women and children in theaters and supermarkets. Any violence is considered legitimate, even heroic, so long as it is committed in the name of some cause or dogma. Some absolutely monstrous régimes, such as those of Pol Pot or Idi Amin, along with Hitler and Stalin unparalleled in genocide since Tamerlane five hundred years ago, either justify their atrocities by reference to some creed or cult or commit them from pure caprice, without rhyme or reason.

Even in the most civilized countries, civility is mocked by violence in the streets and in the homes. The media and the novelists pander shamelessly to the taste for horror and blood. Children are accustomed from their earliest years to daily exposure in television, movies, and real life to the vilest passions of their elders and "betters." The equanimity of whole societies is perturbed and shaken by these assaults on public order and private decency. People feel beset, beleaguered, insecure. What Euripides 2,500 years ago spoke of as "the fear that comes when reason goes" breaks through the comfortable crust of society more and more often in more and more places. One must go back at least to the early seventeenth century and its religious wars to find so pervasive a sense of insecurity.

All these events discompose and disorient the public mind, accustom it to disorder, violence, and fear, and dispose it to extreme responses whenever it feels itself collectively challenged. In such a climate international violence—war—is never far beyond arm's reach.

2. THE CONTROL OF WAR

Under these circumstances the total elimination of nuclear weapons would be by far the wisest course for human beings interested in the survival of their species. It is troubling to recall that never in human history have weapons been perfected and left unused.

Unfortunately the root-and-branch solution of complete elimination is extremely unlikely to occur, at least in the foreseeable future. No international agreement to this effect could be concluded because no one could be sure it would be faithfully carried out. Since even the possession of a few secreted weapons would enable the possessor to dominate the community of nations, no nation would trust the others to do away with them completely. On the contrary, their proliferation is proceeding so that they are likely to fall into more and more hands. Moreover, the increasing use of nuclear energy will disperse weapons-grade materials so widely that even if weapons were improbably banned, they could be easily concocted not only by governments but by factions, gangs, and even individuals. Perhaps the final solution of this apocalyptic problem will come, if ever, only when science devises some authentic "counterforce" to neutralize and nullify nuclear weapons, which will be capable of interrupting and aborting a chain reaction before it takes off.

Pending that happy and no doubt distant day, the best we can do is to curb, to the greatest feasible degree, the manufacture, deployment, and use of these weapons. There are in general three courses to follow to this end. The governments of superpowers now rely mainly on one of them—deterrence by deploying weapons equivalent to those of the adversary. The second is arms control, the third is conflict control.

The paradox of deterrence, as practiced by the United States and the Soviet Union, is that each is feverishly engaged, at enormous and wasteful expense, in improving its ability to deter the other, while laboring to overcome the other's deterrence of itself. In other words, new strategic and tactical nuclear weapons systems designed to ensure invulnerability on one's own side and assured destruction against the other side, are constantly being invented and deployed. Naturally this upside-down game of poker, in which each player depreciates his own hand and exaggerates his opponent's, creates constant anxiety on both sides, which to some extent vitiates deterrence. "Psychological studies tell us," writes A. M. Meerloo, an expert in the psychology of war, "that fear *never* provokes peaceful reactions.... Man reacts to danger and fright by becoming aggressive, not peaceful."*

In any case competition in military technologies and budgets inevitably provokes an ascending ladder of escalation, which may give one or the other side a slight advantage at each successive rung but does not provide one whit more across-the-board security at a higher than at lower levels. The "defense establishment" of each country, immensely powerful yet totally impotent, is helpless to defend its civilian population from decimation and its great cities from almost total annihilation.

To call such a situation "national security" is truly ludicrous, but at the moment we seem to have no other choice. Fortunately, there

Aftermath of War (International Universities Press, 1946).

is little likelihood, despite the frantic screaming of the hawks, that either side in this competition to deter will achieve a "usable superiority," that is, a sufficient superiority in various sorts of nuclear weapons to enable it to launch an attack without fear of fatal retaliation, or to use the threat of such an attack for political blackmail. Both governments, supported by their respective peoples, are determined to prevent the other from achieving superiority and will spend whatever amount, no matter how fantastic or how prejudicial to other national goals, is necessary to do so.

If these arguments are sound, and I am convinced they are, the attention of governments and institutions seeking to diminish the threat of nuclear annihilation should be concentrated, since deliberate attack will almost certainly be deterred, on the other two legs of the defense "triad": arms control and conflict control.

During the past two decades—essentially since the fright caused by the Cuban missile crisis—the superpowers and their allies have moved significantly, though still very modestly, in the area of nuclear and other arms control. The most important successes have been the partial test ban in 1963, the Non-Proliferation Treaty in 1968, the SALT I treaty in 1972 and the unratified and probably lapsed SALT II treaty in 1979. There have also been, at a lower level of significance, prohibitions on the use of biological weapons, and on the placement of nuclear weapons in outer space or on the seabeds. Other serious negotiations have been under way for some time, sometimes for years, but so far without serious result—the multilateral Vienna negotiations concerning reduction of forces in Europe, multilateral negotiations at Geneva under U.N. auspices about control of chemical warfare and other matters, annual debates at the General Assembly and a recent special session on disarmament, several other bilateral negotiations between the United States and the Soviet Union—on arms sales, on a comprehensive test ban, on prohibition of antisatellite weapons, on limitation of military activities in the Indian Ocean, and so on.

It is of the utmost importance that, despite the current frigidity in relations between the United States and the Soviet Union, arising from the invasion of Afghanistan and other factors, these negotiations be continued and invigorated and that others be initiated, not so much because spectacular successes can be expected in the near future as because the continuation of the process itself exerts some restraint over a broad series of technological and geographical escalations which, in its absence, would rise to even higher levels. Moreover, the public debate attendant on these negotiations serves the vital purpose of constantly reminding mankind of the sword of Damocles that it has so carelessly suspended over its own head.

The most important component of the international arms-control process is strategic arms limitation and reduction between the United States and the Soviet Union. The inherent difficulty of this process has been most recently demonstrated by the prolonged negotiations required after SALT I to reach agreement on SALT II—seven years— and by its failure to win ratification in the Senate. Senate opposition arose from a misperception by the hawks that the provisions of the treaty were disadvantageous to the United States, from a correct perception by both hawks and doves that the treaty did not provide for sufficiently substantial reductions to improve significantly the security of either side, but most particularly because of Soviet behavior on other issues not strictly relevant to the terms of SALT but inevitably impinging on them—buildup of Soviet arms in Europe, intervention of Soviet and Cuban forces in Africa and the Middle East, support of Vietnamese aggression in Cambodia and Laos, and finally the invasion of Afghanistan. These ill-conceived activities had so undermined American confidence in détente that the climate was no longer propitious even for mutually profitable arms control.

Indeed the Soviet strategy of attempting to "delink" strategic arms control from military, political, and ideological competition elsewhere has clearly proven, no matter how reasonable it might appear in principle, to be wholly unrealistic in practice. If the Soviets genuinely wish to proceed, as SALT II enjoins its signers, to a prompt negotiation of a more far-reaching SALT III, they will have to be prepared to alter their current policies in two decisive respects; first, to propose much more substantial reductions than were contained in SALT II, perhaps as much as 50 percent of some elements of present strategic arsenals; and, second, to alter the character and lower the level of their unilateral interventions in Third World conflicts. If they are not prepared to modify current policies in these respects, the SALT process may still stumble along, but it is most unlikely to achieve significant results.

I can think of only one eventuality that might dramatically and

instantaneously alter the prospects of nuclear arms control. We have
recently observed the universal alarm that followed an accident at a
nuclear energy plant at Three Mile Island near Harrisburg, even
though the accident was successfully contained and there were no
casualties. Large demonstrations against any further development of
nuclear energy occurred in many countries. Should there ever be a
nuclear accident of catastrophic proportions, either through an explosion in an industrial plant or through the accidental detonation of a
nuclear weapon—particularly should a great city be devastated and
much of its population either killed or subjected to radioactive fallout
—public opinion around the globe could be so appalled by this horror
that it would demand either the total abolition of nuclear weapons or
their submission to international controls of the utmost severity. One
could hardly wish for such a disaster, but, given the stubborn attachment of human beings to the most extravagant and hazardous anachronisms, it might be the only warning that would be heeded and
would spare them far greater disasters at a later time.

If there seem to be almost insurmountable difficulties in the way of
bringing about total or even major nuclear disarmament, equally great
obstacles stand in the way of bringing about significant reductions in
conventional armaments. Never in Europe's troubled two-thousand-
year history have such huge armies with such numerous and destructive weapons been maintained for so long across its vital center.
Efforts over many years to reduce them have proved unavailing.
Indeed the current demand on both sides is that they be substantially
strengthened and "modernized." Similar armies and similar weaponry are drawn up along the Sino-Soviet border and the Korean
demarcation line. Vast navies of the two alliances roam the Seven Seas
with little regard for the wishes of the states whose shores they patrol.

Nor are developing countries, no matter what the destitution and
the needs of most of their peoples, any less insistent on maintaining
military establishments of disproportionate size and on being free to
purchase or obtain whatever arms they wish wherever they can find
them. While their representatives in the U.N. Assembly pay annual
tribute to general and complete disarmament, while they persistently
denounce the selfishness of the great powers in spending vast sums on
armaments rather than on Third World development, these same
governments squander ever larger proportions of their GNP for these
purposes and are quite unwilling to discuss any limitations seriously.

While many have signed the Non-Proliferation Treaty and thus formally renounced nuclear weapons, this self-denial has been primarily a matter of making a virtue of necessity. As the more affluent acquire the technical and industrial capability to manufacture nuclear weapons, more and more of them are likely to do so.

I am myself unhappily inclined to conclude, after observing disarmament negotiations among a great variety of governments for more than fifty years, and indeed participating in some of them at the United Nations, that the prospects of significant conventional arms control and reduction under present circumstances, either among great powers or among the mass of less powerful states, are bleak indeed. The need is so great, the alternatives so horrendous, that the process should be indefatigably pursued, but I should not expect it to achieve results sufficient to safeguard national or international security. An improvement either in mutual confidence among nations, or confidence in the capacity of an international system to keep the peace, will almost certainly have to precede substantial disarmament.

We come therefore to the third alternative—conflict control. This could in principle be achieved in either or both of two ways—by the exercise of much more rigorous self-control by states involved in competition, confrontation, or conflict, or by the generally accepted imposition of effective control at various levels by international institutions.

A contemporary historian of the Roman Empire, Edward Luttwak, has written:

> The firm subordination of tactical priorities, martial ideas and warlike instincts to political goals was the essential condition of the strategic success of the empire. With rare exceptions, the misuse of force in pursuit of purely tactical goals, or for the psychic rewards of purposeless victories, was avoided by those who controlled the destinies of Rome. In the imperial period at least, military force was clearly recognized for what it was, an essentially limited instrument of power, costly and brittle. Much better to *conserve* force and use military power indirectly, as the instrument of political warfare.*

Such prudence and common sense can hardly be expected of statesmen in the twentieth century who have throughout their lives operated in an unhealthy climate of crisis, confrontation, and conflict

The Grand Strategy of the Roman Empire (Johns Hopkins University Press).

more analogous to that of Rome during its wars with Carthage or its civil wars than the triumphant Rome of the empire. It is true that the awesome presence of nuclear weapons has thus far constrained leaders along the margins of disaster and impelled them to find a way out. Unfortunately, neither that presence nor any other consideration has yet deterred them from elbowing their way or from stumbling into confrontations.

Conceivably the premature demise of détente after so short a life may induce in the leaders of the Soviet Union and the United States a mood of greater sobriety, realism, and responsibility. If so, the hard fact may finally sink in that neither can safely take action unilaterally, particularly military action, in an area of major concern to the other —Europe, the Middle East, the Horn of Africa, Northeast or Southeast Asia. They must, if they wish to maintain pacific and constructive relations in some fields, such as arms control and trade, consult and concert before acting in other areas where their interests clash.

It is foolish to suppose, for example, that SALT talks, MBFR (mutual balanced force reductions) negotiations, or commercial arrangements can proceed peacefully in a political vacuum, while Cuban troops with Soviet arms are entering and deciding local conflicts in Africa, while the United States presumes to reorder the Middle East without regard for Soviet interests, if Vietnam should threaten Thailand, North Korea, or South Korea, or if the United States should escalate its legitimate friendship with China into a relationship the Soviets might interpret as an alliance. These would not only be abuses of power but would recoil against the security of the superpower that initiated them or permitted them to be initiated.

"Since the foolish part of mankind," wrote Benjamin Franklin to Edmund Burke in 1781, "will make wars from time to time with each other, not having sense enough otherwise to settle their differences, it certainly becomes the wiser part, who cannot prevent those wars, to alleviate as much as possible the calamities attending them."

This should certainly be the policy of the United States and the Soviet Union in regard to Third World conflicts. Even if one of the superpowers has the capacity by itself to conciliate some of the parties to a conflict, as in the Middle East, it would be wise not to exclude the other party completely. Even if one, by a timely injection of arms, Cubans, and East Germans, has the capacity to determine the outcome of a particular local conflict, it should not forget that a few such "victories" will so alarm the other superpower that their entire relationship will be impaired. The United States and the Soviet Union are indeed an odd couple to be sharing responsibility for world peace; they cannot of course expect to enforce it everywhere. They can certainly be expected, however, jointly and separately, to refrain from action that jeopardizes it.

Though most of the world has been decolonized, some genuine "wars of national liberation," and many civil wars masquerading in this respectable guise, will certainly occur. They may be bloody and harrowing, but they will not be threats to world peace unless the superpowers, even behind a transparent screen, make themselves parties or underwriters. In that case any of these collateral conflicts might become the detonator that sets off World War III.

While self-restraint by the superpowers and timely consultation between them is one essential means of neutralizing local conflicts, it is unlikely to be sufficient. If a fire burns too hot and too long, it will burn some at a distance, even if they honestly seek to keep clear. A superpower can rarely view with indifference the defeat or humiliation of a friend and client. It was primarily for these purposes that the United Nations was established. Only an international organization can be impartial and disinterested, either in forestalling or stopping armed conflicts or in proposing and enforcing peaceful settlements. Such an organization is far and away the best instrument of conflict control—if it can be made effective.

The United Nations has, thus far in its relatively short life, only occasionally and under special circumstances been permitted to carry out its main task—"the maintenance of international peace and security." It played a significant part in the Korean War owing to the fortuitous absence of the Soviet representative from the Security Council on the decisive day. It has successfully organized and carried out peacekeeping operations in the Middle East, Congo, Cyprus, the Indian subcontinent, which either ended, prevented, or delayed more serious wars. It has not, however, because of the breakdown in cooperation between the drafters of its charter, been able to carry out its paramount mandate—to *enforce* peace. It has not been able to *impose* impartial and equitable terms of settlement on the parties to a conflict, either before or after they have gone to war. It has not been able in many cases to prevent their going to war or to stop them after they have done so. It has no army, except as member states lend it contingents, usually with the reservation that they not engage in combat. It has not since Korea dared call on the armies of the great powers, for fear they will seek to enforce the policies of their governments rather than the decisions of the Security Council.

The United Nations has not, therefore, during the past thirty-five years, been a sufficiently effective instrument for conflict control. But is there a better? Is there a prospect for finding any other on which we could rely at all? If not, we have only the two alternatives either of improving the United Nations in the directions intended by its founding fathers or of abandoning all efforts to confront threats to the peace by concerted international action. I am convinced there is no middle course—for example, no regional systems or institutions that can be relied on to maintain peace in their regions.

If and when the great powers can bring themselves to act impartially through the Security Council to end hostilities and support equitable settlements, without prejudice or privilege to either party to a conflict, they will generally be followed by the majority of U.N. members. If they seem simply to be supporting their respective clients, as they have in the Middle East or Southeast Asia, other members will rightly perceive that the United Nations is simply being exploited as a cover for national aims.

Hence the five permanent members of the Security Council—the United States, the Soviet Union, China, Britain, and France—would have to be prepared, if they should come eventually to see that their national interests are better served by international law and order than by international anarchy and conflict, to carry out their responsibilities in the council like judges on the bench rather than like attorneys for the prosecution or defense. If they should do so, the United Nations could eventually come to function as it was intended to do, without any revision of its charter or change in its voting procedure. The great powers often condemn Third World majorities in the General Assembly for "irresponsibility." The charge is sometimes well founded, but the most irresponsible of all are certainly those powerful nations who have prevented the effective operation of the peacemaking and peacekeeping provisions of the charter and who therefore have condemned the world community and their own peoples to perpetual insecurity.

Someone has said that the road to economic development is paved with vicious circles. This is equally true of the road to a more secure world, whether through the better working of the United Nations or otherwise. The prescriptions we have given for more responsible and constructive behavior there by all its members, most of all the great powers, will never be met unless and until public attitudes concerning the duties of nation-states to the international community and the expediency of national use of military force have been radically altered. Probably many more appalling lessons will have to be administered before these simple contemporary truths have been taken to heart.

Maria Montessori, the great educator of children, once wrote: "If we wish to alter the habits and customs of a country, . . . we must take as our instrument the child, for little can be done in this direction by acting upon adults. To change a generation or a nation, to influence it toward either good or evil, we must look to the child who is omnipotent. The truth of this has been demonstrated of late by Nazis and Fascists who changed the character of whole peoples by working on children." From a rather different angle Margaret Mead once said that the modern world is so radically transformed that only the young are natives in it; the middle-aged and old are aliens in a strange land.

Whether those who wish to change the world should address themselves to their contemporaries or should concentrate on the coming generation is a very old question. Those who have striven vainly for years to make an impact on the former often sadly conclude that Montessori was right. But who in fact teaches the children, Montessori or Goebbels or just run-of-the-mill middle-aged pedagogues trying to earn a living and not make waves? Such teachers of course transmit, at best, the conventional wisdom.

Certainly, as Mead pointed out, the young adapt better and are more at home in a given decade than the old, who acquired their attitudes several decades before, but do the two really differ on fundamentals? Life-styles may be transformed with kaleidoscopic rapidity, particularly in times like ours, but beliefs, prejudices, and philosophies move with the majestic deliberation of glaciers; only wars and revolutions accelerate them briefly. There is little reason to suppose that either our generation or the next one will relent in its devotion to the nation-state, which, aside from and sometimes beyond the immediate family, has been the most powerful object of human devotion for at least 300 years.

In the preceding centuries it gradually replaced a welter of warring feudal fiefdoms with a vastly extended zone of security, and so earned the gratitude of its citizens. Most of us have not yet perceived that it is the nation-state itself that has in modern times become the warring fiefdom, that no one of them, even the most powerful, is any longer able to preserve a zone of security, that indeed the only such zone that might in our times become truly reliable and stable would be the whole earth.

"The central question, as I see it," said Adlai Stevenson in 1965 in one of his last speeches, "is whether the wonderfully diverse and gifted assemblage of human beings on this earth really knows how to run a civilization.

"Survival is still an open question, not because of environmental hazards but because of the workings of the human mind. And day by day the problem grows more complex. It was recognized clearly and with compassion by Pope John; to him, the human race was not a cold abstraction. Underlying his messages and encyclicals was this simple thought: that the human race is a family, that men are brothers, all wars are civil wars, and all killing is fratricidal."*

3. CRISIS OF THE DEMOCRACIES

"The more I have brooded upon the events which I have lived through myself," wrote Walter Lippmann in 1955 in his old age, "the more astounding and significant does it seem that the decline of the power and influence and self-confidence of the West has been so steep and so sudden. We have fallen far in a short space of time."†

Lippmann wrote at a time when the United States was at the height of its power, if not its self-confidence. He was speaking, however, of

*Pacem in Terris Convocation, New York, February 1965.
†*The Public Philosophy* (Little, Brown, 1955).

the steep and sudden decline in the power of the West as a whole in the forty years since it had before World War I bestrode the world unchallenged, a complacent colossus sure of its "civilizing mission," conferred upon it by God or manifest destiny. Those were the days the French historian Élie Halévy described as "that great epoch during which the British people cherished the splendid illusion that they had discovered in a moderate liberty, and not for themselves alone but for every nation that would have the wisdom to follow their example, the secret of moral and political stability."

The Americans and the French cherished slightly different but fundamentally similar illusions. The West had been living through and triumphing over successive crises for more than four hundred years, and while doing so had been steadily expanding its capacities and its dominions. Suddenly, before the tired eyes of idealists like Lippmann and H. G. Wells, it seemed to fall apart—the rise of Communism and Fascism, the Great Depression, the loss of nerve in the 1930s, the collapse of the League of Nations, the spiritless drift into the Second World War. Their forebodings appeared to be confirmed, after victory in the second war, by the mortal quarrel between the victors, the sundering from the West of those hereditary domains between the Bug and the Elbe, the Pruth and the Adriatic, the settled confrontation of alien armies in the center of Europe, the breakup of the great European empires, the Cold War projected to every quarter of the globe. These depressing phenomenon seemed to Lippmann and some of his contemporaries to mark unmistakably the "decline of the West" that Spengler had predicted forty years before.

Yet at that same moment Western Europe and Japan, under the leadership and in association with the United States, were rising like a phoenix from the ashes of war and constituting, within a new if still ill-defined community, the most prosperous and most egalitarian society not only Europe but the world had ever known. Its egalitarianism was still far from complete, but the shift of more than half of its "peasants" and "proletarians" into the middle class altered the structure and balance of society so fundamentally as to constitute a revolution as significant as the French or the Russian, to enlarge geometrically the economic welfare and political power of all but the very rich and the very poor.

This social revolution, which had of course been slowly taking shape ever since the industrial revolution began, "took off" among the Western democracies in the quarter-century after World War II. A pragmatic mix of "free enterprise" and "democratic socialism," in different proportions in each country, coupled with new technological discoveries and new markets provided by its own democratization of purchasing power, induced in the West and Japan an absolutely unprecedented surge of prosperity, which even "trickled down" in some modest degree to much of the Third World.

Was Lippmann then wrong in observing both a sudden and a secular decline in the power and self-confidence of the West? Not entirely. Like so many prophets and forecasters, with their eyes on the long curves of social evolution, he underestimated the short swings, the zigs and the zags, that characterize and confuse the behavior of human beings and their collective enterprises. In the 1970s history seemed to be catching up with Lippmann and the Western democracies. Like men swimming in an indoor pool in which the water is steadily rising, their heads began to bump against the ceiling and their complacency to dissolve into chronic anxiety.

For the first time they became aware of physical ceilings: on the number of people the earth could tolerate, on the quantities of food and oil it could produce, on the volume of human and industrial effluents the biosphere could absorb and neutralize. They began to become aware of social limits to growth: of the inability of the system to provide for everyone status and privileges, some of which were attractive because others lacked them; of the need of the system for, on the one hand, a theoretical democratic equality for all and, on the other, a residual reservoir of proletarians to perform the dirty, menial jobs that technology had not yet found a way to bypass. They began, most painfully of all, to become aware of the volatility of their own cherished expectations: of the belief that each year their real standard of living would be a little better than the year before; of the belief that everyone could continue to earn more and more while working less and less, and that everyone is entitled to strike, buy gold, or stop paying taxes if this expectation is frustrated; of the belief that the remedy for inflation is austerity by government and not by citizens.

All these painful perceptions and disillusionments suddenly converging through the 1970s shook the economies, the politics, and the nerve of the Western democracies. Some blamed the politicians and bureaucracies, some blamed the great corporations and banks, some blamed the Communists, some blamed the Arabs, some blamed sin; very few blamed themselves. Those countries in which social custom had best preserved the work ethic and national disaster had compelled the reconstruction of a modern industrial base, like Germany and Japan, suffered less, at least for the time being. Those still mired in traditional and social conflicts and encumbered with swollen bureaucracies and old-fashioned entrepreneurs, like Britain and Italy, suffered most. Which, if either, was the paradigm? Which was farther down the road all were likely to go?

These maladies arise in large part from the disparity between what the democracies are in fact doing and what they say and think they are trying to do, and from the incompatibility of a number of the things they are trying to do at the same time. As suggested above, one of the most admirable achievements of the Western democracies in the twentieth century is their progress toward more equal status and more equal, or at least less unequal, benefits for most of their citizens. Yet both conservatives and liberals, in pursuit of what they call "liberty," are now beginning to assail and sap the institutions through which this progress has been achieved.

"Contemporary Leftists," says Leszek Kolakowski, "are in an untenable position when they demand more equality and less government; in real life more equality means more government and absolute equality means absolute government." It is not only contemporary Leftists who are guilty of this contradiction. Contemporary Rightists clamor even more loudly for less government, though they insist as passionately as anyone on the privileges and benefits it confers on *them.* These lapses in logic, which of course only reflect conflicts of interest, are characteristic of politics in democracies; but, because of the narrowing limits imposed on politics by the physical and social ceilings I have described, to indulge in them becomes more and more hazardous. To quote Lippmann once more: "My hope is that both liberty and democracy can be preserved before the one destroys the other. Whether this can be done is the question of our times, what with more than half the world denying and despairing of it."

The free enterprise system, despite its impressive successes in the past thirty-five years, has its anomalies and its failings. Even in its wealthiest and most faithful devotee, the United States, one only has to stroll through the "inner city" of any of its great metropolises (if one dares) to see how far it falls short, for the inhabitants of these devastated ghettos, of equality, even of equality of opportunity, even of meeting basic needs, and therefore of liberty in any real sense. About 40 percent of the black young people in these inner cities are unemployed and have little prospect of any employment except the most menial and precarious. They are a burden and a disgrace to themselves and to the affluent society, which turns its back on them. Of course they are a small minority but, as William Blake wrote long ago: "A dog starved at his Master's gate/Predicts the ruin of the State." Or, as Martin Luther King more ominously remarked, "Riots are the language of the unheard."

"In a worldwide war of ideologies and ideas," recently wrote Felix Rohatyn, the distinguished businessman who is chairman of New York's Municipal Assistance Corporation, "it will be difficult to claim the virtues of our system if Philadelphia, Washington, New York and Chicago are turned into slums." This is exactly what he fears is happening, and is certain to continue to happen progressively unless drastic remedial measures are undertaken. "None of this is easy," he adds, "but there is still time. Five years from now it will be too late." In other words the drastic action he recommends is required during the term of the President about to be elected as this book appears.

"The notion that economic insecurity is essential for efficiency and economic advance," wrote John Kenneth Galbraith in *The Affluent Society,* "was a major miscalculation—perhaps the greatest in the history of economic ideas. . . . We must find a way to remedy the poverty which afflicts us in public services and which is in such increasingly bizarre contrast with our affluence in private goods. This is necessary to temper and, more hopefully, to eliminate the social disorders which are the counterpart of the present imbalance."

This is the rationale of the welfare state, a rationale inspired both by equity and efficiency. In an economic system animated by private profit and dependent on private profit, whatever does not produce profit, whether essential public services or necessary social security, tends to be neglected. Yet such neglect in a society affluent enough to make it unnecessary is eventually perceived to be morally intolerable and socially dangerous.

The remedy for this neglect has in the Western democracies been in some cases a measure of socialism, that is, government operation of some industries judged to be essential to the public interest. In the United States, however, where state socialism, as distinguished from the "socialism" of great corporations, is identified with sin, relief for undeniable deficiencies has been sought, on the one hand, in government regulation of business to prevent or penalize gross excesses and, on the other, by welfare programs to succor and support those the system has most flagrantly disfavored.

These remedies are inexpedient because, carried to the lengths that Western electorates have jubilantly pursued in recent decades, they have discouraged business initiative and investment in some sectors without providing alternative sources of investment, have absorbed a disproportionate share of the national income to aid the disadvantaged without in the process restoring them to active service, and have created swollen and excessive bureaucracies sometimes more dedicated to their own purposes than to those for which they were designed.

A fundamental dilemma of the free enterprise system is therefore how it can assure the equitable economic security and opportunity for all that the modern social conscience demands, while maintaining sufficient incentives to induce private entrepreneurs to invest and produce.

From another angle the paramount vice of modern industrial society is not the exploitation of man by man, or even the neglect of the poor by the rich, but a disoriented, unplanned, ungoverned technological momentum to which all societies, all nations, and all institutions are subject. In this view, democracies stumble because no one is in charge. A myriad of entities, large and small, busily scheme to their own advantage, greedily seize and exploit the latest brainchild of technology, with little regard for its social utility or disutility or even its compatibility with human health and security. Everyone's reach exceeds anyone's grasp. Everyone insists he must not be impeded in "doing his thing." It is rarely admitted or permitted to be anybody's "thing" to plan for the community, to make society work as rationally and as advantageously for all its members, as any responsible executive of a corporation would insist his corporation work for all its stockholders.

Such are some of the dilemmas of the Western democracies at the pinnacle of their powers and the threshold of their time of troubles.

4. MODERNIZATION OF THE DEMOCRACIES

It is therefore not only the feudal, tribal, autocratic, or oligarchic systems of the Third World that need to be modernized. The political and economic systems of the Western democracies, including those of the United States, which were installed in the eighteenth century, need to be adapted to the conditions of the twentieth and twenty-first. In many ways it is more difficult for those who have succeeded than for those who have not to adjust to inevitable change, which is why great powers rise and fall, and newcomers unburdened with excess ideological baggage overcome older societies staggering under accumulated burdens of that kind.

The essence of modern politics has for many years been a search for an acceptable and relatively equitable balance between the presumed interests of the individual and the presumed interests of society. The central aim of politics, and of education and sociology, should be to narrow the gap between the two, to bring most citizens to believe that the fullest satisfaction of individual interests depends on the satisfaction of the interests of all—to persuade even the "liberty lobbies" that the man who minds only his own business is an impractical man. Thomas Jefferson, Abraham Lincoln, Theodore Roosevelt, Woodrow Wilson, Franklin Roosevelt, and Harry Truman endeavored to institutionalize this belief in the United States. Even they, however, have not been able to make prevail in our competitive and unbuttoned society the principle that, as Simone Weil has put it, "the notion of obligations comes before that of rights." In other words, a citizen cannot expect to have his rights protected by a society in which he himself refuses to assume duties and responsibilities.

Education should aim to produce citizens who (1) can support themselves, (2) have a sense of responsibility toward society and their fellow citizens, and (3) have the knowledge and perspective to judge the probable consequences of their acts and those of their leaders. Unhappily, the American electorate shows as yet few signs of having achieved this ideal. Some of the European democracies are a little closer to it.

Happy the nation whose citizens are secure and whose government is not. This is another criterion of political excellence perhaps met by Sweden and Holland but not by the United States or the Soviet Union. In the USSR, the government is secure but the citizens are not. In the United States and many Western democracies neither is secure. The government because, fortunately, it can be peacefully evicted by democratic processes; the citizens because, despite the protection of the welfare state, they may be suddenly disemployed in large numbers and because, despite the rule of law, no citizen, especially in cities, is safe from lawlessness.

The American definition of that glorious word "liberty" has often been lopsided, claiming for the individual, strong or weak, rich or poor, the right to do almost anything he wants, short of mayhem. Fifty years ago Walter Lippmann proposed a definition more in accord with Simone Weil's balancing of rights and duties. "The war for liberty never ends," Lippmann wrote. "One day liberty has to be defended against the power of wealth, on another day against the dead hand of bureaucrats, on another against the patrioteer and the militarist, on another against the profiteer, and then against the hysteria and passions of mobs, against obscurantism and stupidity, against the criminal and against the overrighteous."

Another perennial contest being waged in modern democracies is that between centralization and decentralization, between bigness and smallness, between concentration and diffusion of power, between monopoly and competition. During the past hundred years the pendulum has swung in the direction of bigness, of imperial concentrations, whether politically in the European empires or in the Soviet Union, or economically in Standard Oil, General Motors, Citibank, or the great, unwieldy, incoherent present-day conglomerates. There are already intimations that the pendulum may be beginning to swing in the other direction—the growing articulateness of states and regions in the United States, the self-assertion of Basques, Scots, Bretons, Kurds, and Ukrainians, decentralization in China and India, reemphasis on small holdings and village life in much of the Third World.

In *The Human Future Revisited,* Harrison Brown has even gone so far as to say: "The probability of survival of peasant-village culture is once again very close to 100%. The probability of survival of industrial civilization is very close to zero." That is an extreme view not widely shared. Many would prefer the position of William James, who wrote: "I am against bigness and greatness in all their forms." He preferred "the invisible molecular moral forces that work from individual to individual, stealing in through the crannies of the world like so many soft rootlets . . . rending the hardest monuments of man's pride, if you give them time."

Still another perennial contest is fought between consolidation and innovation, conservatism and liberalism, in the United States between Republicans and Democrats. In point of fact it is not only possible but desirable to be both a liberal and a conservative—in the best sense in each case. From liberalism one might take commitment to the open mind unfettered by dogma or preconception, to freedom of expression unfettered by law or fear, and to the evolving world in which nothing is static or ideal. From conservatism one might take loyalty to human achievements in religion, culture, and self-discipline, to the essential worth and dignity of the individual, the family, and the community, and to the codes of excellence that the best of civilizations have bequeathed to their delinquent successors.

It is nevertheless true that in an age of such vertiginous technological change as ours, societies have to lean toward innovation if they wish to remain relevant and alive. The dead hands of bureaucracies, priesthoods, and boards of directors, by obstructing necessary adaptations, may prove in the end more destructive and revolutionary than the clumsy hands of radicals. We have not yet found the golden mean between a bureaucracy subject to pressure and purge at each change of political leadership, and a bureaucracy protected in tenure but so entrenched that it accumulates privilege and deadwood to the point of inertia. Perhaps we shall never achieve that mean; nevertheless, we must try.

Free enterprise is both too free and not free enough. It is not free enough because monopoly, concentration, and the vast resources now required to launch a new enterprise in a major sector—steel, autos, energy, banking, newspapers, TV—make it impossible for new competitors without such resources to enter these sectors, and thus in this respect limits "freedom" to the enormously affluent. The system is too free because, despite sectoral concentration and the random association of incongruent enterprises in conglomerates, so little coordination of the economy as a whole is permitted by the conventional wisdom either to democratic government or to oligopolistic enterprise. Technological developments of the past fifty years have made central planning in a riotously centrifugal economy imperative, but the conventional wisdom has consistently and foolishly resisted.

As to the pragmatism of free enterprise, it is hard to demonstrate that an economic system meets contemporary problems efficiently when it periodically succumbs to rampant inflation, painful recession, or, in recent years, to both together. A businessman who managed his business as badly as the economy as a whole is managed would either be fired or go bankrupt. If the inefficiencies of free enterprise, with their political and international side effects, should accumulate and worsen, the competition between capitalism and communism, despite all the shortcomings of the latter, could become less one-sided than it has for the most part been.

Perhaps we need to get away, in this field as in so many others, from old terms and expressions weighed down with the emotional freight of decades of collective identification and intercollective conflict. We might even invent a new term, such as *social enterprise,* which would preserve and embody both the private initiative of capitalism and the collective planning and equity of socialism. Such a system would go with the grain both of history and technology and is indeed what we see gradually evolving before our eyes. The decisive question is whether it is evolving fast enough to spare us either the breakdown Harrison Brown predicts or the foolish and unnecessary tribulations we are now experiencing.

I am closing this subsection with the enumeration of a series of political and economic reforms that I believe, in the light of my half-century of experience and observation, would significantly improve the functioning of the American democracy, and in some cases of other democracies. Since space as we draw near the end does not permit argument or elaboration, and most of these proposals are familiar to those concerned with such matters, I shall merely state them baldly and pass on to my conclusion.

I should declare frankly, however, that, unless many of these reforms are instituted within the next decade or so, I should doubt very much the capacity of the United States to maintain its present position of leadership in a changing world, though in the absence of major catastrophes I believe it can muddle through and survive. The government of a nation aspiring to leadership simply has to be able to act more rapidly and more consistently, and its economy to perform more steadily and reliably, than the government and economy of the United States have done during the past decade.

Elections. U.S. elections are too frequent and electoral campaigns much too long. Representatives should have four-year terms; two-year terms barely allow them to turn around before another election is upon them. In order to remove completely, at least at the federal level, the distraction of the biennial election, Senators should be elected for either four or eight years. Every effort should be made to compress the presidential election campaign into four or five months, as it traditionally was. State primaries should either be eliminated altogether or replaced by several regional primaries taking place on the same date in June or July.

Most financing for presidential, senatorial, and congressional candidates should be provided from federal funds impartially administered. TV networks should be required to provide free time in reasonable amounts to candidates of substantial political parties. Corporations, unions, business, and professional associations should not be permitted to contribute to candidates; contributions from individuals should be limited to $100. Expenditures of wealthy candidates from their own funds should be restricted to small amounts.

Various means should be explored of restoring their traditional strength to political parties. One device might be to designate a "leader of the Opposition," who would be the defeated presidential candidate until a party convention had designated a successor. The leader of the Opposition should be able to address either House of the Congress, though not to vote unless he is a member. The stronger discipline that designation of a leader would provide the opposition would also tend to strengthen corresponding discipline in the President's party.

The Presidency. The President, with his Vice President, is the only federal official elected by all the people and representing all of them. He must be in constant communication with his constituency, using the White House as a "bully pulpit" to inform, stimulate, and mobilize the people behind his programs. A democratic administration must be open in two senses: concealing nothing from the public unless revelation would genuinely and seriously damage national security (not merely the President's own political interests), keeping in as close touch as possible with the needs, moods, and opinions of his whole constituency. The President should be alert to the seductions and hazards of power but should never hesitate to lead. Presidential leadership of the Congress requires assiduous cultivation and tact, but it is essential to effective government.

Formulation of policy should be a matter of mutual reciprocation between the President and his cabinet. Execution should rest with the executive departments and regulatory agencies. White House staff should be limited to the President's essential servants, intimates, counselors, coordinators. The National Security Council staff should be restricted to servicing the President and the council and monitoring the implementation of its decisions; it should not be involved in policy making or execution, since the Departments of State and Defense exist for that purpose. (It is interesting that Henry Kissinger, the only man who has been both Secretary of State and National Security Adviser, expresses in his *Memoirs* a similar judgment.)

On the other hand, the Council of Economic Advisers may properly propose comprehensive policies to the President, since responsibility for economic policy making is so widely diffused through so many departments and agencies that it is prone to flying off in a dozen directions at once. Indeed, as suggested earlier, much more consecutive and authoritative economic planning and policy making by the federal government will be required in the future.

(A cautionary footnote: Too much should not be expected of Presidents. Even Presidents are rarely able to do what they want to do or what they feel needs to be done. Neither audacity nor prudence can guarantee success. In democracies affairs often have to get very bad indeed before sufficient consensus for remedial action can be mobilized.)

Congress. Both Houses of Congress have too many committees and subcommittees, which in many cases duplicate each other and inexcusably complicate and retard legislation. There should be combined committees and subcommittees of the two Houses for most major areas of responsibility. The power of special-interest lobbies needs to be further controlled and limited, perhaps by fuller disclosure and publicity; elimination of their contributions to campaign financing, recommended above, should help reduce their power. Congressional staffs, in the past insufficient, are becoming almost as excessive as those of the executive bureaucracy; their numbers contribute to the volume of legislation and the duration of debate. Members of Congress (and of the Supreme Court) should be obliged to retire at seventy-five, perhaps earlier. The Congress, collectively and individually, should exercise a great deal more self-discipline in refraining from arbitrary, partisan, and often flagrantly irresponsible interference in the conduct of foreign affairs.

Bureaucracies. Federal departments and agencies (probably state and local as well) are far larger than they need be for efficient operation. They tend to burgeon irrepressibly because the prestige of every bureaucrat is measured by his grade, and his grade is determined, in many cases, by the number of his subordinates. The personnel of most departments and agencies could be cut in half, with great advantage to the public business. (In all fairness it should be emphasized that private bureaucracies, that is, the employees of corporations and associations, are as excessive and, contrary to popular myth, no more efficient than public bureaucracies.) Duplicating machines have, not surprisingly, multiplied, not reduced, the volume of paperwork, and computers the volume of statistics and private dossiers, in which errors are multiplied as readily as figures.

The administration and the public have recently become aware of the exorbitant volume of governmental regulations. It is quite true that business is itself responsible for most of the regulation to which it has been subjected, since it has in its pursuit of profit so frequently ignored public health and welfare. Regulation of intemperate free enterprise must continue, indeed probably become more strict, but it need not be so picayune and redundant.

Military. The size of the military bureaucracy is even more grossly excessive than that of the civilian. This is true not only of the civilian employees of the Pentagon but most particularly of the military officer corps. They are maintained at a level vastly disproportionate to the military rank and file on the theory that trained officers would be needed in large numbers to command draftees in time of war. The better way to deal with this problem is through a substantial corps of trained reserve officers. The overstaffing of the peacetime officer corps is at the same time a chief cause and a chief instrument of the military-industrial complex; as the old saying goes, the devil finds work for idle hands to do. A glaring example of such "work" is the extravagant lobbying of the Congress and propagandizing of the public carried out by military officers on active service. These activities should be much more strictly circumscribed. The corps itself, like the civilian bureaucracy, could be advantageously cut in half. National security would profit.

The administration and the Congress should be more conscientious and less reverent in scrutinizing and pruning military budgets. No part of the national budget contains such conspicuous amounts of fat as this one.

National Service Corps. There is much to be said for a requirement that every able-bodied young man and woman should, after high school, devote two years to public service. Those who wished to do so could perform this service in the military, thus helping to meet a growing problem of recruitment without having to resort to a discriminatory draft affecting only part of a generation. The majority of those in the national service corps would, however, be engaged in public works and services valuable to the community not being performed by private enterprise. The corps would relieve unemployment among young people, provide vocational education to facilitate subsequent employment, and, wherever necessary, correct deficiencies in the basic primary and secondary education of the recruits. Training in health care and experience in natural environments would be of particular benefit to urban youth. Those desiring to prolong their service for a third year might be accommodated if funds were available. Such a corps would of course substantially reduce welfare and unemployment benefits, crime and prison costs, drug abuse and traffic in drugs.

Regionalism. Economy and efficiency would suggest that fifty separate state governments and legislatures are excessive. They could reasonably be reduced to fifteen or twenty. Similarly, many counties and other local jurisdictions are anachronistic and unnecessary. At the same time, after all these years in which the federal government has accumulated power, a substantial devolution of powers and responsibilities to state and local jurisdictions, consolidated as suggested above, would be healthy and welcome to most citizens.

Economic reform. I would be so bold as to suggest that during the next decade or two a number of significant reforms in the free enterprise system, several of which have already been adopted in the European democracies, will be found necessary in the United States. Perhaps as a side effect of the impending energy crisis, they will be forced down the collective throat of the American business community, so imaginatively progressive about new industrial technologies, so obstinately backward about new social technologies.

Among these reforms might be: (1) the application of price and wage controls to certain commodities and services as the most rational, effective, and equitable means of checking inflation, a conclusion long since reached, as opinion polls indicate, by a majority of Americans; (2) more objective, consistent, and disciplined management of the money supply; (3) a more effective regulation of monopolies, including a limit to the socially irresponsible conglomeration that more and more inefficiently lumps together not only apples and oranges but oil and water; (4) representation of labor unions on boards of directors and their participation in management, after the German pattern recently introduced to the United States by Chrysler; (5) a respectable array of tax reforms, in the direction of equity, simplicity, and efficiency, long advocated by economists but successfully sabotaged by such paladins of privilege as Senator Russell Long (his father must be weary from turning in his grave); (6) formulation by the federal government, following the French model, of a national economic plan which, without being binding, would serve as a guide for government at all levels and for major components of private enterprise; (7) government readiness to serve as employer of last resort, most of all during depressions, but even in good times for those genuinely seeking work and unable to find it; (8) a much stricter application of zoning by both federal and local authorities to check the further destruction of our precious rural and agricultural heritage in favor of suburban sprawls, supermarkets, highways, and "development"; (9) the time may be approaching when the United States, following all the European democracies, should no longer cringe at the thought of nationalizing certain essential public utilities, such as the railroads, which can no longer be operated profitably by private enterprise, or even other immensely profitable industries if they should consistently ignore the public interest. The sum of these reforms might be called, as I suggested above, "social enterprise."

It goes without saying, unfortunately, that most of these reforms would encounter enormous initial resistance and are unlikely to be accomplished in the near future. Nevertheless, all of them should be placed conspicuously on the national agenda and should appear in party platforms. If we become accustomed to hearing about them over a period of years, we might come to think of them as reasonable, even eventually practical and necessary.

One further element needs to be mentioned before we complete this very imperfect survey of what is required to modernize the democracies.

Civilizations go through periods of self-confidence and ebullience during which great deeds are performed and great works created, because people are inspired to feel their powers are almost limitless. Such was the experience of the Greeks, the Romans, the French, the British in their heyday, such the experience of the Chinese and the Indians under several of their dynasties. On the other hand, once the bubble of confidence has burst, aspiration, hope, and achievement fade rapidly; the civilization succumbs to relatively trivial blows that earlier it would have easily shrugged off.

The democracies in Europe and North America, and their monarchial predecessors in the former, have enjoyed since the Renaissance a quickening of confidence and flowering of civilization that have lasted longer and spread farther than at any time in history since the ascendancy of Rome. That confidence was grievously impaired by World War I and again by World War II but was rather remarkably revived after the second, through the leadership of the United States, through the creation of the European Community, and the resurgence of Japan. There are limits, however, to the number and magnitude of shocks to confidence and to political institutions that any civilization can withstand. The Western democracies do not seem to be approaching those limits, but their social equilibrium is undoubtedly more fragile and precarious than it used to be. They are becoming more vulnerable to many of the ill winds now blowing around the world.

"Mankind cannot survive in anarchy," wrote Arnold Toynbee shortly before his death; "and, if democracy fails to provide stability,

it will assuredly be replaced by some socially stabilizing regime, however uncongenial this alternative regime may be. A community that
has purchased freedom at the cost of losing stability will find itself
constrained to re-purchase stability at the price of sacrificing its freedom. . . . Freedom is expendable; stability is indispensable."

One must therefore add to the powers and practices the democracies will require in order to maintain *their* ascendancy during coming times of troubles the preservation of that most precious asset—
their confidence in themselves and the social cohesion and momentum
that confidence inspires. In the United States, the consecutive shocks
of Vietnam, Watergate, energy vulnerability, and prolonged inflation
have shaken that confidence. Further, perhaps graver, shocks should
be anticipated. Nevertheless, nothing in the objective conditions
should prevent confidence and cohesion from being restored. The
question is whether the necessary psychological and political under-
pinnings can be regenerated. The degree to which the measures of
adaptation and modernization described above can or cannot be carried out will determine the answer.

5. COMMUNISM

Communism as an inspirational creed survives only outside countries
with Communist governments. Inside those countries the dead hand
of totalitarianism, secret police, bureaucracy, censorship, and patently
hypocritical propaganda have killed all genuine belief in Marxist
doctrines and concentrated personal ambitions once more on the
traditional goals of status, privilege, and material comfort. These
observations apply most unequivocally to the Soviet Union, where
Communists have been longest in power. For its present leaders the
"ideological struggle" in the Marxist sense is solely an instrument of
foreign policy and is waged exclusively abroad. The struggle against
dissidence at home is concerned not with ideology but with political
power and represents the determination of the leaders of a Party,
which is no longer communist in a Marxist or even Leninist sense, to
suppress all opposition, no matter how insignificant, even if, perhaps
especially if, it should be a communist opposition.

What is actually happening in the Soviet Union is quite different from what appears to be happening. Inside the emptied carapace of Communism is quietly growing an indigenous throwback, an atavistic, un-Marxist society. It includes the conventional three classes: first, a highly privileged aristocracy, Djilas's new class—the senior party officials, military officers, industrial managers, and the more compliant scientists, journalists, and practitioners of the arts, who enjoy relatively astronomical incomes and fringe benefits and the opportunity to pass on status and privilege to their children; second, a new middle class, below the "aristocracy" but with some hope of access to it—the vast army of second- and third-level bureaucrats, officers, foremen, and ingenious finaglers who keep the system going, all chiefly concerned with entering and bettering themselves in the emerging consumer society; and finally, the eternal, inarticulate mass of proletarians and peasants in farm, factory, services, and military rank and file.

It is worth noting, incidentally, that Djilas in an interview in *Encounter* at the end of 1979 * charged that most of the upper layers of this new society admire Stalin (at least those who did not personally suffer from his atrocities), consider Brezhnev "weak," and are likely to favor a "strong" leader as his successor. If true, this might seem ominous for the West, except that the successor and his colleagues would not be Communists in any real sense. They would simply be traditional Russian nationalists with whom, if national aims could be mutually accommodated, no ideological pretensions or impediments need bar the "peaceful coexistence" that is in the vital interest of both sides.

Nevertheless, the Soviet Union as the current embodiment of Russian nationalism is more extensive and more powerful than Russia ever was before. Its empire now extends from the Elbe to the outer islands of Japan. The role of Stalin in winning the "Great Patriotic War" and expanding so significantly territories under Soviet dominion assures him, despite his gulags and great purges, an exalted place in the Russian pantheon. Russians have never objected to monstrous rulers so long as they were successful. Ivan the Terrible and Peter the Great were equally feared and are equally admired. Moreover, the nations of Eastern Europe, through which during the seventeenth, eighteenth, and nineteenth centuries some elements of the Western Enlightenment percolated to Russia and inspired not only Tolstoi but

Lenin, have now unwillingly become, for the most part, transmitters of Soviet mystification to the West rather than of Western illumination to the East.

However, the military and political threat of the Soviet Union as a great power is no doubt exaggerated, as was the threat of the czarist empire by Britain, Germany, and other Western nations during the nineteenth and early twentieth centuries. The Russian empire has always expanded when resistance was feeble and halted or recoiled when resistance was strong. Muscovy won its European domain from the Tartars, the Turks, and the Poles after the decadence of the former and the disorganization of the latter were well advanced. The obstacles to its absorption of Siberia were little more than those confronting U.S. absorption of the territories west of the Mississippi. Russia never gratified its ancient dream of annexing Constantinople or any significant part of the Balkans; it was turned back easily by the Japanese in Manchuria; it was disastrously defeated by the Germans in World War I; it owed its victory in World War II, certainly to the valor and endurance of its people, but also to the folly of Hitler in challenging most of the world at the same time.

It is true that the Soviet Union is today one of the two most formidable military powers on earth and that it has an economic infrastructure and a political system capable of maintaining and even expanding that power in peacetime. The usefulness of such military power, however, except as an instrument of defense and prestige, is questionable. The Soviet leaders know that for them to start either a nuclear or a major conventional war (which would soon become nuclear) would almost certainly result in the destruction of most of the great cities and industries that they have so painfully constructed and reconstructed. They suspect that in such a holocaust not only their reluctant European allies but even the vast national minorities inside the Soviet Union would revolt, that indeed the survival of the régime and of its leaders and their families would be in gravest doubt. Under these circumstances they are not only unlikely intentionally to risk a war but also pragmatically unable, against resolute adversaries, to gain political advantages by threats so obviously empty. The situation of the Soviet Union supports the modern axiom that nuclear weapons are unusable for any rational political purpose, and that their only utility is as a deterrent. Nevertheless the recent invasion of

Afghanistan has reminded the rest of the world that not only the Soviet Union but Mother Russia has immemorially had the disposition to seep or penetrate across its frontiers, allegedly, sometimes genuinely, for defense reasons. Defense, however, is an implausible excuse for acquiring and holding the largest land area on the planet. In a dispatch to the State Department on September 20, 1944, while World War II was still in progress, Ambassador Averell Harriman wrote from Moscow: "What frightens me is that when a country begins to extend its influence beyond its borders under the guise of security it is difficult to see how a line can be drawn. If the policy is accepted that the Soviet Union has a right to penetrate her immediate neighbors for security, penetration of the next immediate neighbors becomes at a certain time equally logical." It is that engrained and self-righteous disposition to territorial aggrandizement that has extended Russia from the Elbe to the Sea of Japan, that makes her such a frightening and dangerous neighbor and that, if the world and the Soviet Union itself are to escape catastrophe, must be curbed either from within or without.

In the competition for influence in the Third World the ability of the Soviet Union and its allies to supply large quantities of weaponry and, in recent times, some military contingents certainly does confer advantages. On the other hand, judging by the experience of the last quarter-century, these advantages seem to be far from overwhelming or durable. The only two countries beyond the immediate reach of Soviet armies that have remained attached to it are Vietnam, which has needed and continues to need its help in resisting French, Americans, and Chinese, and Cuba, which has since 1960 felt and still feels threatened by the United States. Others where for a time it has seemed that Soviet influence was predominant—Egypt, Indonesia, Ghana, Guinea, Algeria, Iraq, not to mention China—have all slipped back into nonalignment or open hostility. There is no reason to believe that the eventual evolution of Angola, Ethiopia, even South Yemen will be much different. Of course the Russians can invade and "occupy" Afghanistan, which is adjacent to them, but it seems doubtful that they, any more than the British in the nineteenth century, can settle comfortably down there. Moreover, any war against a Muslim people further weakens Soviet influence throughout the Muslim world and may indeed have disturbing repercussions in Soviet Asia itself.

The appeal of the Soviet Union to the Third World is confined almost entirely to military assistance. The Soviets have never been willing or able, except in a few spectacular cases, to give developing countries the massive economic aid they need and demand, and to the limited extent they do so their terms are usually onerous. Third World students, soldiers, and technicians who tarry in the Soviet Union find surveillance by the police oppressive, the unavailability of consumer goods uncomfortable, and Russian social attitudes racist. The eminent Egyptian journalist Mohammed Heikal has noted, "Of the 200,000 Arabs who have been to the Soviet Union—from the armed forces, or for training as engineers and other specialists, or as negotiators for trade and other bilateral agreements—fewer than a hundred have married Russian girls, while of the 15,000 Arabs who went to the United States as students in the late fifties and sixties 7000—almost half—married American girls."

No great faith, religious or secular, has had so short a shrift as Marxism. It was its misfortune to triumph first in Russia, where it became infected with Byzantinism and where its application soon became totally arid and uninspiring even to its protagonists. "The heaven on earth of modern man," wrote the American theologian Reinhold Niebuhr, "turned out to be more incredible than the old heaven; and much more dangerous." But the incredible does not long remain dangerous.

Had Marxism first come to power in China, the story might have been different. They would have transformed it into something essentially Chinese, as they are now in the process of doing. They would have made it function more successfully than the Russians, as they are likely to do. They would have been, as they are, less interested in propagating it abroad than, as was the case with Buddhism, in assimilating it to the Middle Kingdom, where the barbarians might come to admire its works if they were so disposed.

China will soon have a billion inhabitants, almost a quarter of mankind. While the Chinese are subject to occasional paroxysms of rage and violence, particularly when driven to despair, they are constitutionally an equable, moderate, diligent, well-disciplined people. They tend by osmosis to flow across thinly populated frontiers but are not ordinarily expansionist. China's national minorities, in striking contrast to Russia's, constitute only about 5 percent of the population and are encouraged to multiply, whereas the Chinese themselves are sternly discouraged from doing so. China will wish to resume its ancient role as a great power, accidentally interrupted by its technologically lagging behind the West and Japan, but it is unlikely, certainly for the balance of this century, to be a serious threat to its neighbors, even to the Russians, not to mention those farther away. China may become a paradigm for the Third World, but it is doubtful that it will have the hubris or the appetite to become its master.

6. INTERNATIONAL POLITICAL RELATIONS

As long as international relations are external relations among economically interdependent but politically independent and often hostile states, rather than internal relations among autonomous components of a single political system, the central factor in these relations will be the use and abuse of power by the strongest nations and the balance of power among them.

The significance of balance of power has, however, been traditionally exaggerated. Unless one state has such a superiority of power that it has no effective rivals, as was true of Rome for three hundred years after the fall of Carthage, balances of power among strong and ambitious nations are precarious and short-lived. From the consolidation of modern nation-states around 1500 until the present day, no single nation or group of nations has been able to maintain either preponderance or stability for more than a relatively short time. The most recent example is the startling fashion in which the predominance of the United States after World War II was successfully challenged by the Soviet Union, and thereafter the predominance of the two superpowers was checked by the growing strength and self-assertion of their own allies and by the vigorous nationalism of the Third World. Balance of power has become a euphemism for barely contained anarchy.

The Congress of Vienna has often been praised for establishing a balance of power that prevented a general European war for one hundred years. The achievement of Castlereagh, Tallyrand, and Metternich was certainly admirable, but it was not enduring. The "Concert of Europe" they established broke down within seven years and, while it was revived in shadowy form from time to time, was not able to prevent a series of revolutions and of substantial wars throughout the century. As the Italian historian Guglielmo Ferrero wrote about the Holy Alliance and its architects: "One of the gravest mistakes committed by human indolence is the belief that order is best preserved by keeping it as it stands. It can only be preserved by continually reconstructing it. The only real guardians are those who reconstruct it. Unfortunately nothing is as necessary and yet as fruitless, so useful and yet so arduous, as the construction and reconstruction of world order."*

There are some signs in some places today of a more coherent regional structure and order. The European Community has for twenty years been moving gradually toward a considerable degree of economic integration, a lesser degree of military integration, and even some primitive forms of political association. This coalescence, so surprising after the two savage European civil wars of this century, has no doubt been partly motivated by the Soviet threat, but it may too reflect the overwhelming needs of national societies too small under modern conditions to provide security and satisfaction to sophisticated populations.

This is certainly not to say that stability in Europe is assured. A continent split down the middle, reluctant host to two rival ideologies and two hostile armies, can hardly be stable. Each side will certainly continue to gnaw politically at the structure and unity of the other, in the hope of causing its ties to loosen and break. Each is to some degree vulnerable to this process.

The East is vulnerable because Soviet dominion is detested among its satellites; their lively nationalisms are ready to flare up if provoked by too stern oppression or encouraged by too lax control. The West is vulnerable because its autonomous and idiosyncratic members are inclined, particularly when Soviet pressure relaxes, to fly off in different directions. Policies of the United States, which is far from the scene, tend to be more militant and sometimes provocative, while those of its European allies, who have to live cheek by jowl with the East in a small continent, tend to be more cautious and accommodating. These discrepancies could conceivably cause the Western alliance to fracture and split, if its members do not approach their respective

The Reconstruction of Europe (Putnam, 1941).

concerns with deep mutual respect and understanding. A stubborn persistence by either in imposing its views, military or political, on the other would serve more effectively than any Soviet machinations to pry the Western alliance apart.

Peaceful regional integration has not proceeded far outside Europe. Where integration has taken place by force and submerged nationalisms have been affronted rather than indulged, as in Eastern Europe and Indochina, integration is brittle and insecure. Nothing is more certain than that the Soviet and Vietnamese empires, unless they can transform themselves into freely accepted federations of autonomous parts, will sooner or later fall apart.

Elsewhere regional integration has made little or no progress. The Latin American nations, despite their common culture and relatively harmonious history, seem unable to draw closer together in any significant way. India, united by Moghul and then British conquest, already split in two in 1947, maintains its present unity only precariously. It will be a miracle if it does not sooner or later break up further. The countries of the Association of Southeast Asian nations are wisely cooperating more closely together, but there is no sign of any intention actually to federate. Even the tiny islands of the Caribbean and the South Pacific, which one would think had everything to gain by seeking strength in unity, remain blindly insistent on a separate national existence which, in many cases at least, has not the means to resist either foreign cupidity or domestic turmoil.

This brings us finally to the anomalous behavior of most Third World countries which, ardent and meticulous in the protection of their newly won independence, are yet, because of domestic instability or territorial disputes with their neighbors, constantly tempted to invite the intervention of great powers to help them solve their problems. The consequences are rarely a solution but more often, both for the developing country and the great power, a joint excursion onto political quicksands from which it may take years for both to extricate themselves. Yet the fascination for great powers of "global balance of power," "strategic advantage," and "imperial glory" is still so compelling that, throwbacks to the nineteenth century, they continue unchastened to plunge into the most dubious and costly adventures.

Meanwhile, they grossly neglect the real needs of the developing countries, either for the necessities of life, the tools of development, or a greater share in the decisions that determine their fate. Under these circumstances it is not surprising that the relations between North and South are on the whole poor, that communication between them is more often over loudspeakers than over coffeetables, that the Middle East and much of Africa are no less turbulent than when they supposedly achieved independence, and that therefore "the construction and reconstruction of world order" is for the most part stalled.

More than sixty years ago, just after World War I, Albert Einstein wrote to Max Born: "I don't believe that human beings as such can really change but I am convinced that it is possible, and indeed necessary, to put an end to anarchy in international relations, even if it were to mean sacrificing the independence of various countries."

Of course such a solution would, if it ever came about, mean sacrificing the independence of *all* countries, if by independence is meant the license to act unilaterally, each having regard only to its own interests. Actually, the heart of the matter is that it is no longer in the interest of any nation to act *solely* in its own interest, any more than it is or ever has been in the interest of an individual to act solely in his or her own interest. The current interdependence of nations means that any substantial action by one nation against essential interests of others rebounds sooner or later to its own disadvantage. The Soviet occupation of Eastern Europe has not enhanced but placed in constant jeopardy the security of the USSR. The security network that the United States flung around the world during the Cold War meant that it could be wounded not only by an attack on its homeland but by an upheaval anywhere in this troubled world, in Korea, in Vietnam, in the Middle East, in Cuba. Realism in international affairs today consists less in imposing limits on others than on oneself, less in containing communism or capitalism than containing one's own excessive ambitions and unwarranted fears.

Idealism is so often misinterpreted and misapplied that it is a poor guide for statesmen. The pursuit of, even worse the imposition of, "justice" is the cause of many wars. One people's justice is another people's dishonor. Justice for the Israelis is injustice for the Palestinians; justice for the Irish Catholics or Greek Cypriots is injustice for the Irish Protestants or Turkish Cypriots. Where there is no law, there can be no impartial justice. Territorial claims can never be equitably settled by reference to who occupied the territory a hundred or a thousand years ago, but only by a compromise consolidating both interests.

George Santayana in his last book, *Dominations and Powers*, made a wise comment about the benevolent neutrality that would have to characterize any world government. "If any general domination is to be established and successfully maintained over mankind," he wrote, "it must needs be in the name of physical necessities and physical conditions. The universal government must have no arbitrary moral tradition, no gospel of its own; it must nowhere seem, or in fact be, a foreign government."

In the meantime, in all the years that must pass before there is a universal government, how should we seek to direct the policy and behavior of our own national government? How can our patriotism best express itself? Alan Paton, the South African writer and exile, gave one answer in a commencement address at Harvard in 1971. "In what way can one's highest loyalty be given to one's country?" he asked. "Surely only in one way, and that is when one wishes with all one's heart and tries with all one's powers, to make it a better country, to make it more just and more tolerant and more merciful, and if it is powerful, more wise in the use of its power."

7. THE THIRD WORLD

Asia and Africa have been almost entirely liberated from the yoke of Western colonialism. There are now more than 150 members of the United Nations, as compared with 50 when the organization was founded in 1945. The latest surprising beneficiary of peaceful liberation is Zimbabwe, the embattled Rhodesia.

A few territories remain under one or another sort of domination: first, in Southern Africa, Namibia dominated by South Africa, and South Africa itself, still wholly dominated by a large white minority; second, a multitude of small islands in the Caribbean and the South Pacific, whose "independence" would be nominal but who nevertheless may seek it and U.N. membership, as a number of their neighbors successfully have; third, some ethnic groups encapsulated for longer or shorter periods by stronger neighbors, like the Eritreans, the Palestinians, the Kurds, even the Basques or the Scots, who are now striving for statehood or autonomy; and finally, dare one mention it, some of the numerous non-Russian "republics" of the Soviet Union and "democracies" of Eastern Europe in which the fires of separate nationalism are by no means extinguished.

Many of the newly independent countries still have great difficulty in creating a national identity. Some have no history as nations. Many are artificial creations of colonialism with boundaries cutting across tribal or economic realities. Even the nations of Latin America, independent for a century and a half, still seem uneasy with their separateness and uncertain of their image. Since any nation is in some sense a figment of a collective imagination, artificially homogenized and speciously separated from the rest of mankind, several generations may be required before a new national ethos can be fully assimilated and become second nature.

A second formidable problem confronting Third World countries is self-government. Many have never practiced it. Some were long under colonial masters who permitted no vestige of it. Others, like the former British possessions, for example India, had in a wise process of devolution been afforded some experience in parliamentarianism, but it is by no means clear how deeply such alien usages grafted on ancient civilizations have taken root. Even the Latin American countries, heirs of an authoritarian Spanish tradition but mimics of North American republicanism, have rarely been able to reconcile the two satisfactorily or to provide themselves with stable governments.

Inexperienced and confused elites, often educated abroad and culturally severed from their own people, some idealistically pursuing the public welfare through some alien creed, others greedily seizing the sweet perquisites of power they had watched their masters enjoy, all busily climbing up to precarious seats atop lopsided pyramids, are more often than not unable to manage public affairs either democratically or autocratically. Rapid alternation between civil and military governments is likely to ensue, as it has for more than a century in Latin America. Leaving aside the perennial hazard of assassination, prison, or exile, elites tend to prosper relatively because they are in a position to skim the thin cream off thin economies, but the mass of the people generally remain sunk in a poverty as abject as any they experienced under colonialism.

A third problem is the "wrenching and tearing" experience to which Heilbroner referred, the process of transition from medieval, feudal, peasant societies through the industrial and communications revolutions to late-twentieth-century postindustrial society, a great leap forward having to be performed, or at least simulated, in a few decades with grossly inadequate preparation. The inevitable clash between modernization and traditional culture, the natural appetite for instant and spectacular feats of industrialization and the consequent neglect of agriculture and rural majorities, the importation of capital-intensive systems into countries where the paramount problem is employment, all these skew economies and poison politics in the Third World, producing revolutions as various as those of Khomeini in Iran, Qadaffi in Libya, Perón in Argentina, and Pinochet in Chile.

No doubt the gravest Third World problem, indeed the gravest problem after nuclear weapons for humanity as a whole, is the inordinate increase in population in the twentieth century, which I have repeatedly emphasized in these pages.

"The great difficulty in bringing population growth to a halt quickly," writes Lester Brown, "must be weighed against the social costs of failing to do so in time to avoid collapse of the earth's major ecological systems. On balance, the sum of the social stresses on both sides might be minimized if population growth could be brought to a halt somewhere around six billion. . . . Adequately supporting even six billion people will not be possible without greatly improved management of biological systems, widespread rationing, stringent energy conservation measures, recycling programs, and a more equitable distribution of vital resources such as food, land and petroleum."*

It is in the developing countries, particularly since over half the people of many of them are under twenty, that the bulk of future growth is anticipated. Yet they can least support such growth in numbers; it thwarts their efforts to raise standards of living, to meet basic human needs, to develop prosperous economies and stable political systems. Improvements in nutrition, health care, and education, more steady employment and greater equality of opportunity, which Pope John Paul II, for example, rightly demands, will not be forthcoming until population growth is checked. Excellent beginnings have

---

*Worldwatch Paper 29, "Resource Trends and Population Policy."

been made in many countries, but the prevalence of the nubile is still so enormous that only the most prodigious efforts, national and international, could possibly bring global growth to a halt at or near the figure Brown considers imperative, about 6 billion.

Of course this dichotomy is far more than a question of population. The hundred-odd developing countries are more and more insistently demanding a "new international economic order," under which the world's resources, technologies, and wealth would be more equitably shared among nations. Since they control at least some of these resources, they are not wholly without leverage. So far, however, the response of the developed countries has been more rhetorical than real. They have for the most part done the least they could get away with. However, in John Donne's famous words, they are not "an island, entire of itself" but "a part of the main"; the bell tolls for them as well as for the poorest. If the Third World, because its revolutions of rising expectations are brought to naught, because it cannot shore up the foundations even of traditional minimum standards of living, falls into further anarchy and violence, it will not be that world alone that will suffer. Iran is a melodramatic example. Anarchy is as contagious as plague and less easy to control.

The Third World, therefore, is not only its own problem but ours. Yet, except among a handful of experts and idealists, few in rich countries are prepared to acknowledge this fact or to take remedial actions that cost them anything. The 1980s are, therefore, likely to be characterized by confrontations between North and South, arising from increasingly imperative demands by the South for more equitable international economic arrangements; by confrontations *inside* countries of the South, arising from increasingly imperative demands for more equitable distribution of limited quantities of goods among growing numbers of people; and by confrontations between East and West, arising from conflicts in the South from which the great powers seek to extract strategic, political, or economic advantage.

The United Nations system of agencies—not only the U.N. proper but the International Monetary Fund and the World Bank, the International Labor Organization, the Food and Agriculture Organization, the World Health Organization, the U.N. Development Program, the U.N. Environmental Program, the U.N. Conference on Trade and Development, and a host of other related international institutions—

were established to deal with many of these problems. The preamble to the United Nations Charter affirms that the organization is designed not only "to save succeeding generations from the scourge of war" but equally "to promote social progress and better standards of life in larger freedom." The human rights it champions are not only the political rights dear to the democracies but the even more fundamental economic rights demanded both by poor countries and the poor in the rich countries.

The United Nations in its relatively short career has accomplished much more in these respects than might have been expected. As Dag Hammarskjold used to say, "If the U.N. did not exist, we would have to invent it." A panoply of diverse international agencies and a multitude of dedicated international civil servants span the globe and serve its peoples in an extraordinary variety of ways. Their accomplishments, however, are far less than the crises they confront demand, not so much because of their shortcomings, which certainly exist, as because of the inherent limitations on the performances of any international institutions in a world dominated by sovereign nations.

I have often had occasion to remind my fellow citizens, when they condemn or reproach the United Nations for this or that action, error, or omission, that the organization is not in any sense a sovereign entity but merely an instrument of its member governments. No U.N. organ or agency can act without the consent of a majority of its members, in the case of the Security Council without at least the acquiescence of its five permanent members. No U.N. organ or agency can function without the funds provided by its members, for the most part voluntarily and at their discretion.

The United States, as its most powerful and wealthy member, has always played a predominant role in the United Nations. This predominance is sometimes masked by symbolic defeats in the General Assembly, where a majority of members can pass resolutions binding on no one, not even those who voted for them. On substantive matters, however, the policy and posture of the United States is likely to be decisive. If we decide action should be taken and provide the necessary support, action is taken; if we decide to withhold support, only a flood of rhetoric is unleashed. If the United States supports the United Nations in deed as well as in word, as it did generally under Truman, Eisenhower, and Kennedy, it prospers; if we withhold support, as we have for the most part under Johnson, Nixon, and Carter, and the more inwardlooking Congresses of their administrations, it withers and contracts. When we criticize the U.N. for its substantive failures and omissions, we are in fact criticizing our own neglect of it.

In a larger sense, however, the failures of the United Nations in both peacemaking and economic development stem inevitably from the collective disorganization of the peoples of the world, from the compelling appeal of parochial nationalisms, which are so contradictory to the practical demands of relentlessly growing economic interdependence.

Speaking to a PEN Congress in September 1939, the month that World War II broke out, H. G. Wells, the old warrior for world order, uttered a cry of anguish and despair. "The whole intellectual life of man," he said, "revolts against this intolerable, suffocating, murderous nuisance, the obsolescent national State. A world revolution to a higher social order, a world order, or utter downfall lies before us."

Such an agonized jeremiad from a modern Cassandra, who had predicted many of the horrors his century produced and found himself time after time unheeded, might have been expected. What is more startling is not that Wells or Edward Grey or Woodrow Wilson or Franklin Roosevelt or Dag Hammarskjold have been for half a century warning of the perils of unbridled nationalism and calling for international institutions commensurate with the global nature of the challenges we face, but that this idea has been around so long. Who would have imagined that Prince Metternich, the paladin of reaction and immobility, should have been one of its prophets? Yet he wrote in the early nineteenth century: "Politics is the science of the vital interests of States, in its widest meaning. Since, however, an isolated State no longer exists and is found only in the annals of the heathen world . . . we must always view the Society of States as the essential condition of the modern world. The great axioms of political science proceed from the knowledge of the true political interests of *all* States; it is upon these general interests that rests the guarantee of their existence."

Alas, we are far from having learned that lesson even a hundred and fifty years later when the "general interests" of all states are so much more self-evident and compelling than they were in Metternich's time.

Perhaps as long as governments are solely responsible to a national constituency and can be thrown out of office by that constituency, they will not subordinate national interests, as perceived by that constituency, to common general interests, no matter how overriding those general interests are. In that sense we are once again inescapably confronted with H. G. Wells's "race between education and catastrophe"—which he, when he died in 1946, was inclined to believe had been lost.

8. THE WORLD ECONOMY

Whatever North and South, East and West, rich and poor countries may think of each other, their survival and progress are as inextricably linked as the lives of castaways in a lifeboat. That poor countries cannot prosper and develop, indeed in many cases even meet the basic needs of their populations and maintain stable governments, without substantial help from rich countries is obvious. That developed countries cannot prosper and maintain high standards of living without importing essential resources and exporting surplus production to less developed countries is less obvious but equally true.

Santayana in the passage quoted earlier argues that if any world order is ever to be established, it must be done "in the name of physical necessities and physical conditions." That is precisely what is happening, not by any single charter or treaty but by the materialization of a vast network of uncoordinated and overlapping arrangements among nations and groups of nations. These arrangements vary all the way from bilateral trade agreements between two governments or contracts for the sale of technology by a multinational corporation, to powerful institutions like the International Monetary Fund, which exercises extensive powers over national and international economic relations. This network is both enlarging and drawing tighter. No nation could any more escape from it than it could escape from the biosphere.

Two other aspects of this interdependence, if and when they are sufficiently apprehended by governments and peoples, will deepen and alter its impact. The first ought by this time to be obvious but still is not—national security, about which we agonize and pontificate so constantly, depends in this day and age much more on the unimpeded flow of goods, services, and credit among nations than on the level of armaments or balance of power. As Lester Brown remarks, "In the late 20th century the key to national security is sustainability.... The traditional military concept of 'national security' is growing ever less adequate as nonmilitary threats grow more formidable. At some point, governments will be forced either to realign priorities in a manner responsive to the new threats or to watch their national security deteriorate."*

The second, complementary aspect of economic interdependence worth mentioning, one that more and more dominates the international dialogue on this subject, is both a pragmatic and a moral consideration. In a speech to the United Nations General Assembly in October 1979 Pope John Paul II said:

> It is no secret that the abyss separating the minority of the excessively rich from the multitude of the destitute is a very grave symptom in the life of any society. This also must be said—with even greater insistence —with regard to the abyss separating countries and regions of the earth. Surely the only way to overcome this serious disparity between areas of satiety and areas of hunger and oppression is through coordinated cooperation by all countries.

Similar exhortations had been voiced by the pope's predecessors, John XXIII and Paul VI. The disparity of levels of development between rich and poor countries increasingly envenoms the dialogue between them and tempts the poor to use both their economic resources and their capacity for political violence as weapons against the rich. The disparity of standards of living between rich and poor people *inside* both rich and poor countries accentuates the moral imperative that far more concerted national and international effort must be directed to meeting basic human needs.

In the perspective of this enlarging international economic interdependence, of the disastrous impact on national security that interruptions in or mismanagement of this interdependence could have, and of the moral imperative that poverty in the midst of plenty poses for both individual and collective consciences, I set forth below a few of the more essential measures which, in my view, national govern-

The Twenty-Ninth Day (W.W. Norton).

ments and the international community must concert and carry out in one form or another.

Population. I have already said so much about population growth because it is one of the two modern phenomena which, if uncurbed in time, could be fatal to civilization. At this point we need only recall that, by the year 2000, there will almost certainly be more than 6 billion human beings on the planet, and that that was the figure Lester Brown cited as the maximum the biosphere might be able safely to tolerate.

Food. However large aggregate populations may become, the one indispensable daily requirement of the human beings that compose them is food. In many parts of the world, including some in which population has grown most rapidly, food production has not kept pace. Hundreds of millions of people are dependent for survival from day to day on food imported, very largely, from the United States, Canada, and Australia. Such dependence is unhealthy and precarious, both because a series of poor crop years in North America could cause appalling famines around the globe and because means of payment by less developed countries for these mammoth imports are in many cases steadily shrinking.

This unhealthy situation has arisen not only because of rapid population growth but also because most developing countries have in recent years concentrated on industry and neglected agriculture, and because it served American economic and political interests to export vast quantities of food. The cure resides in drastic and rapid measures by the importers to expand agricultural production. This has to be done, moreover, for reasons of social and political stability, not by consolidation of land holdings and their "efficient" operation by agribusinesses, which might be the most immediately productive means but would accelerate depopulation of the land and further concentration of unemployed millions in great cities. What is required is the revival and reenforcement of the village, of small landholdings, of peasant farms as the main unit of production, and all those measures of cooperation, instruction, credit, water supply, storage, and distribution needed to make such means of production viable and attractive in the modern environment. It is significant and timely that two distinguished exponents of paramount emphasis on village agriculture in developing countries, Sir Arthur Lewis and Theodore

Schultz, were awarded the Nobel Prize for Economics in 1979. Here indeed is a case where small is not only beautiful but indispensable—because employment is, for both economic and psychological reasons, at least as important as production.

It is generally thought immoral to speak of food and politics in the same breath. Nevertheless a heavy responsibility, which is more than philanthropic, rests on the shoulders of the states able to provide or withhold the staff of life to hundreds of millions in other nations. There is certainly a moral obligation to provide food, without cost if necessary, in case of exceptional famines. In order to ensure that this recurring need can be met substantial food reserves, preferably under international and hence impartial auspices, should be built up, as has been repeatedly promised at international conferences. These promises have for the most part not been kept because farmers fear the effect of reserves on prices. There is no reason why these fears cannot be met and overcome.

So much for occasional famines, but what of the gross undernourishment, separated from famine by only a hair's breadth, which occurs chronically in so many countries? I should not myself feel that surplus food producers like the United States have a moral obligation to satisfy hunger wherever it exists. Indeed, as suggested above, their prodigality, motivated more by domestic political pressures than by generosity, has encouraged many developing countries to neglect their own agriculture and reduce or limit their own food production.

It is true, however, that if food is sold to all who can pay the market price and donated or provided on concessionary terms only to those the donor favors politically, injustice is inevitably committed. Huge quantities of grain are sold to the Soviet Union, which is thus enabled to supply its population with more meat without reforming its grossly inefficient agricultural system. Large quantities of grain are supplied on generously concessionary terms to Egypt, which neither limits its population nor develops its own agriculture with necessary zeal and effectiveness. At the same time the poor of many other countries are inadequately fed. These policies call for urgent reexamination. Food as an instrument of power, as well as a symbol of compassion, is likely to become for the United States more decisive than nuclear weapons.

Biosphere. Certain unmistakable and unacceptable outrages against the environment have been identified, and agreement in principle has been reached internationally that common preventive measures are necessary. However, enforcement of these measures depends on national governments. Since their concern with the problem is sporadic and subject to a host of countervailing pressures, pollution of the seas and atmosphere, intrusion of toxic substances into many foods, threats to the stability of global climate still far outstrip national or international action against them.

It is already clear that these offenses against nature could sooner or later so contaminate or subvert the biosphere as to threaten human life on a vast scale. We are not yet clear which might do so or when. More and more people are more deeply concerned, but not deeply enough. No one can be sure whether the toxins we manufacture and the waste we accumulate may not at some point reach a critical mass beyond our power to contain. Measures to prevent their reaching such a mass become with each year of neglect more crucial.

Resources. Since the oil embargo of 1973–74 it has gradually begun to dawn on the general public that material resources are finite, that expanding and industrializing populations cannot go on using up more and more of them faster and faster without risking eventual exhaustion of some or many. The implications for the popular philosophy of unceasing growth and progress are far from having been fully assimilated, but they are beginning to penetrate the public consciousness, particularly among the younger generation.

For the past seven years the peoples of the West, particularly the United States, have obstinately sought to close their eyes to the fact that oil shortages and price escalations are not solely an invention of OPEC and the petroleum multinationals but also reflect an approaching exhaustion of readily available oil supplies. When this unpalatable fact is finally swallowed, the first recourse—in accordance with the conventional and convenient conviction that technology will eventually come up with an answer to every problem—is to turn to alternative sources of energy, synthetic fuels derived from coal, nuclear, even solar. All of these, however, except solar, have side effects that have not been fully calculated but are already beginning to be realized. These side effects will impose ceilings, quite unpredictable levels, on the use of these alternative sources of energy.

Similar situations will undoubtedly arise during coming decades in regard to the supply and exploitation of many other raw materials.

Technology is miraculous, but it cannot always be summoned, like Aladdin's genie, to perform on command. A hundred years from now the economy of the world may be based on sunlight, sand, and the sea, which seem inexhaustible, but that economy will not be available to the next several generations. They will have to find other ways to economize.

Two developments can be predicted. The power of nations possessing acutely desired raw materials in large quantities—the United States, the Soviet Union, OPEC, a few other developing countries—will grow, and efforts of other nations to persuade or oblige them to share their treasures will grow correspondingly. These inequalities and demands could lead to a sharply exacerbated, though confused and inconclusive, struggle for raw materials between nations and blocs, a struggle in which arms, food, nationalism, and psychological frustrations would all play their part. On the other hand, these same dichotomies and imperatives could lead to radically improved international management of access to dwindling raw materials, if all or most nations should finally perceive that impartial and efficient international management better served their interests than economic warfare, always teetering on the brink of armed conflict.

The second development emerging from the slowly dawning recognition of the finiteness of industrial materials was foreshadowed several years ago by the Club of Rome in its proclamation of limits to growth. We can see taking shape all around us a new paradigm, a revolution in perceptions and expectations, an acceptance, among the young sometimes an embracing of a simpler life based less on material comforts and display and more on interpersonal and intellectual satisfactions. Such an opportune philosophy, making a virtue of necessity, stressing conservation, recycling, austerity, and nearness to nature rather than affluence and conspicuous consumption, could much more quickly and certainly respond to the limits we suddenly confront than could the dubious expenditure of billions of dollars for synfuels, nuclear fusion, or mines on the moon.

Development. The second most passionate preoccupation of the less developed countries, after national independence, is economic development and modernization. Even the rich among them are moved by a profound perception of injustice, inequality, and prejudice because, whatever their status now, they were until so recently treated by the West as primitives and inferiors. Such treatment leaves scars for several generations.

Nevertheless, their relationship with the West remains a love-hate relationship. Elites of developing countries have rarely questioned Western values, and their ambition has been to share and match Western affluence, institutions, and manners. In so doing they have aped the worst of the West as well as the best. Even when they have tried to reproduce "the best"—advanced technology, grandiose industry, university education—they have often done so in a way quite inconsistent with their own best traditions, their stage of development, and their real needs.

The objectives that, from the perspective of an outsider, would seem most appropriate to them in their present condition would be: first, meeting the basic needs of the mass of their people for a life-sustaining diet, health care including family planning, regular employment, and primary and vocational education; and, second, accommodation and harmonization of their traditional cultures with a sufficient measure of modernization to permit peaceful economic and political progress. Unfortunately, elites in developing countries all too frequently insist on moving away from traditional culture into modernization either too quickly or too slowly and, in either case, in reserving the first fruits of modernization mostly for themselves.

Developed countries, on the other hand—both capitalist and communist—are increasingly resistant to providing the economic assistance poorer countries so desperately need and at the same time increasingly insistent that what they do provide be applied primarily to ends they, not the recipients, judge most urgent. That insistence is at present directed to meeting basic human needs, which in practice means promoting social revolutions. Such revolutions may be necessary and long overdue, but for Northerners to promote them in the South is likely to seem subversive to Southern elites, whether the Northerners are capitalist or communist. Recurring tensions and clashes over this central issue may be confidently expected.

Monetary management. International monetary management, abstruse and technical as it may seem, is too critical to the welfare of practically everyone to be left to *national* money managers, whether public or private. Second only to the need for an international institution with sufficient authority to control armed conflict is the need for an international institution with sufficient authority to manage, or at least to supervise, the rise and fall, the excesses and the deficiencies, of currencies and credit. The first prerequisite for both such institutions, however, is that they be impartial and disinterested.

It is unlikely that such far-reaching authority would be explicitly granted to any international agency by national legislatures, but the very obscurity of the subject of money affords managers the opportunity to exercise an authority in this field considerably beyond their nominal mandate. This will remain the case only if the International Monetary Fund is able to retain the confidence of financial authorities, public and private, in the principal developed countries. It is of the utmost importance, therefore, that the IMF remain primarily responsible to those nations that provide its resources, that it not be politicized and emasculated by the application of the superficially attractive principle of one member, one vote.

This is not to claim, however, that the directors of the IMF and of national financial institutions associated with it are at present necessarily impartial and wise. They are men like all others who "see what is behind their eyes." Their prescriptions are often too cautious and conventional to remedy new infirmities, their economic counsels, derived from their experience in rich countries, often politically inapplicable to countries with weak governments and turbulent populations. Sometimes the scrupulous enforcement of their requirements triggers political and social revolution. Austerity is admirable, but not when applied to the necessities of life.

Nevertheless, this is without question an area where only an increasing exercise of centralized management over multilateral policies and practices can offer any prospect of equilibrium and progress. If the result is a larger measure of world government than national governments authorize or want, the justification is that, as a single world economy grows up silently and swiftly around us, only a single international authority can hope to manage it successfully. The alternative is an ungoverned and ungovernable ebb and flow of uncoordinated national policies, some contradictory and mutually neutralizing, others compounding each other's errors by sharing a common hubris or a common panic. Under such circumstances there would eventually occur globally what in 1929 occurred in the United States and in Europe—a collapse of credit and confidence and an economic depression with disastrous political consequences.

Seas and seabeds. It is often said that the seas and seabeds are the one remaining relatively untapped resource available on earth. That statement is rapidly losing its validity. A combination of inappropriate technology, demand for protein for growing populations, and assertions of national sovereignty 200 miles from coastlines is jeopardizing the sea's traditional and most available resource—fish. Whales and dolphins are already endangered species; all marine life that cannot be domesticated may soon become so.

The admirable effort to preserve the produce of the sea and seabeds as "a heritage of all mankind," launched and patiently pursued by the United Nations, has fallen afoul of jealous and ambitious national sovereignties and bids fair to bring forth little more than a minnow. New imperialisms are dividing up the seas as arrogantly and thoroughly as the old ones divided up the continents, and of course provoking new international conflicts in the process. Soon nothing may be left from which to extract the heritage of mankind but the very deepest seas, from which most of mankind has not the means to extract anything. Perhaps eventually all that will remain of unpartitioned and inviolate international waters, which once embraced three-quarters of the globe, will be a few international parks, where swarms of tourists and ichthyological relics will be permitted to observe each other.

Needless to say, this should not be allowed to happen. The international community should find means, even at this late date, to preserve the freedom of the seas from national appropriation, from overexploitation, from destructive contamination, from progressive degeneration into a monstrous dead sea. That would be a shameful fate for the element that has since the dawn of history been one of the chief theaters of man's adventure and his inspiration, of the voyages of Odysseus, Columbus, Magellan, and Cook, of the dreams and poetry of so many generations.

International institutions. We have spoken of the astonishing fact that during the last thirty-five years—the merest instant in the passage of history—there have grown up under the aegis of the United Nations, no doubt its most significant achievement thus far, a vast network of multilateral economic organizations dealing internationally for the first time with almost every aspect of our growing interdependence—health, population, children, food and agriculture, industry, labor, money and credit, aid for development, trade, resources, education, aviation, even the weather.

All these agencies are infant or adolescent, their powers feeble and precarious compared with those of national governments, on which they depend for whatever authority and funds they have. Yet manifest necessity has brought them into being, is confronting them daily with new and broader responsibilities, and is extending their reach into every nook and cranny of the globe and into every facet of peoples' lives.

However, they must be given more authority and more independence. These will come, but they will come slowly. Independent sources of financing would serve them best and free them most from servitude to partial and parochial interests. It was hoped that the minerals of the seabeds would provide one such source, but these are being maldistributed before they are even available. What may be required is a tax, small in its units, large in its aggregates, on international transactions, on trade, on tourism, on shipping and aviation. Governments will resist losing the control of international organizations that control of the purse provides, but this will be an essential element in moving from international feudalism even to that degree of international economic association the European Community now enjoys.

These international agencies, moreover, provide both the most constructive forum for the North-South dialogue and the most practical instrument for carrying out whatever conclusions it reaches. In so doing, as we have pointed out earlier, they sustain both North and South in the pursuit of satisfactions that are more and more becoming necessities. They enrich each one without impoverishing the other. They provide the cement that counteracts the centrifugal forces of chauvinism, parochialism, fanaticism, primitivism, and indifference. They are becoming a partial insurance against the political instability that plagues one half the world and the seductions of hegemony that tempt the other. They are, like the coral polyps beneath the surface of the sea, quietly laying the foundations for the synergetic ecumenical structure which human society at its present stage of development will soon require to survive.

9. SURVEILLANCE OF SCIENCE AND REVIVAL OF EDUCATION

The last areas in which I should like to submit one or two propositions are those of science and education.

As we have remarked earlier, human society and human life in the twentieth century have been transformed by science in ways and to a degree that would seem both miraculous and frightening to our forefathers. Indeed, they should be miraculous and frightening to us, when we reflect that new miracles of similar kinds are being performed or prepared around us daily and that the transformations of the future, for both good and ill, are likely to dwarf those of the past.

For good or ill—those are the fateful words. The boons science has brought us are legion and manifest; they need not be enumerated again. The accompanying afflictions, the unhealthy or unsavory spinoffs and sideeffects, have been less readily recognized. Some have been with us for more than a century, since the Industrial Revolution first sent children into coal mines for twelve-hour days and poured soot over the British Midlands to such an extent that white caterpillars evolved into black ones. Other injuries were brought to our attention only a few years ago by Rachel Carson's *Silent Spring.* Now, in one guise or another, they provoke almost daily popular demonstrations throughout the developed world.

The problem, both an ethical and a technical one, is how to distinguish the good from the ill at the time of conception, or at latest birth, how to monitor the labor pains of science without aborting them, how to curb its indiscriminate exuberance without stifling its inventive genius.

Scientists, like journalists, are inclined to be infuriated at any sort of supervision and to equate freedom of fantasy with freedom of speech. Certainly there is no reason why human imaginations should not run riot, but there may be every reason why the incarnation of all their fantasies should not. Scientists have rights, but so do other people, and both have obligations as well. We are not obliged docilely to submit to every dynamic disruption of our social equilibrium, every mind-blowing and mind-boggling drug, every insinuating and mischievous gadget that some scientist finds it irresistible to devise and some entrepreneur profitable to produce.

As Philip Slater has remarked: "While we think of ourselves as people of change and progress, masters of our environment and our fate, we are no more entitled to this designation than the most superstitious savage, for our relation to change is entirely passive. We poke our noses out of the door each day and wonder breathlessly what new disruptions technology has in store for us."*

Where and how should we draw the line, even if we should decide, as we have begun to do, that a line should be drawn? A key to the answer is provided by a great modern scientist, Werner Heisenberg, who wrote in his old age: "I venture to formulate the task confronting us in more general terms, as follows: It will be a matter of conceding to technology only so much space for expansion as will serve the real interests of human society, and of filling out that space as rationally as possible. We should, however, no longer do everything we are capable of doing."

If scientists and their technological disciples would exercise self-discipline as Heisenberg suggests, society would not have to discipline them. Unfortunately, professions and priesthoods, while regulating themselves internally for their own purposes, rarely discipline as conscientiously their interface with society. The final proof of many a scientific discovery—whether it does more good than harm—is carried out today simply by extending the experiment from the laboratory to the general public. Society, therefore, represented by the harassed and maligned politicians and bureaucrats, has in self-defense to discipline the scientists. That is the lesson we are now painfully learning. Just how we should proceed, and how far we should go, remain open questions, but there is no question at all that exorbitant science, the most revolutionary and subversive agent in our lives, must be controlled.

On the other hand, the sobriety and objectivity, the unflinching openmindedness of the scientist at his best, are qualities that the

---

***The Pursuit of Loneliness* (Beacon Press, 1970).

statesman, the sociologist, and the citizen need much more conscientiously to imitate. A world governed occasionally by a scrupulous passion for intellectual honesty would be a safer, saner place to live in and more likely to prosper. How would demagogues earn their living if demagoguery was treated by the public not with homeopathic doses of similar nostrums but with the penetrating impartiality of the scientific mind? Indeed why do not scientists more frequently lend their minds to social causes instead of reserving them so jealously for professional enthusiasms and private profit?

Perhaps passion and objectivity can never be happily married, but, to the extent they can be, it will be as a consequence of patient, lifelong application, that is, education in its broadest and deepest sense. We need to perfect and prolong our education at all levels, beginning with those most sensitive and susceptible receptors, the minds of small children. If we choose to confide these precious charges not to Maria Montessori and her successors but to the inanities and chicaneries of commercial television, we should not be surprised if we bring forth generations too "cool" for democracy.

Too many of our schools, particularly the public schools that used to be our pride and joy, that indeed have the charge of those young people most in need of education, have succumbed to a variety of contemporary pressures that make it easier to turn out illiterates than citizens. While we slept, dedication, discipline, and diligence have been insidiously drained away from much of our public school system, as though by some slow, invisible internal bleeding.

Many young people "complete" their schooling more bereft of the skills on which their future livelihood depends, less prepared to make the slightest contribution to society, emptier of all but the crudest values, than are young savages who have at least been socialized if not civilized through their tribal customs.

No aspect of our society is more in need of reform, inspiration, and rigor than is education. Without it there can be no civilization and no solid social structure.

Here indeed is a proper and a creative role for conservatism. No aspect of Western enlightenment through the centuries, from Abelard through Erasmus to Horace Mann, has been more decisive in determining its success than has its transmission of values, knowledge, and curiosity from generation to generation. These qualities will be desperately needed in the decades immediately before us. They must not be depreciated, diminished, or allowed to slip away.

10. CONCLUSION

In the radiant high noon of the Renaissance, Shakespeare has Miranda exclaim: "How beauteous mankind is! O brave new world, that has such people in it."

In the battered 1930s Aldous Huxley published a best-seller foreshadowing a "brave new world" of joyless robots. A little earlier Franz Kafka had been writing novels and stories—later praised for their intuitive reflection of things to come—in which his characters were the bewildered, helpless victims of anonymous powers who seemed to act, or fail to act, wholly without rhyme or reason.

These contrasting literary devices reflect not so much the differing moods of two eras as differing ways in which dissimilar temperaments see similar events. After all, life in Shakespeare's time was at least as troubling as in ours; his tragedies reflect that part of reality also.

On the other hand, the period just before the First World War was a time of the most ebullient optimism in which, as a consequence of the industrial and scientific revolutions, uninterrupted progress in every field of human endeavor was complacently foreseen. Yet there were even then those whose observation of human contraieties caused them to reserve judgment. "The difference between us is fundamental," Joseph Conrad wrote to H. G. Wells at that time. "You don't care for humanity but think they are to be improved. I love humanity but know they are not."

In fact, as a Victorian poet wrote, man *is* to a remarkable degree "the master of his fate." Most of his present predicament is self-inflicted and, as we have insisted throughout this chapter, could be alleviated or remedied if he could bring himself to act rationally, resolutely, and collectively.

What has changed from past times of troubles is the presence of the five factors described at the opening of this chapter, which have the capacity, if not much more strictly controlled than they have been, to wreak fatal damage on human civilization in a relatively short space of time. Whether or not these hazards are contained, however, rests almost entirely, not with "fate" or the deity, but with men and women —ourselves.

It is true that things are happening to us that we don't understand. The upholstered way of life most of the West has grown accustomed to since World War II seems threatened from many sides, mostly by our own prodigality and parochialism. Our age seems to be suddenly encountering, indeed creating, more discontinuities than history can recall since the transition from the Middle Ages to the Renaissance. It is possible that in the 1980s or 1990s men and women may find themselves in an environment in some respects as inhospitable as that of some science fiction Mars. If they do, it will be an environment they themselves have made.

Any such deterioration would be quite unnecessary. Neither East nor West could defeat the other in war without destroying itself, but the two together could put away their unusable weapons and grudgingly coexist. Neither can dominate or manipulate the Third World, but both could join with it in managing their interdependence to common advantage. None of the works of man, including himself, can be allowed to grow exponentially and indefinitely without running out of space and air, but all of them could be prudently programmed, like man himself, to grow to an optimum size for survival and well-being.

A few years ago the scientist and humanist, Jacob Bronowski, wrote: "The dilemma of today is not that human values cannot control a mechanical science. It is the other way about: the scientific spirit is more humane than the machinery of government. We have not let either the tolerance or the empiricism of science enter the parochial rules by which we still try to prescribe the behavior of nations. Our conduct as states clings to a code of self-interest which science, like humanity, has long left behind."

The purpose of this book has been in fact to propose a redefinition of self-interest in terms of the situation contemporary man confronts. If we can be persuaded that self-interest now demands much more sophisticated, forbearing, and harmonious accommodations with nature and with our fellow men of all colors and creeds than has been necessary in the past, there is no reason why we and our civilization should not go on to develop the almost magical capacities science promises. If, however, we persist in defining self-interest and national interest in terms relevant to more primitive eras, but incompatible with our own, we risk creating a world in which, not some distant generation, but our own grandchildren will become an endangered species.

I have no doubt we are capable of the bold effort of will and imagination which is required, but I wake at night wondering if we realize how fast the hands of the clock are moving.

Index

Index